DEMOCRACY
AWAKENING

DEMOCRACY AWAKENING

Notes on the State of America

Heather Cox Richardson

VIKING

VIKING
An imprint of Penguin Random House LLC
penguinrandomhouse.com

LIBRARY OF CONGRESS CATALOGING-IN-PUBLICATION DATA
Names: Richardson, Heather Cox, author.
Title: Democracy awakening: notes on the state of America / Heather Cox
Richardson.
Description: First edition. | [New York]: Viking, [2023] | Includes
bibliographical references and index.
Identifiers: LCCN 2023006034 (print) | LCCN 2023006035 (ebook) | ISBN
9780593652961 (hardcover) | ISBN 9780593652978 (ebook)
Subjects: LCSH: Democracy—United States—History. | Elite (Social
sciences)—United States. | Rich people—Political activity. | United
States—History—Errors, inventions, etc. | Common fallacies—United
States. | Conspiracies—United States. | Authoritarianism—United
States—History.
Classification: LCC JK1726 .R535 2023 (print) | LCC JK1726 (ebook) | DDC
320.47309—dc23/eng/20230501
LC record available at https://lccn.loc.gov/2023006034
LC ebook record available at https://lccn.loc.gov/2023006035

Printed in the United States of America
1st Printing

Set in Stempel Garamond LT Std
Designed by Cassandra Garruzzo Mueller

*To the people who have joined me in
exploring the complex relationship between history,
humanity, and modern politics—this book is
yours as much as it is mine.*

We have frequently printed the word Democracy. Yet I cannot too often repeat that it is a word the real gist of which still sleeps, quite unawaken'd.

WALT WHITMAN
DEMOCRATIC VISTAS, 1871

Contents

Part 3 **RECLAIMING AMERICA**

Foreword

America is at a crossroads.

A country that once stood as the global symbol of democracy has been teetering on the brink of authoritarianism.

How did this happen? Is the fall of democracy in the United States inevitable? And if not, how can we reclaim our democratic principles?

This crisis in American democracy crept up on many of us. For generations of Americans, grainy news footage from World War II showing row upon row of Nazi soldiers goose-stepping in military parades tricked us into thinking that the Adolf Hitlers of the world arrive at the head of giant armies. So long as we didn't see tanks in our streets, we imagined that democracy was secure. But in fact, Hitler's rise to absolute power began with his consolidation of political influence to win 36.8 percent of the vote in 1932, which he parlayed into a deal to become German chancellor. The absolute dictatorship came afterward.[1]

Democracies die more often through the ballot box than at gunpoint.

But why would voters give away their power to autocrats who inevitably destroy their livelihoods and sometimes execute their neighbors?

In the aftermath of World War II, scholars invested a great deal of energy in trying to explain how, in the 1930s, ordinary Germans whose constitution was one of the most democratic in the world had been persuaded to stand behind a fascist government whose policies led to the destruction of cities, made millions homeless, and created such a shortage of food that Germans were eking by on less than fifteen hundred calories a day. That government also ultimately murdered six million Jews and millions more Slavs, Roma, sexual minorities, disabled individuals, and dissenters.[2]

Social scientists noted that the economic and political instability in Germany after World War I was crucial for Hitler's rise. But it took writers, philosophers, and historians to explain how authoritarians like Hitler harnessed societal instability into their own service.

The key to the rise of authoritarians, they explained, is their use of language and false history.[3]

Authoritarians rise when economic, social, political, or religious change makes members of a formerly powerful group feel as if they have been left behind. Their frustration makes them vulnerable to leaders who promise to make them dominant again. A strongman downplays the real conditions that have created their problems and tells them that the only reason they have been dispossessed is that enemies have cheated them of power.

Such leaders undermine existing power structures, and as they collapse, people previously apathetic about politics turn into activists, not necessarily expecting a better life, but seeing themselves as heroes reclaiming the country. Leaders don't try to persuade people to support real solutions, but instead reinforce their followers' fantasy self-image and organize them into a mass movement. Once people internalize their leader's propaganda, it doesn't matter when pieces of it are proven to be lies, because it has become central to their identity.

As a strongman becomes more and more destructive, followers' loyalty only increases. Having begun to treat their perceived enemies badly, they need to believe their victims deserve it. Turning against the leader who inspired such behavior would mean admitting they had been wrong and that they, not their enemies, are evil. This, they cannot do.

Having forged a dedicated following, a strongman warps history to galvanize his base into an authoritarian movement. He insists that his policies—which opponents loathe—simply follow established natural or religious rules his enemies have abandoned. Those rules portray society as based in hierarchies, rather than equality, and make the strongman's followers better than their opponents. Following those "traditional" rules creates a clear path for a nation and can only lead to a good outcome. Failing to follow them will lead to terrible consequences.

Those studying the rise of authoritarianism after World War II believed these patterns were universal. Yet scholars in the United States noted that while countries around the world were falling to authoritarianism in the 1930s, the United States, sailing between the siren songs of fascism on the one side and communism on the other, had somehow avoided destruction.

This was no small thing. The U.S. was as rocked as any country by economic trouble and the collapse of authority it revealed and, in the 1930s, it had its own strong fascist movement with prominent spokespeople. Things had gone so far that in February 1939, in honor of President George Washington's birthday, Nazis held a rally at New York City's Madison Square Garden. More than twenty thousand people showed up for the "true Americanism" event, held on a stage that featured a huge portrait of Washington in his Continental Army uniform flanked by swastikas.[4]

And yet, just two years later, Americans went to war against fascism. Within six years the United States was leading the defense of democracy around the world, never perfectly—indeed, often quite badly—but it had rejected authoritarianism in favor of the idea that all people are created equal.

Scholars studying the U.S. suggested that Americans were somehow different from those who had fallen to authoritarianism. They were too practical, too moderate, to embrace political extremes. They liked life in the middle.

It was a lovely thought, but it wasn't true.

America took a different course in the 1930s not because Americans were immune to authoritarianism, but because they rallied around the language of human self-determination embodied in the Declaration of Independence.

They chose to root the United States not in an imagined heroic past, but in the country's real history: the constant struggle of all Americans, from all races, ethnicities, genders, and abilities, to make the belief that we are all created equal and that we have a right to have a say in our democracy come true. People in the U.S. had never lost sight of the promise of democracy because marginalized people had kept it in the forefront of the national experience. From the very first days of the new nation, minorities and women had consistently, persistently, and bravely insisted on their right to equality before the law and to a say in their government.

In the 1930s their insistence translated into a defense of democracy around the world. President Franklin Delano Roosevelt clearly and repeatedly spelled out the difference between a society based on the idea that all people are equal and a society based on the idea that some people are better than others and have a right to rule.

Americans chose a free future by choosing a principled past. But they could have chosen differently.

In the 1930s the struggle between equality and inequality took shape as a fight between democracy and fascism. But while fascism was a newly articulated ideology in that era, the thinking on which it was based—that some people are better than others—had deep roots in the U.S. From the nation's beginning, the Founders' embrace of equality depended on keeping women, people of color, and Black Americans unequal.[5]

That paradox had in it the potential for the rhetoric that authoritarians use, and in the past, those determined to undermine democracy have indeed gone down that road. Whenever it looked as if marginalized people might get an equal voice, designing political leaders told white men that their own rights were under attack. Soon, they warned, minorities and women would take over and push them aside.[6]

Elite enslavers had done this in the 1850s and had come close to taking over the country. "We do not agree with the authors of the Declaration of Independence, that governments 'derive their just powers from the consent of the governed,'" enslaver George Fitzhugh of Virginia wrote in 1857. "All governments must originate in force, and be continued by force." There were eighteen thousand people in his county and only twelve hundred could vote, he said, "but we twelve hundred . . . never asked and never intend to ask the consent of the sixteen thousand eight hundred whom we govern."[7]

During the Civil War, the majority of Americans worked to defeat the enslavers' new definition of the United States. Their victory on the battlefields made them think they had made sure that "government of the people, by the people, for the people, shall not perish from the earth."

But the thinking behind the Confederacy—that people are inherently unequal and some should rule the rest—persisted.

That thinking has once again brought us to a crisis. In the 1950s, business, religious, and political leaders insisted that the federal government's defense of civil rights was an attempt to replace white men with minorities and women. To stay in control, politicians ramped up attacks on their perceived enemies and began to skew the machinery of government to favor their interests. Wealth surged upward.

In the years after 1980, a political minority took over Congress, the state legislatures, the courts, and the Electoral College, and by 2016 the Economist Intelligence Unit had downgraded the U.S. from a "full democracy" to a "flawed democracy." By 2021, warnings had become more dire. Freedom House, a nonprofit that charts the health of democracies internationally, "urgently" called for reforms after a decade in which "US democracy has declined significantly."[8]

The election and then the presidency of Donald Trump hastened that decline. When the nation's rising oligarchy met a budding authoritarian, the Republican Party embraced the opportunity to abandon democracy with surprising ease. In the four years of Trump's presidency, his base began to look much like the one post–World War II scholars had identified: previously apathetic citizens turned into a movement based in heroic personal identity. Trump discarded the idea of equality before the law and scoffed at the notion that Americans had the right to choose their government. He and his followers embraced the false past of the Confederates and insisted they were simply trying to follow the nation's traditional principles. Eventually, they tried to overturn the results of the 2020 presidential election to stay in power. And even after Trump had tried to undermine the principle of self-government on which the United States was founded, his followers stayed loyal.

Those justifying their embrace of authoritarianism as the future of government in the twenty-first century say that democracy is obsolete. Some argue that popular government responds too slowly to the rapid pace of the modern world and that strong countries need a leader who can make fast decisions without trying to create a consensus among the people.

Critics of liberal democracy say that its focus on individual rights undermines the traditional values that hold societies together, values like religion and ethnic or racial similarities. Religious extremists in the U.S. have tried to tie their destruction of democracy into our history by insisting that the Founders believed that citizens must be virtuous and that religion alone can create virtue. By this line of thought, imposing religious values on our country is exactly what the Founders intended.

I don't buy it.

The concept that humans have the right to determine their own fate remains as true today as it was when the Founders put that statement into the Declaration of Independence, a statement so radical that even they did not understand its full implications. It is as true today as it was when FDR and the United States stood firm on it. With today's increasingly connected global world, that concept is even more important now than it was when our Founders declared that no one had an inherent right to rule over anyone else, that we are all created equal, and that we have a right to consent to our government.

This is a book about how a small group of people have tried to make us believe that our fundamental principles aren't true. They have made war on American democracy by using language that served their interests, then led us toward authoritarianism by creating a disaffected population and promising to re-create an imagined past where those people could feel important again. As they took control, they falsely claimed they were following the nation's true and natural laws.

This book is also the story of how democracy has persisted throughout our history despite the many attempts to undermine it. It is the story of the American people, especially those whom the powerful have tried to marginalize, who first backed the idea of equality and a government that defended it, and then, throughout history, have fought to expand that definition to create a government that can, once and for all, finally make it real.

Part 1

UNDERMINING DEMOCRACY

CHAPTER 1

American Conservatism

Today's crisis began in the 1930s, when Republicans who detested the business regulation in President Franklin Delano Roosevelt's New Deal began to flirt with the idea of making a formal alliance with two wings of the Democratic Party to stand against it. They turned to southern Democrats, who hated that New Deal programs were not overtly segregationist, and westerners who disliked the idea of the federal government protecting land and water. Those contemplating the alliance used the word *conservative* to signify their opposition to the New Deal. They insisted that a government that answered to the needs of ordinary Americans was a dangerous, radical experiment.

This was not an accurate description of conservatism: it was a political position. In the 1920s, Republicans had taken control of both Congress and the White House from Progressive Era Democrats. They turned the government over to businessmen, believing that they would reinvest their money as only they knew best, providing jobs for workers and exciting products for a new middle class. At first, as the nation's new glossy magazines advertised refrigerators and radios, stockings and speedboats, those policies seemed miraculous.

But then the Great Crash of 1929 and the Great Depression that followed it revealed how poorly distributed the nation's paper prosperity had been. FDR, then the Democratic governor of New York, warned that the Republican system worked only for those at the top.

"Democracy is not safe if the people tolerate the growth of private power to a point where it becomes stronger than their democratic state itself," he later explained. "That, in its essence, is Fascism— ownership of Government by an individual, by a group, or by any other controlling private power." He told the American people they deserved a "New Deal."[1]

Desperate to break out of the Depression, Americans embraced FDR's promise to use the federal government to protect ordinary Americans. In 1932 they elected him president and put Democrats in charge of Congress. In place of businessmen, Democrats brought into the government new voices like law professors and economic advisors—a so-called Brain Trust.

Crucially, FDR also turned to Frances Perkins, who brought to the table the idea that the federal government should protect workers and women and children. A well-educated social worker, Perkins was a descendant of a colonial family and had spent significant time in a small town in Maine. In 1911, she had witnessed New York City's horrific Triangle Shirtwaist Factory fire, in which 146 workers, mostly young women, leaped to their death from a burning building after their bosses had locked the doors to keep them from sneaking breaks on the fire escapes. The catastrophe inspired Perkins to bring the idea of old-fashioned community responsibility to the government, ad- dressing the working conditions in rapidly growing cities, with their immigrant populations and their unregulated industries.

Recognizing the growing power of women in the Democratic co- alition and eager to understand the needs of marginalized Americans, FDR named Perkins to his cabinet as secretary of labor. The first woman in a presidential cabinet, she served from 1933 to 1945, making her the longest serving labor secretary in U.S. history.

To get rid of the financial free-for-all that had sparked the Great Crash and the Great Depression, Congress regulated the stock market and limited the ability of bankers to use depositors' money to speculate in stocks. It also set maximum weekly hours and minimum wages for workers—forty-four hours and twenty-five cents an hour—and prohibited child labor. It guaranteed workers the right to join unions. It provided jobs for the unemployed, and it raised tax rates on the wealthy.

Congress also provided jobs programs for workers thrown into the streets by the Depression and created a basic social safety net—the centerpiece of which was Perkins's Social Security Act—for women and children and workers out of a job from unemployment or retirement. Finally, the government invested heavily in infrastructure, bringing to ordinary Americans new opportunities previously available only to the wealthy.

From the first, FDR's New Deal included—imperfectly, but included—Black Americans and women.

Racist southern Democrats hated the new system. So did a rump group of Republicans, despite the fact that their own utter failure to manage the economy had left people living in packing boxes and eating out of garbage cans. In 1937, after Roosevelt's triumphant reelection, members of these two groups set out to organize against the New Deal. They agreed that the growing power of the federal government threatened what they called "traditional values": individual hard work, private property, a balanced federal budget, and local control of politics.[2]

In early December 1937, a coalition of anti–New Deal lawmakers of both parties wrote a formal declaration of their principles and quietly circulated it to likely sympathizers. On December 15, 1937, their Conservative Manifesto leaked to the press. Called "An Address to the People of the United States," it rejected the idea of public spending and called private investment the bedrock of the economic health of the nation.

To free up capital, the manifesto demanded tax cuts and cuts to social welfare spending. It called for an end to government support for labor, which, it claimed, "injures all." It called for "states' rights, home rule and local self-government," by which it meant that federal laws must not disrupt southern states' racial codes. It called for an end to public support for able-bodied individuals with a "view to encourage individual self-reliance," trusting "kinship and benevolence" to provide a social safety net. "We propose," the manifesto read, "to preserve and rely upon the American system of private enterprise and initiative. . . ."[3]

The declaration received little congressional support. Republicans preferred to attack FDR without tying themselves to Democrats, and Democrats criticized those around FDR rather than be seen publicly undermining their president. But the manifesto caught the attention of whites-only citizens' organizations and chambers of commerce, which endorsed it, and business and manufacturing organizations republished and circulated almost two million copies. Anti–New Deal newspapers continued to reprint it. The Conservative Manifesto was a blueprint for those who stood against FDR's New Deal, and it's this declaration of values that makes today's radicals claim to be "conservatives."[4]

But this is not the historical meaning of conservatism in America.

The idea of a "conservative" stance in politics emerged during the French Revolution, when Anglo-Irish statesman Edmund Burke recoiled from what was happening on the other side of the English Channel. As revolutionaries in France abolished the traditional hierarchies of government and the church, Burke took a stand against radical change driven by people trying to make the government enforce a specific ideology. Ideologically driven government was radical and dangerous, he thought, because the ideology quickly became more important than the reality of the way society—and people— actually worked.

In 1790, Burke argued that the role of government was not to impose a worldview, but rather to promote stability, and that lawmakers could achieve that stability most effectively by supporting traditional structures: social hierarchies, the church, property, the family. "Conservative" meant, literally, conserving what was already there, without reference to an ideology. Those in charge of government should make changes slowly, according to facts on the ground, in order to keep the country stable. This idea also meant that government could be a positive force in society, rather than a negative one.

That "conservative" political identity did not translate particularly well to America, where, because leaders were still creating the new government out of whole cloth, there was nothing long-standing to conserve. Until the 1840s, the word rarely appeared in the political realm, and when it did, it referred to someone who rejected the "radical" ideas of abolitionists, who wanted to end human enslavement, or of women's rights activists, who wanted to give women the vote.

The word *conservative* began to take on specific political meaning in the U.S. when antislavery northerners refused to honor the Fugitive Slave Act that was part of the Compromise of 1850. That law required federal officials, including those in free states, to return to the South anyone a white enslaver claimed was his property. Black Americans could not testify in their own defense, and anyone helping a "runaway" could be imprisoned for six months and fined one thousand dollars, which was about three years' income.[5]

Enslavers and their Democratic colleagues began to call those speaking out against the Fugitive Slave Act "radicals" because they rejected a law. Charges of "radicalism" spread more widely four years later when northerners of all parties organized against the 1854 Kansas-Nebraska Act, under which Congress allowed the spread of slavery into lands that had for more than thirty years been set aside for free labor.

In December 1855, Democratic president Franklin Pierce used his annual message to Congress to accuse Americans who opposed the spread of slavery of trying to overturn American traditions. He described the United States as a white man's republic and claimed that the Founders had believed in a hierarchy of races, in which "free white men" ruled over "the subject races . . . Indian and African."[6]

The editor of the *Chicago Tribune*, lawyer and staunch abolitionist Joseph Medill, was outraged. He accused Pierce and his Democratic supporters, not the antislavery men, of attacking American laws. "There are perversions of historical facts, and false statements, in Gen[eral] Pierce's Message, which cannot fail to arrest the attention and shock the feelings of the most conservative among us," he wrote.

Medill had claimed the word *conservative* for the cause of equality.

The editor called out as "False all through!" Pierce's declaration that the Founders had established "a Federal Republic of the free white men of the Colonies." In fact, he wrote, the Founders had enshrined the nation's principles in the Declaration of Independence. Where in that document was the discussion of "free white men," the editor asked. In it, he continued, "Is there an intimation about 'the subject races,' whether Indian or African? . . . Their 'one guiding thought,' as they themselves proclaimed it, was the inalienable right of ALL men to Freedom, as a principle."[7]

As the Republican Party took shape over the next few years, its members worked to undercut charges that they were wild-eyed radicals, "Black Republicans," and "N****r worshippers." They embraced the idea that opposing slavery was a conservative stance. When Democratic Illinois senator Stephen A. Douglas tried to portray his political opponent Abraham Lincoln as a "radical abolitionist" in 1858, Lincoln hammered home the idea that it was Douglas and his supporters, not the Republicans, who were radicals. Lincoln claimed to be fighting against slavery "on 'original principles'—fighting . . . in the Jeffersonian, Washingtonian, and Madisonian fashion."[8]

Lincoln did not use the word *conservative* in the Lincoln-Douglas debates, but on February 27, 1860, at New York City's Cooper Union, he claimed the mantle of conservatism for the Republicans. Much as Pierce had done in his controversial 1855 message, Lincoln retold the history of America. In his version, though, that history was one in which the Founders opposed slavery, and the new Republican Party stood on their side.

"You say you are conservative—eminently conservative—while we are revolutionary, destructive, or something of the sort," he said, addressing Democrats. "What is conservatism? Is it not adherence to the old and tried, against the new and untried? We stick to, contend for, the identical old policy on the point in controversy which was adopted by 'our fathers who framed the Government under which we live'; while you with one accord . . . spit upon that old policy, and insist upon substituting something new. . . . Not one of all your various plans can show a precedent or an advocate in the century within which our Government originated."[9]

When voters elected Lincoln president later that year, his centering of the Declaration of Independence led the Republican Party to create a new, active government that guaranteed poorer men would have access to resources that the wealthy had previously monopolized. They put men onto homesteads, created public universities, chartered a transcontinental railroad, invented national taxation (including the income tax), and, of course, ended Black enslavement in America except as punishment for crime. As Lincoln wrote, "The legitimate object of government, is to do for a community of people, whatever they need to have done, but can not do, at all, or can not, so well do, for themselves—in their separate, and individual capacities."[10]

By 1865 the party of Lincoln had put into practice their conservative position that the nation must, at long last, embrace the principles embodied in the Declaration of Independence: that all men are created equal and must have equal access to resources to enable them to work hard and rise. That was the same position underpinning the New Deal, and those taking a stand against its business regulation and racial advances in the 1930s were not true American conservatives; they were the same dangerous radicals Lincoln and the Republicans of his era warned against.

CHAPTER 2

The Liberal Consensus

The New Deal did not immediately end the Depression or level the nation's racial playing field, but it won the loyalty of Americans who blamed the rich for having manipulated the economy until the Great Crash revealed its hollow core. Still, Americans were wary enough of what Republicans called "socialism" to make FDR's program precarious. In 1937, worried about deficits and attacks from the right, FDR began to cut federal spending, ultimately by about 17 percent. Unemployment shot back up, and the stock market, which had begun to recover, fell again. It was not at all clear that the New Deal system would survive.

Then, on the sunny Sunday morning of December 7, 1941, in a surprise attack, 353 Japanese aircraft bombed the U.S. naval base at Pearl Harbor, in Honolulu, Hawaii, killing or wounding more than 3,500 Americans and destroying U.S. aircraft and ships. Two hours later, Japan declared war on the United States. The next day, the U.S. declared war on Japan, and on December 11, 1941, four days after the bombing of Pearl Harbor, both Italy and Germany declared war on America. "The powers of the Pact of Steel, fascist Italy and national-socialist Germany, ever more closely united, stand beside heroic Japan against the United States of America," Italian leader Benito Mussolini said. "We will be victorious!"[1]

The steel pact was the vanguard of a new political ideology. Mussolini had been a socialist as a young man and had grown frustrated with how hard it was to organize people. No matter what socialists tried, they seemed unable to convince their neighbors that they must rise up and take over the country's means of production. The efficiency of World War I inspired Mussolini to give up on socialism and develop a new political theory.

He rejected the equality that defined democracy and came to believe that some men were better than others. Those few must lead, taking a nation forward by directing the actions of the rest. They must organize the people as they had during wartime, ruthlessly suppressing all opposition and directing the economy so that business and politicians worked together. Logically, that select group of leaders would elevate a single man, who would become an all-powerful dictator. To turn their followers into an efficient machine, they demonized opponents into an "other" that their followers could hate.

This hierarchical system of government was called "fascism." Italy adopted it, and Mussolini's ideas inspired others, notably Germany's Adolf Hitler. When Hitler became chancellor in 1933, he claimed that Germany was the successor to the Holy Roman Empire that had dominated Central Europe for a thousand years. These leaders believed that their new system would reclaim the past with the ideology of the future, welding pure men into a military and social machine that moved all as one, while pure women supported society as mothers. They set out to eliminate those who didn't fit their model and to destroy the messy, inefficient democracy that stood in their way.

Before Pearl Harbor, there were Americans who believed that the new Democratic coalition was driving the economy and the political system into chaos. They had embraced fascism as a way to reassert traditional power structures. But after the Pearl Harbor attack their movement collapsed as Americans embraced the war effort, sustained by FDR's clarion defense of democracy and the media's focus on stories of popular heroism.

One of the first of those stories featured Black messman Doris Miller of Waco, Texas, who was stationed on the U.S.S. *West Virginia* at the time of the attack. Assigned not to fight but to serve the white officers on the ship, Miller abandoned the laundry he was collecting when the first of nine torpedoes hit. He helped rescue the ship's mortally wounded captain and then took over an abandoned antiaircraft machine gun.

Miller immediately became a national sensation. Congressional support eventually led Admiral Chester W. Nimitz, the commander of the Pacific Fleet, to personally award him the Navy Cross, then the third-highest Navy award, for gallantry during combat. Throughout the war, reporters, generals, and lawmakers praised the ordinary Americans like Miller, the G.I. Joes, as the backbone of the American war effort.

While Axis powers emphasized the heroism of their leaders and Hitler championed a hierarchical society in which a superior race ruled subject races, FDR and the media reminded Americans again and again that democracy, based on the principle that all men are created equal, was the best possible government.[2]

But for all that leaders were talking about democracy, it was ordinary Americans who were defending it. Thanks to armies made up of men and women from all races and ethnicities—a mixed population Nazi leaders disdained—the Allies won the war for democracy against fascism.

Of the more than 16 million Americans who served in the war, more than 1.2 million were Black men and women, 500,000 were Latinos, and more than 550,000 Jews were part of the military. Native Americans served at a higher percentage than any other ethnic group who fought—more than a third of able-bodied men between 19 and 50 joined the service—and among those 25,000 soldiers were the men who developed the famous "code talk," based in tribal languages, that Axis codebreakers never cracked.[3]

At home, men and women from all backgrounds threw themselves into war work in the factories and fields, cementing their loyalty to the nation, while the economy, bolstered by extraordinary deficit spending to fight the war, boomed. If Americans had not been totally sold on the New Deal government in the 1930s, its victory in World War II seemed to confirm that FDR's approach to governance was right. By 1945, most Republicans joined with Democrats to embrace a government that regulated business, provided a basic social safety net, and promoted investment in infrastructure.

The national celebration of equality during the war had the effect of highlighting that all Americans were not actually treated equally. Black Americans fought in segregated units, race riots broke out between white gangs and their Black and Brown neighbors in cities across the country, women generally had to play secondary roles in the military, and the government incarcerated Japanese Americans.

In 1944, an especially horrifying sexual assault brought national attention to racial inequality. Six white men gang-raped a twenty-five-year-old Black woman in Abbeville, Alabama, and two grand juries refused to indict the men despite their confessions. Black leaders in Abbeville took Recy Taylor's case to the National Association for the Advancement of Colored People (NAACP). Founded by journalists, reformers, and scholars on February 12, 1909, the hundredth anniversary of Abraham Lincoln's birthday, "to promote equality of rights and eradicate caste or race prejudice among citizens of the United States," the NAACP worked to secure voting rights, education, jobs, and "complete equality before the law."[4]

The NAACP had long focused on challenging racial inequality by calling popular attention to racial atrocities and demanding that officials enforce laws already on the books. The attack on Mrs. Taylor as she walked home from church was particularly newsworthy. The secretary of the NAACP's Montgomery, Alabama, chapter, Rosa Parks, investigated the assault on Mrs. Taylor and then pulled women's organizations, labor unions, and Black rights groups together into a new "Committee for Equal Justice for Mrs. Recy Taylor" to champion Mrs. Taylor's rights. As a child, Parks had watched her grandfather guard the family's house with a gun as the Ku Klux Klan marched down their Montgomery street, and since 1943 she had traveled across Alabama making records of rapes, assaults, murders, and voter intimidation motivated by race. Her new organization expanded across the United States, calling attention to what unequal laws wrought.[5]

Neither FDR nor his successor, Harry S. Truman, could move civil rights legislation through Congress because of the segregationist southern Democrats in their party. But after he took office in 1953, Republican Dwight D. Eisenhower took up the cause. He appointed former California governor Earl Warren, a Republican, as chief justice of the Supreme Court. Warren set out to use the power of the federal courts to enforce American equality, and under his watch the landmark 1954 *Brown v. Board of Education of Topeka* decision began the process by declaring racial segregation in public schools unconstitutional.

In 1956, Republican Arthur Larson explained that modern Democratic policies and traditional Republicanism had come together in a system he called "Modern Republicanism." Echoing Lincoln, Larson explained, "Our underlying philosophy . . . is this: if a job has to be done to meet the needs of people, and no one else can do it, then it is a proper function of the federal government." Americans had, "for the first time in our history, discovered and established the Authentic American Center in politics. This is not a Center in the European sense of an uneasy and precarious mid-point between large and powerful left-wing and right-wing elements of varying degrees of radicalism. It is a Center in the American sense of a common meeting-ground of the great majority of our people on our own issues, against a backdrop of our own history, our own current setting and our own responsibilities for the future."[6]

CHAPTER 3

Bringing the Declaration
of Independence to Life

I n the first years after the Supreme Court's 1954 *Brown v. Board* decision recognizing racial segregation as unconstitutional, that faith in American equality was mostly aspirational. But Black Americans and people of color who had fought for the nation all over the world during World War II were not content with promises; they demanded actual equality. To generate the kind of public attention and political pressure that would finally enshrine minority rights into law, they mobilized organizations like the interracial NAACP, with its publicity savvy and legal talents.

In February 1946 a brutal attack on Isaac Woodard, a returning World War II soldier, jump-started the process of engaging white lawmakers in protecting civil rights. Still in his uniform, the decorated veteran was on a bus making its way from Georgia, where he had been honorably discharged, to his home in North Carolina. The soldiers on the bus, both Black and white, were socializing and drinking, and Woodard asked the bus driver to pull over at a rest stop so he could relieve himself. The driver at first refused, calling Woodard "boy." Woodard told him not to talk that way: "I'm a man, just like you."

When they reached the next stop, in Batesburg, South Carolina, the driver found a police officer to get Woodard off the bus. Chief

Lynwood Shull arrested Woodard and beat him, plunging a billy club into each of his eyes, then threw the semiconscious man in jail overnight. The next day, he hauled Woodard before a local judge, who found him guilty of disorderly conduct and fined him fifty dollars. Woodard was free to go, but he could not see to leave. He went back to the jail to lie down, telling Shull he felt sick. A doctor Shull fetched recommended Woodard be moved immediately to the nearest Veterans Administration hospital, thirty miles away in Columbia. There, doctors confirmed that Shull's attack had left Woodard permanently blind.[1]

When the South Carolina government refused to charge Shull, the NAACP spread Woodard's story to those with a public voice. In July, actor Orson Welles read the wounded soldier's affidavit on his popular radio show, and for the next four shows he called out South Carolina officials for refusing to prosecute. On September 19, 1946, Walter Francis White, the executive secretary of the NAACP, met with President Harry S. Truman in the Oval Office to direct the president's attention to the case.

Truman was born in Missouri in 1884 and reared as a southern Democrat. His early letters were thoroughly racist. But the Woodard case changed something in him. He later said, "When a Mayor and City Marshal can take a . . . Sergeant off a bus in South Carolina, beat him up and put out . . . his eyes, and nothing is done about it by the State authorities, something is radically wrong with the system."[2]

Truman ordered the Department of Justice to open an investigation, and less than a week later, a federal U.S. district court indicted Shull and his accomplice. But local rule triumphed in the trial: the audience applauded as an all-white jury acquitted Shull after just a half hour of deliberation, accepting his explanation that he hit the unarmed Woodard in the eyes in self-defense.

Presiding judge Julius Waties Waring, the son of a Confederate veteran, was disgusted by the jury's verdict, and by the cheering crowd. He began to stew on how to challenge racial discrimination legally when white juries at the state level could simply decide to nullify the law. For his part, Truman didn't have to stew: on December 5, 1946, he put together the President's Committee on Civil Rights, directly asking its members to find ways to use the federal government to protect the civil rights of racial and religious minorities in the country.

The committee's final report recommended new federal laws to address police brutality, end lynching, protect voting—including for Indigenous Americans—and promote equal rights, accounting for the incarceration of Japanese Americans as well as discrimination against Black Americans. It called for "the elimination of segregation, based on race, color, creed, or national origin, from American life" and, as the NAACP had done, also called for a public campaign to explain to Americans why ending segregation was important.

Truman knew he couldn't raise enough congressional votes to pass the kinds of legislation the committee recommended. Instead, he found a workaround, starting the process of establishing that the military, the civil service, and defense contractors could not discriminate on the basis of race. In 1948, after the Democratic National Convention approved a platform plank in favor of civil rights—prompting a walkout of southern "Dixiecrats" led by South Carolina governor Strom Thurmond—Truman shocked the political world by campaigning in the Black neighborhood of Harlem, in New York City. Pundits assumed that Truman's move toward civil rights would destroy his hopes of reelection, but voters confounded conventional wisdom by putting him back in office, giving us the famous picture of a victorious Truman holding the *Chicago Daily Tribune* over his head with the editor's wishful thinking in the headline: DEWEY DEFEATS TRUMAN.[3]

Before Truman's second inaugural, another civil rights case blew up, one that would help to shift battle lines over race in Congress. In the segregated town of Three Rivers, Texas, the widow of decorated soldier Felix Longoria, who had been killed in Luzon, Philippines, in 1945, wanted to hold a wake for her husband when his body came home in January 1949. The local funeral director refused, saying "the whites won't like it."

About an hour away in Corpus Christi, Mexican American doctor Héctor P. García took up Longoria's case. García had organized the American GI Forum the previous year to emphasize that Hispanic veterans were Americans who were fully entitled to their constitutional rights. *The New York Times* picked up Longoria's story and, at García's urging, brand-new Texas senator Lyndon B. Johnson intervened to arrange Longoria's burial in Arlington National Cemetery with full military honors. The ceremony was symbolic not only for what it said about the present but also for what it said about history. The Arlington cemetery had been established during the Civil War on the grounds of Confederate general Robert E. Lee's plantation. An official ceremony for Longoria there explicitly rejected the South's history of white supremacy.[4]

In Johnson, the civil rights movement now had a powerful congressional voice, but even with the support of Democrats like Truman and Johnson, the movement could not overcome the power of racist southern Democrats. By virtue of the fact that they tended to be reelected for decades, these senators held crucial committee chairs in Congress that were awarded on the basis of seniority. It fell to Republican Dwight D. Eisenhower, whom voters elected in 1952, to find a way around the racist rump.

Eisenhower preferred not to upset the nation's racial status quo dramatically, but he respected the men who had fought and died for democracy. He also recognized that racial discrimination gave international communists a powerful argument for disparaging the idea that American democracy was a superior form of government. In January 1954, Eisenhower put the power of the Supreme Court behind civil rights by appointing Earl Warren as its chief justice.

Immediately after his confirmation to the Supreme Court, Warren faced a case argued by NAACP lawyer Thurgood Marshall, along with civil rights lawyer Constance Baker Motley and other civil rights advocates. In 1934, as a young Baltimore lawyer, Marshall—who had learned to love the law because his father, who was a waiter, loved following court cases—had begun to work with the NAACP. In 1940 he founded the affiliated NAACP Legal Defense and Educational Fund in New York City. Six years later, Motley joined him; she would become the first Black woman to argue before the Supreme Court and the first Black woman to become a federal judge. They were a powerhouse team.

Marshall had previously won discrimination cases by relying on the 1896 *Plessy v. Ferguson* decision that allowed "separate" accommodations for Black and white Americans so long as they were "equal." Marshall would point out how much poorer the conditions were in Black schools as compared to white schools, proving those conditions violated the "separate but equal" requirement in the decision condoning racial segregation. But in 1952, with the support of Judge Waring, Marshall and Motley opposed segregation in public schools outright by arguing that racial segregation violated the equal protection clause of the Fourteenth Amendment.

This formula would enable the federal government to restrain white juries at the state level. The Supreme Court listened. In May 1954 it handed down two key decisions: *Hernandez v. Texas* declared that all-white juries denied Mexican American defendants equal protection of the law, and the *Brown v. Board of Education* decision declared the same about segregated schools. Relying on the Fourteenth Amendment, the Supreme Court declared racial discrimination unconstitutional. The decisions were unanimous.

Now the fat was in the fire. The Supreme Court demanded that the federal government protect the equal rights of citizens within the states. It said that the equal protection clause and the due process clause of the Fourteenth Amendment meant that the protections in the Bill of Rights applied to the states, continuing a process that the court had begun in the 1940s through the efforts of several of FDR's appointees. Discriminatory state laws were unconstitutional.

White southerners promptly set up all-white schools known as segregation academies, often funded with public money, and Black and Brown Americans who stood up for their right to equality lost jobs, homes, and sometimes their lives. Mounting white reactionary violence exploded into view in August 1955, when Roy Bryant and J. W. Milam murdered fourteen-year-old Emmett Till, a Chicago boy who was visiting relatives in a small Mississippi town known even then for its brutality toward Black people. After Bryant's wife accused the boy of flirting with her, the two men kidnapped Till, brutally beat him, mutilated him, shot him in the back of the head, and dumped his body in the Tallahatchie River.

NAACP leaders Ruby Hurley, Medgar Evers, and Amzie Moore demanded that Mississippi conduct an investigation. Till's mother, Mamie, insisted on an open-casket funeral for her son, and pictures of the child's mutilated body exposed the vulnerability of American lives if states looked the other way when white men took the law into their own hands. When an all-white jury acquitted Bryant and Milam, outrage built. NAACP workers organized mass demonstrations across the country. Then the two men admitted their guilt and sold the story of the murder to *Look* magazine for cash, making the fragility of American democracy clear even to those who hadn't previously been paying attention.

The pressure for racial equality built. In December 1955, Rosa Parks refused to move to the Black section of a bus in Montgomery, Alabama, and for the next year, Black Montgomery citizens and their white allies organized carpools, taxis, bicycles, and even horse-drawn buggies to enable Black Americans to stay off segregated public transportation. Members of the White Citizens' Council attacked supporters of the Montgomery bus boycott and firebombed the homes of two ministers leading the boycott: Ralph Abernathy and Martin Luther King Jr. When authorities arrested King and eighty-eight other leaders for conspiring to cause a business (the bus company) financial harm, the boycott became national news. In December 1956 the Supreme Court ruled that state laws segregating public transportation were unconstitutional.

In 1957, when nine Black students tried to enroll at Central High School in Little Rock, Arkansas, massive resistance prompted Eisenhower to federalize the National Guard and send the 101st Airborne Division to defend their constitutional right to do so. The president pushed Congress to protect Black voting, using its authority under the Fifteenth Amendment. Lyndon B. Johnson, now the Senate majority leader, signed on to the Civil Rights Act of 1957, strengthening Black voting rights. Even though Johnson permitted southern Democrats to water down the bill, Strom Thurmond—by now a senator from South Carolina—took advantage of the fact that the Senate had never developed a rule to make people quit talking. He launched the longest filibuster in American history in an attempt to stop the measure.[5]

Thurmond's drama didn't work. The federal tide was turning.

The Civil Rights Act passed with a bipartisan vote of 285 to 126 in the house, and 71 to 18 in the Senate. A majority of both parties had swung behind it. Going forward, the federal government would protect the rights of American citizens from states that refused to recognize the American principle that all people are created equal and have a right to a say in their government.[6]

CHAPTER 4

Race and Taxes

From 1946 to 1964 this "liberal consensus" was so popular that its opponents were immortalized by Foghorn Leghorn, a ridiculous Looney Tunes rooster with a southern accent. By 1960 the consensus seemed so widely shared that political scientist Philip Converse advised political candidates to nail together coalitions based on promises of government spending. There was no longer any point in trying to attract voters with appeals to principled visions of American society, he wrote, because almost everyone was on board the liberal consensus.[1]

But the Supreme Court's 1954 *Brown v. Board of Education* decision exposed a crucial vulnerability in that consensus. The decision tied the active federal government not just to economic equality for white Americans but also to civil rights. That link enabled opponents of the liberal consensus to resurrect a different American history than the one that had been uppermost since World War II. And this one, constructed by former Confederates during the Reconstruction years, was based not in equality but in a racial hierarchy.

Those who had been trying to unwind the legislation enacted since FDR took office argued that the newly active federal government was misusing tax dollars taken from hardworking white men to promote civil rights for undeserving Black people. The troops President Eisenhower sent to Little Rock Central High School in 1957, for example, didn't come cheap. The federal government's defense of civil rights redistributed wealth, they said, and so was virtually socialism.

This argument had sharp teeth in the 1950s as Americans recoiled from the growing influence of the communist Soviet Union and the rise of Communist China, but the American fear of socialism in the 1950s was not at all a product of its time. Instead, it resurrected a false history of the nation, written by white supremacists after the Civil War.

The use of the word *socialism* by those opposed to the liberal consensus had virtually nothing to do with actual international socialism, which developed in the late nineteenth century and burst into international prominence when the 1917 Bolshevik Revolution in Russia overthrew Czar Nicholas II. International socialism is based on the ideas of mid-nineteenth-century political theorist Karl Marx, who believed that as the wealthy crushed the working class during late-stage capitalism, people would rise up to take control of the means of production: factories, farms, utilities, and so on.

That theory has never been popular in America. While the U.S. had a few Socialist mayors and even two avowed Socialist congressmen—Wisconsin's Victor Berger and New York's Meyer London—in the early twentieth century, the best a Socialist Party candidate has ever done in a presidential election was when Eugene V. Debs won about 6 percent of the popular vote in 1912 with 900,000 votes. Even then, while Debs called himself a socialist, it is not clear he was advocating for the national takeover of industry so much as calling for the government to work for ordinary Americans rather than the very wealthy.

In America the use of the word *socialism* came long before the Bolshevik Revolution. In 1871, during the period of Reconstruction after the Civil War, white supremacist southerners seized on a word that had been a general term for utopian communities and gave it a political definition that was specific to the United States.

During the Civil War, the Republicans in charge of the government had both created national taxation and abolished legal slavery (except as punishment for crime). For the first time in U.S. history, voting had a direct impact on people's pocketbooks, and the Democrats opposed to the Lincoln administration insisted that taxation would destroy white workers. Then, in 1867, Congress passed the Military Reconstruction Act expanding state voting to include Black men and, in 1870, protected that right with the Fifteenth Amendment to the Constitution.

White southerners who hated the idea that Black men could use the vote to protect themselves started to terrorize their Black neighbors. Pretending to be the ghosts of dead Confederate soldiers, they dressed in white robes with hoods to cover their faces and warned formerly enslaved people not to show up at the polls. But in 1870, Congress created the Department of Justice to enable the federal government to protect the right of Black men to vote. President U. S. Grant's attorney general set out to destroy the Ku Klux Klan.

The next year, in 1871, unreconstructed white southerners began to argue that they objected to Black rights not on racial grounds—which now was unconstitutional and ran the risk of jail time from a Department of Justice prosecution—but rather on economic grounds. They did not want Black men voting, they said, because formerly enslaved people were poor and were voting for leaders who promised to build things like roads and hospitals. Those public investments could be paid for only with tax levies, and the only people in the South with property after the war were white. Thus, they said, Black voting amounted to a redistribution of wealth from white men to Black people, who wanted something for nothing.

Black voting was, one popular magazine insisted, "Socialism in South Carolina."[2]

Immediately after the war, those Republicans who had fought alongside Black colleagues and those who saw Black Americans as the only reliably loyal people in the South insisted that Black Americans must be equal before the law. But the argument that poor workers were dangerous resonated with northerners who had previously supported Black rights, as native-born Americans began to worry about a new wave of immigration from southern and eastern Europe. The newcomers—Italians, Poles, Catholics, Jews, people who wore the costumes of their homelands and spoke unfamiliar languages—seemed alien to older inhabitants of the northern cities where many of them settled. Many upwardly mobile native-born Americans agreed that cutting poor people, in this case, immigrants, out of the vote was a good idea.

And so, with a growing distrust of poor voters who wanted public investment that would cost tax dollars, Republicans who had previously recognized the right to vote as crucial for Black Americans to protect their interests began to look the other way as former Confederates kept their Black neighbors from the polls. Black voting slowed. And then it stopped.[3]

Seeking a contrast to the government action they called socialism, southern Democrats after the Civil War celebrated the American cowboy, who began to drive cattle from the border of Texas and Mexico north across the plains to army posts and railheads in 1866. In their view, cowboys were real Americans who wanted nothing from the government but to be left alone. The Democratic press mythologized these cowboys as white men (in fact, a third of the cowboys were men of color) who worked hard for a day's pay independent of the government—although the government bought the cattle, funded the railroads, and fought Indigenous Americans who pushed back against the railroads—all the while fighting off warriors, Mexicans, and rustlers who were trying to stop them.[4]

That mythological cowboy caught the nation's imagination in the 1870s as the antithesis of what southern Democrats insisted was government-backed socialism in the East. He lived on with Buffalo Bill and his Wild West Show and in literature and films that defined true Americans as independent men, erasing the townspeople building the communities the cowboys theoretically fought to protect. The cowboy would be an effective propagandist for those standing against the liberal consensus in the 1950s and 1960s.

And they needed something that ordinary voters would find attractive, because in the years after World War II, those eager to tear down the liberal consensus were finding their ideas a difficult sell. In 1951, William F. Buckley Jr., an oilman's son fresh out of Yale, was so frustrated that voters kept choosing leaders who reinforced the principles of government regulation of the economy, provision of a social safety net, and promotion of infrastructure (the government was not at that point doing much to protect civil rights) that he took a stand against the Enlightenment principles on which the United States had been founded.

Enlightenment thinkers had rejected leadership based on religion or birth, arguing instead that society moved forward when people made good choices after hearing arguments based on fact. But this Enlightenment idea must be replaced, Buckley argued in *God and Man at Yale: The Superstitions of "Academic Freedom,"* because Americans kept choosing the liberal consensus, which, to his mind, was obviously wrong. He concluded that the nation's universities must stop using the fact-based arguments that he insisted led to "secularism and collectivism," and instead teach the values of Christianity and individualism. His traditional ideology would create citizens who would vote against the "orthodoxy" of the liberal consensus, he said. Instead, they would create a new orthodoxy of religion and the ideology of free markets.[5]

Buckley and his brother-in-law L. Brent Bozell Jr. inherited a strand of Catholic thought that divided the world into Christians and communists—the latter aided by Jews, according to the antisemites who embraced this theory—who were at war for control of the world.

In their minds, the liberal consensus was operating on the evil side, and they laid out a plan to destroy it. In *McCarthy and His Enemies*, their 1954 book defending Wisconsin senator Joseph McCarthy for his attacks on alleged communists in government, Buckley and Bozell divided America into two groups.[6]

On one hand were the "Liberals," who they insisted were basically communists (they capitalized the word to make it look like the Chinese Communist Party, which was on everyone's mind after its 1949 takeover of China's government). This was not some limited group of conspirators; it was the vast majority of Americans: anyone, Republican or Democrat, who believed that the government should regulate business, protect social welfare, promote infrastructure, and protect civil rights, and who believed in fact-based argument.

On the other hand were the very few people Buckley and Bozell called "conservatives" in an echo of the 1937 Conservative Manifesto. They wanted America to return to the world of the 1920s to protect the ability of businessmen to run the economy as they saw fit. According to Buckley's argument, businessmen could gain the support of religious traditionalists, who were less interested in deregulating business than they were in overturning the trend toward liberal values. Traditionalists thought that liberalism in government undermined religion by weakening traditional family structures and social hierarchies that put men in charge of their families the same way that God oversaw the world. Thus, they believed, the liberal consensus served evil. Government must stand firm behind what they called "free enterprise" and "religion"; those values were not negotiable.

Buckley and Bozell acknowledged that they were trying to overturn the shared belief system that had stabilized the country and that they were doing so on the basis of ideology. This was the opposite of true conservatism, which Edmund Burke had conceived to stand against ideologically based government, and readers at the time noted that the plan was, in fact, radical. It was a political movement, one that would come to be known as "Movement Conservatism."[7]

Most Americans didn't buy it. They knew what businessmen would do to the economy unless they were checked: they had seen people homeless and hungry during the Depression. Americans scoffed at the idea that the New Deal system, which had managed to keep the country afloat during the 1930s and then bankroll World War II, was a bad idea. They looked around at their homes, at the candy-colored cars that they drove on the new interstate highways built under what was at the time the biggest public works project in U.S. history, and at their union-boosted paychecks in a nation with its highest gross domestic production ever, and dismissed the Movement Conservatives as a radical fringe.

But the 1954 *Brown v. Board* decision resurrected the mythological cowboy, now backed by the extraordinary power of television, as a brilliant vehicle for Movement Conservatism. By 1959, there were twenty-six Westerns on TV, and in one week of March 1959, eight of the top shows were Westerns. September 1959 introduced viewers to *Bonanza*, the first television show filmed in color, which sprinted up the charts and went on to run for fourteen seasons. *Bonanza* told the story of Ben Cartwright, a patriarch on a half-million-acre ranch, overseen by his three sons from different mothers, all of whom had died, leaving the hotheaded youngest, Little Joe, played by Michael Landon, motherless at age four. Westerns like *Bonanza* showed a male world of hardworking cowboys protecting their land from evildoers. The cowboys didn't need help from their government; they made their own law with a gun. They even helped keep order in nearby towns that had a government.[8]

Cowboy mythology quickly permeated politics on the right. In 1958, Republican senator Barry Goldwater of Arizona rocketed to prominence after he accused his party's standard-bearer, President

Dwight Eisenhower, of embracing "the siren song of socialism." Goldwater had come from a wealthy background after his family of storekeepers cashed in on the boom of federal money flowing to Arizona dam construction, but he presented himself to the media as a cowboy, telling stories of how his family had come to Arizona when "there was no federal welfare system, no federally mandated employment insurance, no federal agency to monitor the purity of the air, the food we ate, or the water we drank," and how "everything that was done, we did it ourselves." Goldwater opposed the *Brown v. Board* decision and Eisenhower's decision to use troops to desegregate Little Rock Central High School.[9]

In Goldwater, Movement Conservatism and the racist mythology of the post–Civil War years came together. Hoping to boost Goldwater for president in 1960, his supporters hired Bozell to write a position platform for him. Published as a book under Goldwater's name, it was titled *The Conscience of a Conservative*. Joining opposition to the federal defense of civil rights with Movement Conservative hatred of business regulation, it was more than a party platform. It was a general manifesto against the liberal consensus.[10]

Like the 1937 Conservative Manifesto, *The Conscience of a Conservative* defended states' rights against federal power. It also denied the Supreme Court's ability to use the Fourteenth Amendment to protect civil rights or, for that matter, to use the Constitution's Commerce Clause to regulate business. But in 1960, unlike in 1937, those determined to destroy the liberal consensus had racism on their side.

CHAPTER 5

Nixon and the Southern Strategy

D emocrats, too, were trying to figure out how to respond to the nation's shifting ground on race. Goldwater had declined to run for president in 1960, and Republicans turned instead to Eisenhower's vice president, Richard M. Nixon, who lost to Democrat John F. Kennedy. When Kennedy took office in January 1961, his powerful inaugural address called for Americans to rally for a new era, looking back to the Declaration of Independence by promising to bring freedom to the world. But careful observers noted that he didn't mention racial justice at home.[1]

Black veteran James Meredith of Mississippi was a careful observer. He was also "firmly convinced that only a power struggle between the state and the federal government could make it possible for me or anyone else to successfully" enroll, and complete a course of study, at a state university, he later recalled. So he vowed to test the resolve of the young president who talked so inspirationally about the torch being passed "to a new generation of Americans" whom Kennedy described as "unwilling to witness or permit the slow undoing of those human rights to which this nation has always been committed."

The day after Kennedy took office, Meredith started the process of applying to study at the whites-only University of Mississippi. Twice denied admission, Meredith began to work with Medgar Evers, the head of the NAACP in Mississippi, and with the NAACP Legal

Defense and Educational Fund. On May 31, 1961, Meredith sued for admission to the school.

The U.S. Court of Appeals for the Fifth Circuit decided that Meredith had the right to enroll at Ole Miss in fall 1962, putting Kennedy on the spot. He would have to pick between northern urban Democrats who embraced the liberal consensus and southern white supremacists. His attorney general (and brother), Robert F. Kennedy, told him the government had no choice: it must enforce the decision of the Supreme Court requiring racial desegregation.

The Department of Justice ordered the school to register Meredith. Mississippi governor Ross Barnett physically barred Meredith from registering. White supremacists rushed to the campus to "rally to the cause of freedom," as one of their sympathizers, Major General Edwin Walker, said. They became increasingly violent, killing two men, wounding others, and destroying property. After close to a day of rioting, the military arrived and arrested three hundred people, breaking the resistance.

Meredith registered at Ole Miss on October 1. His first class was on American history.

Kennedy had put the muscle of the federal government behind desegregation, and Movement Conservatives promptly called him and his attorney general communists: "The Castro Brothers"—a reference to the communist revolutionaries in Cuba—were at Ole Miss, a bumper sticker read.[2]

That conflation of Black rights and communism stoked such anger in the southern right wing that Kennedy felt obliged to travel to Dallas, Texas, in November 1963 to mend some fences in the state Democratic Party. On the morning of November 22, *The Dallas Morning News* contained a flyer saying the president was wanted for "treason" for "betraying the Constitution" and giving "support and encouragement to the Communist inspired racial riots." Kennedy warned his wife, Jacqueline, that they were "heading into nut country today." They were, and he paid with his life for that attempt to enforce the liberal consensus.[3]

When Meredith returned to Ole Miss for the second semester, he noted that he was doing so not as a Black man but on his own terms as "an American citizen." Meanwhile, those protecting Black rights ramped up their efforts to register voters and to organize communities to support political change in what became known as the "Freedom Summer" of 1964. Because only 6.7 percent of Black Mississippians were registered, Mississippi became a focal point. Under Bob Moses, a New York City teacher who began voting work in Mississippi in 1961, volunteers set out to register voters. Just as they were getting under way, on June 21, three voting rights workers disappeared near Philadelphia, Mississippi. They were James Chaney, 21, a Black organizer from Mississippi; Michael Schwerner, 24, a white Jewish civil rights activist from New York who had sparked the wrath of the local Ku Klux Klan for organizing in Mississippi; and Andrew Goodman, 20, another New York City Jewish civil rights worker, who had arrived in town just the day before, sending a postcard to his parents saying "This is a wonderful town and the weather is fine."[4]

No one knew where they had gone, but no one—except for the white supremacists claiming the men had deliberately gone into hiding to create news—imagined it was anywhere good. President Lyndon B. Johnson, who had stepped into the presidency after Kennedy's murder, and Attorney General Kennedy ordered the Federal Bureau of Investigation (FBI) to find the missing registration workers. They failed to find these three at first, but their search turned up eight murdered Black men, at least two of whom had also been registering voters. As popular rage over the disappearances grew, Johnson pressured Congress to pass the Civil Rights Act of 1964, in part to make it easier to register to vote. He signed the measure into law on July 2.[5]

On July 16, Goldwater struck against government protection for Black rights when he officially launched his 1964 run for the presidency. A little more than three weeks after Chaney, Schwerner, and Goodman disappeared and while they were still missing, Goldwater strode across the stage at the Republican National Convention to accept the nomination. He told delegates that "extremism in the defense of liberty is no vice. And . . . moderation in the pursuit of justice is no virtue."[6]

Prominent South Carolina segregationist senator Strom Thurmond, who had filibustered the 1957 Civil Rights Act, publicly backed Goldwater, and the votes of the delegates from South Carolina were the ones that put his nomination over the top. White delegates to the convention set a Black delegate's coat on fire. Horrified by the turn in the Republican Party, Jackie Robinson, who had been the first Black major league baseball player in generations and faced everything from physical abuse to death threats, later said: "I now believe I know what it felt like to be a Jew in Hitler's Germany."[7]

On August 4 the missing bodies of Chaney, Schwerner, and Goodman were found buried in an earthen dam near Philadelphia, Mississippi. Ku Klux Klan members, at least one of whom was a law enforcement officer, had murdered them.[8]

Those defending the liberal consensus and the power of the federal government to enforce it saw themselves as directly challenging the power of the dangerous Foghorn Leghorns of the South. Three weeks after the men were found, the Democrats nominated Lyndon B. Johnson for president, declaring, "America is One Nation, One People. The welfare, progress, security and survival of each of us reside in the common good . . . [and] democracy . . . rests on the confidence that people can be trusted with freedom." They dismissed "those who traffic in fear, hate, falsehood, and violence" and invited all Americans "who believe that narrow partisanship takes too small account of the size of our task," to vote for Johnson.[9]

They did, by a landslide. Goldwater won only his own state of Arizona and, ominously, five states of the Deep South: Louisiana, Mississippi, Alabama, Georgia, and South Carolina, which had not voted for a Republican since Reconstruction. In those states, white supremacists had kept Black residents from registering to vote.

After the election, Black Americans were determined to bring the voting rights provisions of the Civil Rights Act of 1964 to life. Voting rights activists who had been trying to register voters for years stepped up their efforts. In Selma, Alabama, Black Americans outnumbered white Americans among the 29,500 people who lived there, but the city's voting rolls were 99 percent white. White law enforcement officers regularly harassed and arrested activists. And on February 18, 1965, local police, sheriff's deputies, and Alabama state troopers beat and shot an unarmed twenty-six-year-old, Jimmie Lee Jackson, who was marching for voting rights at a demonstration in his hometown of Marion, Alabama, about twenty-five miles northwest of Selma. Jackson died eight days later.[10]

Hoping to defuse the community's anger, Black leaders in Selma planned a march. They would walk the fifty-four miles from Selma to the state capitol in Montgomery to draw attention to the murder and to voter suppression.

On March 7, 1965, the marchers set out. As they crossed the Edmund Pettus Bridge, named for a Confederate brigadier general, grand dragon of the Alabama Ku Klux Klan, and U.S. senator who stood against Black rights, state troopers and other law enforcement officers met the unarmed marchers with billy clubs, bullwhips, and tear gas. They fractured the skull of young activist John Lewis and beat voting rights leader Amelia Boynton unconscious. A newspaper photograph of the fifty-four-year-old Boynton, seemingly dead in the arms of another marcher, illustrated the depravity of those determined to maintain the nation's racial hierarchy.

Images of "Bloody Sunday" on the national news horrified the country. On March 15, Johnson addressed a nationally televised joint session of Congress to ask for the passage of a national voting rights act. "Their cause must be our cause too," he said. "All of us . . . must overcome the crippling legacy of bigotry and injustice." He paused and then stared sternly ahead. "And we shall overcome."[11]

Two days later, he submitted to Congress proposed voting rights legislation, and on August 6 he signed the Voting Rights Act of 1965. He recalled "the outrage of Selma" when he said, "This right to vote is the basic right without which all others are meaningless. It gives people, people as individuals, control over their own destinies."[12]

The Voting Rights Act authorized federal supervision of voter registration in districts where Black Americans were historically underrepresented. Johnson vowed to uphold the law.

The Democrats' swing behind Black voting orphaned the southern white supremacists like Thurmond who had organized as the Dixiecrats in 1948 and backed Goldwater in 1964. After the Voting Rights Act passed, the most extreme among them organized their own political party behind Alabama governor George Wallace, who in 1963 had called for "segregation now, segregation tomorrow, segregation forever."[13]

But others from the old solid South were open to switching parties. And when he ran for president in 1968, Republican candidate Richard M. Nixon recognized that he needed to win some of those disaffected Democrats in order to have a fighting chance. Embracing what later became known as the "southern strategy," Nixon traveled to South Carolina personally to ask Thurmond to make his switch to the Republican Party permanent. In exchange, he promised to stop using the federal government to enforce desegregation in the states, and to look the other way as southern whites established segregation academies, which were so successful that, in 1974, 3,500 academies in the South enrolled 750,000 white children. As white students left the public schools, funds followed them. The schools educating the remaining students, mostly Black but including a few white children, were left with very few resources.[14]

The southern strategy marked the switch of the parties' positions over the issue of race. Johnson knew what that meant: that the nation's move toward equality would provide a weapon for a certain kind of politician to rise to power. In a hotel in Tennessee after a day spent seeing racial slurs scrawled on signs and an evening of bourbon, Johnson explained the signs to his young aide Bill Moyers: "I'll tell you what's at the bottom of it," he said. "If you can convince the lowest white man he's better than the best colored man, he won't notice you're picking his pocket. Hell, give him somebody to look down on, and he'll empty his pockets for you."[15]

The stage was set, with rhetoric and policy, for the rise of authoritarianism.

CHAPTER 6

Positive Polarization

Courting white supremacists began the process of appealing to voters' fears, effectively dividing the country between allegedly good Americans and those allegedly seeking to destroy it. Nixon's media handlers vowed to reach voters by emotion rather than reason. "Voters are basically lazy," one wrote. "Reason requires a high degree of discipline, of concentration; impression is easier. . . . The emotions are more easily roused, closer to the surface, more malleable."[1]

Those handlers needed to create an "other," and they had an obvious foil not only in Black activism but also in the rise of the New Left in the 1960s. College campuses were flooded with young adults born after World War II—the so-called baby boomers—and many were horrified by the excesses of communism in Joseph Stalin's purges in the Soviet Union and as disgusted by the liberal consensus as the Movement Conservatives were. Witnessing racial turmoil at home and colonial struggles abroad, all the while living under the threat of nuclear war, they had given up hope that workers would ever usher in a more just form of government.

Instead, leaders of the New Left called for "a democracy of individual participation," one that valued individualism and the creativity of work rather than political organization, to overthrow the nation's unjust systems. In 1964, students at the University of California, Berkeley, demanded the right to advocate for racial equality and opposition to direct U.S. involvement in the Vietnam War. On December 2, 1964, more than two thousand students entered Berkeley's Sproul Hall to "put [their] bodies upon the gears and upon the wheels, upon the levers, upon all the apparatus [of the machine] and . . . make it stop."[2]

The deputy district attorney for Alameda County, Edwin Meese III, got authorization from California's governor for a mass arrest of the protesters, and in the early hours of December 4, police arrested about eight hundred students. Berkeley officials eventually backed down and let students set up information tables about various causes on the steps of Sproul Hall, but the image of students occupying the building worried voters who couldn't imagine what had happened to turn America's white, prosperous children into lawbreakers calling for individual expression their parents couldn't fathom. In 1966, Ronald Reagan won the California governorship by promising to "clean up the mess in Berkeley."[3]

In 1968, Nixon's team offered voters a candidate weak on policy but big on carefully curated images of traditional America under siege from "others." His campaign contrasted powerfully with the chaos of the 1968 Democratic National Convention in Chicago, where the New Left squared off against the Democratic establishment. There, in August, Chicago police working for the city's mayor, Richard Daley, covered their badges and launched a "police riot" against the protesters.

Nixon pulled together a coalition of pro-business Republicans, southern racists, traditionalists, and "law and order" voters to win the White House despite the fact that more Americans voted for other candidates than voted for him. *Time* magazine said Nixon's "Middle Americans" prayed, loved America, and hated protesters and the "angry minorities" who got the government's attention while all they got was condescension and tax bills. They worried they were losing their country to liberals, intellectuals, radicals, and defiant youngsters helped by a lying communications industry. They liked traditional family structures and worried about women working outside the home. They liked Goldwater and politicians like Reagan, who promised to end protests even "if it takes a bloodbath."[4]

This polarization of voters led to a logical next step: keeping the government in safe hands meant winning elections, and to win elections it might be necessary to cheat. While he was cultivating a public image as a statesman, behind the scenes Nixon and his men were undermining the peace talks in Vietnam to hurt the Democrats. The notion that members of a presidential campaign had worked with a foreign government to affect an election was so unthinkable that it was not until the 2017 discovery of notes from Nixon aide H. R. Haldeman that longtime rumors became accepted as fact. The logic, though, was simple: if Democrats were dangerous "others," extraordinary measures to keep them from office were justified.[5]

Nixon began his presidential term by trying to appeal to Movement Conservatives without undermining the liberal consensus. But his vague promises of "peace with honor" in Vietnam caught up with him when instead of ending the war, he escalated it. Protesters called him out, and he responded by conflating loyalty to America with loyalty to the president.

In 1947, Congress had passed the National Security Act to concentrate foreign policy and military action in the executive branch, largely cutting out Congress from debates over military intervention overseas. Nixon used that authority to manipulate foreign affairs to solidify domestic support, as Americans tend to rally around the flag during wartime. In November 1969, despite mounting opposition to the increased U.S. presence in Vietnam, he insisted that a "silent majority" agreed with his Vietnam policy. His language tied national pride to a Republican president.[6]

At the end of April 1970, the president announced that he had sent ground troops into Vietnam's neighbor, Cambodia, and protests in the wake of the announcement led to the May shooting of four college students at Ohio's Kent State University. After he clumsily suggested the shooting was the fault of the students themselves, voters in his key demographic—middle-class white Americans—were ready to abandon him.

Before the midterm elections of 1970, it was pretty clear to Nixon's advisors that they needed a Hail Mary plan to rally voters around the increasingly beleaguered president. Patrick Buchanan and Lee Atwater quite deliberately turned against what they called "the media, the left, [and] the liberal academic community," drawing voters to Nixon by accusing their opponents of being lazy, dangerous, and anti-American.

They called their strategy "positive polarization" because it stoked the anger they needed voters to feel in order to bother to show up to vote, a development they saw as good. Buchanan wrote a memo to Nixon urging him to manipulate the media and warning: "We are in a contest over the soul of the country now and the decision will not be some middle compromise—it will be their kind of society or ours."[7]

Nixon's primary scapegoats in 1969 had been anti–Vietnam War protesters and college students, but after Kent State he expanded the list to include Black and Brown Americans and other "special interests" who, Nixon's team insisted, wanted a redistribution of wealth so they wouldn't have to work. On the one hand were hardworking, taxpaying individuals. On the other were "detractors of America"—lazy people who wanted a government handout.[8]

This theme tied into the historical trope about Reconstruction: the idea that minority voting was simply a way to redistribute wealth to the undeserving. It revived an intellectual argument for the backlash against the civil rights movement, and Nixon worked to bring voters who didn't want to think of themselves as old-fashioned bigots to his standard. But the old-fashioned bigots came, too. White Americans opposed to civil rights had resurrected the Confederate battle flag, and in May 1970, Nixon's vice president, Spiro Agnew, attended the dedication ceremony for the Confederate monument at Stone Mountain, Georgia, a project from the Reconstruction years that had been abandoned and then resurrected after *Brown v. Board.*[9]

The administration's strategy of polarizing the country to pick up voters began to shatter the liberal consensus.

In 1971, lawyer Lewis Powell wrote a confidential memo for the U.S. Chamber of Commerce warning that corporate America needed to work harder to counter the liberal consensus and defend what he called "free enterprise." Angry that activists like Ralph Nader had forced safety regulations onto automobile manufacturers and the tobacco industry, he believed that businessmen were losing their right to run their businesses however they wished. Any attack on "the enterprise system," he wrote, was "a threat to individual freedom."

Powell believed that business interests needed to advance their principles "aggressively" in universities, the media, religion, politics—and the courts. "The judiciary," he wrote, "may be the most important instrument for social, economic and political change." He wrote that civil rights activists and "left" institutions like the American Civil Liberties Union (ACLU) and labor unions were winning cases that hurt business. "It is time for American business—which has demonstrated the greatest capacity in all history to produce and to influence consumer decisions—to apply its great talents vigorously to the preservation of the system itself."[10]

The following year, Nixon appointed Powell to the Supreme Court. While Justice Powell proved to be far more moderate and consensus minded than lawyer Powell, what he had advocated came to pass: right-wing organizations began to push against the liberal consensus. The Heritage Foundation, the Hoover Institution, the

American Enterprise Institute, the United States Chamber of Commerce, the Business Roundtable, and the National Association of Manufacturers all began to argue that the economic dislocations of the 1970s could be laid at the door of regulation and taxation and that the country demanded "market-based" solutions.

In that same year, Nixon turned the issue of abortion into another political wedge. Abortion was not yet legal nationally, but it had been decriminalized in many states in the 1960s after U.S. doctors called attention to the deadly health crisis of 200,000 to 1.2 million illegal abortions annually. By 1971, even the evangelical Southern Baptist Convention agreed that abortion should be legal in some cases, and by 1972, Gallup pollsters reported that 64 percent of Americans agreed that abortion should be between a woman and her doctor. Sixty-eight percent of Republicans, who had always liked family planning, agreed, as did 59 percent of Democrats. In 1970, Nixon had directed U.S. military hospitals to perform abortions regardless of state law.

Worried that Nixon would lose reelection, Pat Buchanan saw an opportunity to attract antiabortion Catholic Democrats, and at his urging, the president in 1971 reversed course, citing a personal belief "in the sanctity of human life—including the life of the yet unborn."

Nixon's supporters used abortion to stand in for women's rights in general, which were under assault in the Southern Baptist Convention as fundamentalists were working to take over the largest Protestant denomination in the U.S. In her first public comment on abortion, activist Phyllis Schlafly said: "Women's lib is a total assault on the role of the American woman as wife and mother and on the family as the basic unit of society. Women's libbers are trying to make wives and mothers unhappy with their career. . . . They are promoting Federal 'day-care centers' for babies instead of homes. They are promoting abortions instead of families."[11]

This sleight of hand rhetorically turned those who embraced the liberal consensus and its defense of equal rights for women into anti-family agitators.

By 1972, Nixon had so internalized his own division of the nation into good and bad Americans that he became convinced that he must win the election to save America. (And possibly he worried that if he lost, his people's undermining of the Vietnam peace talks in 1968 would be exposed.) The Committee to Re-elect the President—aptly nick-named CREEP as its operations came to light—embarked on a course of campaign sabotage. They planted fake letters in newspapers, hired vendors for Democratic rallies and then ran out on the unpaid bills, planted spies in opponents' camps, and tapped opponents' phones. Young operative Roger Stone claimed to be a socialist as he donated to one of Nixon's Republican challengers, then took the donation receipt to a reporter as proof that the opponent was a tool of the political left. One of their legal advisors called their methods "ratf*cking."[12]

Their actions came to light on June 17, 1972, when security guard Frank Wills at the fashionable Watergate office complex found a door propped open and called the police. They caught five burglars bugging the headquarters of the Democratic National Committee.

The Watergate story didn't really catch on until after the election, so Nixon's divisive approach to politics worked in the short term. He won the 1972 election with an astonishing 60.7 percent of the popular vote and by 520 to 17 in the Electoral College. After the election, the involvement of key figures in his administration in the Watergate break-in gradually came to light, and Nixon's cover-up of the attempt to rig the election shocked the nation, including members of his own party. On August 9, 1974, Nixon became the first—and, so far, only—president to resign.

But while Nixon paid a price for his attempt to cheat in an election, his division of the world into good and evil began to take hold, perverting American politics by convincing his loyalists that putting their people in office was imperative, no matter what it took. Watergate eventually backfired on them, but Nixon's people had more luck when they experimented with "ratf*cking" elections in other countries.

Under Nixon, the U.S. launched a successful operation in Chile that would be a laboratory for overturning a democratically elected leader without leaving obvious fingerprints. When voters in Chile elected moderate socialist Salvador Allende to the presidency there, Nixon's administration worked with the Central Intelligence Agency (CIA) to promote a nationwide truckers' strike that lasted twenty-six days in fall 1972 and started a labor crisis for the new president. Right-wing dictator Augusto Pinochet seized power in September 1973. The United States supported his reign of terror, including his infamous practice of throwing opponents out of helicopters.

Nixon operative Roger Stone, who had a picture of Nixon tattooed on his back, later told a reporter: "What I admire about Nixon was his resilience. . . . It's attack, attack, attack."[13]

CHAPTER 7

The Reagan Revolution

I n 1974, most Americans thought they had put Nixon and his crimes behind them, but six years after Nixon resigned, Ronald Reagan would travel the road to the White House that Goldwater and Nixon had paved. This would include sabotaging the previous administration's efforts at diplomacy, in this case delaying the release of fifty-two American diplomats and private citizens being held hostage in Iran.[1] He would also use Nixon's rhetorical strategy to continue the process of rolling back the liberal consensus and re-creating a nation based on the idea that some people are better than others.

A big fan of Goldwater, Reagan had been an actor, and he honed Nixon's rhetoric with a soft voice and made-up stories that pitted hardworking white men against a grasping government that served "special interests" and nonexistent Black people living it up on the taxpayer's dime. His language brought together images of race and class that Movement Conservatives had taken from the Reconstruction years. He promised to defend hardworking white Americans and cultivated an image of himself as a cowboy, with the antigovernment, racist, and traditionalist saddlebags that image carried.

Reagan had been an early supporter of William F. Buckley Jr.'s *National Review*, which promised to "tell the violated businessman's side of the story." Much as Buckley advocated, Reagan constructed a world based on a deliberately false image of people who believed in using the government to create an equitable society, especially Democrats.[2]

Movement Conservatives described the U.S. as if it were in dire economic straits, but that image was rooted in racial and cultural complaints rather than in reality. In fact, the economy had boomed in the 1950s and continued to grow in the 1960s, with the Dow Jones Industrial Average—a common way of measuring the stock market—breaking 1,000 for the first time in January 1966. Stocks continued to rise. Economic growth, along with the new social welfare programs, meant that the poverty rate fell fast: from 1959 to 1966, the number of people living below the poverty line fell from 39 million to 30 million even as the population grew by about 2.5 million a year.

The picture was not uniformly rosy. Family income for all Americans trended upward, but the gaps between Black and white families were still wide—in 1968, Black families made only about 59 percent of the income of white families, though that ratio was declining. At the same time, corporate mergers were wiping out small businesses, and manufacturing was moving to the South or overseas. This change was hollowing out northern industrial cities, frustrating the Black Americans who had moved to cities in the past decades, and workers in general.[3]

Attempting to address persistent inequality and urged on by the New Left, Democratic leadership sought to include more voices directly in their party apparatus. After the 1968 debacle at their national convention, a committee concluded that the party must work to include minorities and women at the national level.[4]

But that doubling down on inclusion helped Movement Conservatives to court white workers who had been left behind by the changing economy. They painted the Democrats as a party of grievance and special interests who simply wanted to pay off lazy supporters, rather than being interested in the good of America as a whole.

Manufacturing jobs continued to disappear, driving unemployment upward, just as inflation soared because of the massive cost of the Vietnam War and new social programs, as well as the oil embargo launched against the U.S. by the Organization of Petroleum Exporting Countries. Suddenly, the economic model of the liberal consensus could be interpreted as a grave error.

In his campaign for president in 1980, Reagan, whose advisors included some of Nixon's, such as Paul Manafort and Roger Stone, spun the story of a "welfare queen" from the South Side of Chicago—code words for "Black"—who lived large on government benefits she stole. Reagan launched his presidential candidacy at Philadelphia, Mississippi, sixteen years and three miles from where civil rights workers James Chaney, Andrew Goodman, and Michael Schwerner had been found murdered by members of the Ku Klux Klan. "I believe in states' rights," Reagan said, and the Republican platform promised to protect the private segregation academies organized to prevent desegregation.[5]

Reagan's coalition also picked up those traditionalists appalled by the growing public role of American women. In 1974, the cowboy Little Joe of *Bonanza* had turned into Pa Ingalls in the popular television series *Little House on the Prairie*, which would stay on the air until 1982. Played by actor Michael Landon, Pa was a benevolent patriarch who loved and cared for his wife and daughters while they lived homebound and moral lives.

The series echoed the hugely popular books by Laura Ingalls Wilder, which had been shaped and edited by her daughter, libertarian Rose Wilder Lane, to be an anti–New Deal screed. The real life of the Ingalls family was one in which the women and girls—not Pa—supported the family, and the West depended on the federal government. But the image of the traditionalist family gripped the country; prairie dresses were the rage in the late 1970s.[6]

Reagan also married the Republican Party and Movement Conservatism to right-wing religious groups. By 1979 the fundamentalists had successfully taken over the Southern Baptist Convention, electing their candidate to be its president. Under him, the Southern Baptists abandoned their previous willingness to include women and minorities and to support reproductive rights. They became active in politics, staunchly supporting the Republican Party, and in the 1980s numbered about fifteen million people. A televangelist, Reverend Jerry Falwell, formed the Moral Majority, and Reagan made it clear he was one of their number.

As it gathered those angry at the modern world, Reagan's campaign invited voters to remember a time before Black and Brown voices and women began to claim equal rights. His campaign passed out buttons and posters urging voters to "make America great again."[7]

Democratic president Jimmy Carter, who was running for reelection, accurately challenged Reagan's record, but the press bought into Movement Conservatives' complaints that they were victims of a "liberal media." That term originally referred to a media that required fact-based argument, but it quickly became a code word for political bias.

When Carter called out the racism in Reagan's states' rights speech, the press attacked him for being mean, although the Mississippi Republican chair had deliberately set up an appearance at the Neshoba County Fair to attract George Wallace's pro-segregation voters. More powerfully, in a late October debate, when Carter accurately explained Reagan's opposition to Medicare and Social Security, Reagan retorted with sarcastic weariness, "There you go again." The quip became shorthand for the idea that Reagan's opponents were scolds or were exaggerating when they cited facts.[8]

The campaign worked. Voters put Reagan into the White House. In his inaugural address, he promised to protect "a special interest group that has been too long neglected: 'We the people,' this breed called Americans." He warned that "in the present crisis, government is not the solution to our problem, government is the problem."[9]

After years of rhetoric, the Reagan administration set out to unwind the laws that had brought the liberal consensus of the post–World War II years to life.

Reagan's belief in "supply-side economics" overturned the economic justification of the liberal consensus, which was based on the idea that helping poorer people, those on the "demand side," would expand the economy. Instead, Reagan's people argued that cutting taxes on wealthier Americans would free up capital for them to reinvest in businesses that would, in turn, hire more American workers. A rising tide would lift all boats. They promised that their new booming economy would produce record amounts of tax money and thus would pay for itself. According to this theory, voters could have both low taxes and expanded services.

It was an extraordinarily attractive theory, but when the computers at the Office of Management and Budget projected that rather than balancing the budget, Reagan's proposed cuts would create budget deficits of up to $116 billion by 1984, Reagan's budget director, David Stockman, simply reprogrammed the computers. "None of us really understands what's going on with all these numbers," he told a reporter. "The whole thing is premised on faith," he explained, "on a belief about how the world works."[10]

That faith was divorced from reality, and the gap between ideology and reality would only get wider over time. By every measure, 1981 marked a dramatic change in the distribution of American wealth. From the beginning of the New Deal in 1933 until the election of Reagan in 1980, while the economy expanded dramatically for all, the gap between rich and poor in America got smaller. Economists call this "the great compression." In the years after 1981, the economy continued to grow, but wealth moved dramatically upward in what's known as "the great divergence."

Massive tax cuts in 1981 and 1986 cut top income tax rates from

70 percent to 30 percent, cut estate taxes, and cut windfall profit taxes. At the same time, the administration slashed spending on public welfare programs while pouring money into defense spending, raising it from $267.1 billion in 1980 to $393.1 billion in 1988, from 22.7 percent of public expenditure to 27.3 percent.

The national debt tripled from $738 billion to $2.1 trillion, turning the United States from the world's largest creditor nation to the world's largest debtor nation. But that huge government spending— for the military now, rather than for social welfare programs—boosted the economy effectively enough that Republicans claimed their system worked. The jobs their spending created, though, were in defense, where minority workers had less traction.[11]

Although Black and Brown Americans, women, and organized workers warned they were falling behind, American voters reelected Reagan in 1984. But they did not give Republicans control of Congress. Indeed, they left Democrats with a commanding majority in the House of Representatives and switched two Senate seats to the Democrats, although Republicans still held the Senate. The American people appeared to be turning against the Reagan experiment: in 1986, Democrats picked up five seats in the House and eight in the Senate, regaining control of the upper chamber.

So the administration increased the volume of Movement Conservative rhetoric, using new microphones to amplify their message.

In 1987, members of the Federal Communications Commission appointed by Reagan ended the Fairness Doctrine, which had protected public information since the earliest days of radio, in the 1920s. In order to get a public license, a radio station had to agree to present information honestly and fairly and to balance different points of view. Movement Conservatives demanded an end to the Fairness Doctrine so they could push their ideology of "individualism" and Christianity.[12]

Reagan's FCC obliged just as the higher quality of FM radio had sent AM radio operators searching for profitable new formats. Those operators turned to talk radio, whose hosts soon realized that shocking political talk won listeners. By 1988, hosts like Rush Limbaugh had gone national. His attacks on "feminazis," liberals, and Black Americans and his insistence that socialism was creeping through America attracted like-minded listeners. Their opponents, who were portrayed as the country's enemies, kept their heads down.

The 1988 presidential election demonstrated the growing hold that Movement Conservative thinking had over the Republican Party. The party's nominee, Vice President George H. W. Bush, who had generally embraced the liberal consensus, capitulated to the extremist faction of the party when his poll numbers fell seventeen points below those of his Democratic opponent, Massachusetts governor Michael Dukakis. Bush's campaign manager, former Nixon operative Lee Atwater, and media advisor Roger Ailes, who had promoted Nixon in 1968, produced the infamous Willie Horton ad, laying the groundwork for a new kind of right-wing television in which ideological propaganda would be filmed as if it were a news story, making it hard for viewers to tell the difference.

The ad showed a mug shot of Horton, a Black criminal who had been allowed out of prison for a weekend and, while out, had raped a white woman and stabbed her boyfriend. Although Horton had been released under a program established by Dukakis's Republican predecessor, the narrative of a Democrat putting white people at risk to cater to Black criminals overrode reality. (Making amends at the end of his life, Atwater apologized for the "naked cruelty" of his actions and acknowledged that Bush won handily "in part because of our successful manipulation of his campaign themes.")[13]

Bush also allowed Atwater and his allies Roger Stone and Paul Manafort to tar Dukakis for obeying the law by refusing to require teachers to lead students in saying the Pledge of Allegiance. Dukakis pointed out that his state supreme court had advised against it on the basis of a U.S. Supreme Court ruling. But Bush attacked him anyway.

Once in office, Bush tried to regain control of the party, but its weight had shifted irrevocably. In 1990, GOPAC, the Republican state and local political training organization under the direction of Georgia representative Newt Gingrich, distributed a memo titled "Language: A Key Mechanism of Control" to elected Republicans. The paper urged them to refer to Democrats with words like *corrupt, cheat, disgrace, endanger, failure, hypocrisy, intolerant, liberal, lie, pathetic, sick, steal, traitors, waste, welfare,* and *abuse of power.*[14]

In 1992, after losing a presidential bid, talk show host and former Goldwater speechwriter Pat Buchanan gave a barn-burning speech at the Republican National Convention in Houston. He credited Reagan both with creating a booming economy and with winning the Cold War. In contrast, he denigrated Democrats as "liberals and radicals" who engaged in "the greatest single exhibition of cross-dressing in American political history" when they called themselves "moderates and centrists." He attacked "the discredited liberalism of the 1960s and the failed liberalism of the 1970s," claiming that Democrats wanted "unrestricted abortion on demand" and "homosexual rights" and that they objected to religious schools and supported "radical feminism."

There was a "culture war" under way, Buchanan said: "My friends, this election is about more than who gets what. It is about who we are. It is about what we believe, and what we stand for as Americans. There is a religious war going on in this country. It is a cultural war, as critical to the kind of nation we shall be as was the Cold War itself, for this war is for the soul of America." In his telling, American values centered not on democracy, but on "freedom." "And in that struggle for the soul of America," Buchanan made clear, Democrats were the enemy and Republicans were on the side of the angels.[15]

Republicans had created an underclass of Americans increasingly falling behind economically. And, crucially, they had given that underclass someone to hate.

CHAPTER 8

Skewing the System

There was a key psychological advantage to the rhetoric that turned Democrats into the enemy: it put Democrats on defense, forcing them to explain themselves instead of counter their opponents. This made it easier for the Republican Party, captured now by Movement Conservatives, to skew the nation's political system in their favor. Reagan's people had to reckon with the reality that Americans liked the liberal consensus, and Republicans could not win control of Congress to put their vision into place. Disillusioned when voters refused to embrace the ideology that seemed so fundamental to them, they began to weaken the actual mechanics of democracy.

In 1986, concerned that voters in the future might overturn their tax cuts, Republicans took a more proactive approach to mobilizing their evangelical support. Chamber of Commerce economist Grover Norquist formally brought together Nixon's alliance of big business, evangelicals, and social conservatives into Americans for Tax Reform. "Traditional Republican business groups can provide the resources, but these groups can provide the votes," he said.[1]

While the votes he was marshaling were for tax cuts and pro-business legislation, Republicans usually defended those measures in terms of family values. Activist Phyllis Schlafly, for example, protested vehemently against tax deductions for poor families, because such a benefit was "just an idea of liberal bureaucrats who want to redistribute the wealth." Deductions were "anti-growth" and therefore "anti-family" by definition.[2]

Republicans also started talking of "ballot integrity" measures that party operatives privately hoped would knock Black voters off the rolls. When Americans elected a Democratic president, Bill Clinton, to the White House in 1992, Republicans' sense of mission escalated. After Democrats made it easier to register to vote by passing the so-called Motor Voter Act in 1993, permitting voters to register at certain state offices, Republicans accused them of turning to "illegal," usually immigrant, voters.

Republican candidates who lost in the 1994 midterm elections began to claim that Democrats had won only through "voter fraud." In 1996, Republicans in both the House and the Senate launched yearlong investigations into what they insisted were problematic elections, one in Louisiana and one in California. Ultimately, they turned up nothing, but keeping the cases in front of the media for a year helped to convince Americans that Democratic voter fraud was a serious issue.

The House began to talk of passing a voter identification law, but the Florida legislature beat them to it. After a corrupt 1997 Miami mayoral race between a Republican and an Independent, the Florida legislature passed a law that purged up to a hundred thousand Black voters, presumed to be Democrats, from the system. This purge paid off in 2000 when Democratic presidential candidate Albert Gore Jr., running against Republican George W. Bush, won the popular vote by more than half a million votes but was four votes short of a win in the Electoral College. The contest came down to Florida, where a confusing ballot siphoned off to far-right Reform Party candidate Pat Buchanan about ten thousand votes meant for Gore.

A hand recount had reduced Bush's lead from 1,784 to 537 when Republican operatives—with the approval of Bush advisor and longtime Republican establishment figure James Baker, and including Roger Stone—attacked the recount venue in Miami-Dade County to stop the recount. As the "Brooks Brothers riot" made clear, Republicans now saw politics as a street fight for victory. Black voters who had been kept from the polls recognized that what was happening was a Jim Crow confrontation, but Democratic leaders tried to preserve the calm reason of the democratic system.[3]

They lost. The Supreme Court—led by five Republican-appointed justices and headed by Chief Justice William Rehnquist, who started in politics by questioning Black voters at Arizona polling sites in the 1960s—stepped in to decide the winner. Later, after widespread reports of irregularities, an investigation by the United States Commission on Civil Rights revealed "an extraordinarily high and inexcusable level of disenfranchisement," primarily of Democratic African American voters. Republicans' work to reduce voting under cover of "voter fraud" and then taking to the streets to sway the courts by creating chaos had given them the White House.[4]

The country was shifting away from democracy in other ways, too. In February 1986, Samuel A. Alito, a thirty-five-year-old lawyer for the Office of Legal Counsel in the Department of Justice, offered up a plan to revise the lawmaking power the Constitution gave to Congress, giving the president more authority. He claimed that the president should not simply sign or veto a law passed by Congress, but shape the law as he wished.

Alito proposed the use of "signing statements" to give the president the power to "interpret" the laws. He recognized that this idea would be controversial, so he proposed beginning by quietly establishing a precedent that would "convince the courts that Presidential signing statements are valuable interpretive tools." He acknowledged that Congress would not welcome this "new type of signing statement," because it would increase the power of the president relative to

Congress and would give the president the last word on the interpretation of laws.[5]

The next year, on September 29, 1987, Reagan attached a signing statement to a debt bill, declaring his right to interpret it as he wished, saying the president could not be forced "to follow the orders of a subordinate." While few people paid attention to it, this statement was a shot across the bow of American democracy. It advanced the theory of the unitary executive, which says that because the president is the head of one of the three unique branches of government, any oversight of that office, by Congress, for example, or the courts, is unconstitutional. Presidents since George Washington had accepted congressional oversight of the government; Republicans were setting up the idea that a president could act alone.

Meanwhile, Republicans also turned their attention to the courts. Since the 1950s, the Supreme Court had used the Fourteenth Amendment to apply the first ten amendments to the Constitution to the state governments, outlawing racial discrimination, laws prohibiting married couples from buying birth control, and, in 1973, laws prohibiting abortions in the first trimester of a pregnancy.

Opponents of these decisions insisted that the court was engaging in "judicial activism," taking away from voters in the states the right to make their own decisions about how society should work. They said that justices were "legislating from the bench" and insisted that the national government can do nothing that is not explicitly written in the 1787 Constitution. This would mean it cannot regulate business, provide a social safety net, promote infrastructure, or protect civil rights, all hallmarks of the liberal consensus.

Reagan's attorney general, Edwin Meese, said he planned to "institutionalize the Reagan revolution so it can't be set aside no matter what happens in future presidential elections" and began to examine candidates for judgeship for their ideological purity. In 1986, Reagan nominated Antonin Scalia, the intellectual leader of these "original-ists," for the Supreme Court, and the following year he signaled his determination to overturn the liberal consensus when he nominated to the Supreme Court extremist Robert Bork.[6]

Bork had called the ban on whites-only lunch counters "unsur-passed ugliness." Massachusetts senator Ted Kennedy, a Democrat, warned that "Robert Bork's America is a land in which women would be forced into back-alley abortions, Blacks would sit at segregated lunch counters, rogue police could break down citizens' doors in mid-night raids, schoolchildren could not be taught about evolution, writ-ers and artists could be censored at the whim of the Government, and the doors of the Federal courts would be shut on the fingers of millions of citizens for whom the judiciary is—and is often the only—protector of the individual rights that are the heart of our democracy." Bork was so extreme that six Republicans joined Democrats in rejecting his ap-pointment to the Supreme Court, but the Republican push to stack the courts was under way.[7]

Reagan's team advanced their flirtation with authoritarianism through foreign affairs. The 1947 National Security Act brought to-gether the U.S. Army, Navy, and Air Force under the Department of Defense and established the National Security Council to advise the president on national security and foreign policy. The NSC included the president, vice president, secretary of state, secretary of the trea-sury, secretary of energy, the attorney general, the president's chief of staff, the chair of the Joint Chiefs of Staff, and other senior advisors. It centered foreign policy in the White House and made much of it secret.

Nixon's advisors had taken advantage of this secrecy in their sup-port for Pinochet in Chile as well as their actions in Vietnam, Laos, and Cambodia. They had also insisted that supporting America in the world required supporting the president.

In 1985, Reagan launched his own experiment in promoting American "freedom" overseas. Six years before, the socialist Sandinista National Liberation Front won control of the Nicaraguan government. Afraid that communism would spread across Latin America and seeing the struggle as a proxy battleground in the Cold War with the Soviet Union, Congress began to fund the Contras, an opposition group. Quickly, though, congressional Democrats came to oppose U.S. meddling in another country's political system and noted that the Contras, whom Reagan called "the moral equal of our Founding Fathers," were no prizes: their tactics included kidnapping, rape, arson, and murder. In 1985, Congress prohibited any further aid to the Contras.

But members of Reagan's National Security Council ignored the new law. Using a plan concocted by Lieutenant Colonel Oliver North, an evangelical military aide to National Security Council advisor John Poindexter, the administration illegally sold arms to Iran and funneled the profits to the Contras.

When the story of the Iran-Contra affair broke in November 1986, government officials were unrepentant. They continued to break the law, shredding documents that Congress had subpoenaed. Democrats condemned the administration's "secrecy, deception, and disdain for the law," but to many Republicans, North was the face of what America should be: a strong, moral man taking military action to spread American freedom over the objections of socialist-sympathizing Democrats. Rather than condemning North, they questioned the patriotism of the investigating committee's chair, Senator Daniel Inouye, who had lost his right arm in World War II fighting in a Nisei combat unit.

Fourteen administration officials were indicted and eleven convicted in the Iran-Contra affair, but on the advice of his attorney general, William Barr, George H. W. Bush—himself implicated in the scandal—pardoned them before he left office in 1992. Lawrence

Walsh, the independent prosecutor in the case, worried that the pardons weakened American democracy. They "undermine . . . the principle . . . that no man is above the law," he said. "It demonstrates that powerful people with powerful allies can commit serious crimes in high office, deliberately abusing the public trust without consequences."[8]

CHAPTER 9

A New Global Project

On December 25, 1991, Soviet president Mikhail Gorbachev resigned, marking the end of the Union of Soviet Socialist Republics. The fall of the USSR meant the end of the Cold War, and those Americans who had come to define the world as a fight between the dark forces of communism and the good forces of capitalism believed their ideology of radical individualism had triumphed. With the USSR vanquished, they set out to destroy what they saw as socialist ideology at home.

The breakup of the Soviet Union gave political operatives and the politicians in the United States for whom they worked a new, crucial tool to undermine American democracy: money, and lots of it, from international authoritarians, especially those from Russia and other former republics of the USSR. Republican politicians and foreign authoritarians began to make alliances over money, influence, and plots to gain power.

Since the 1980s, authoritarian governments had figured out they could score U.S. foreign aid by claiming they were standing against communists. Political consultants Charles Black, Paul Manafort, and Roger Stone, who had come together in 1980 to work on Ronald Reagan's campaign, racked up clients by touting their connections to the Reagan and Bush administrations. They represented so many authoritarian governments—in Nigeria, Kenya, Zaire, Equatorial Guinea, Saudi Arabia, and Somalia, among others—that a 1992 report from the Center for Public Integrity called their firm the Torturers' Lobby. They brought under one roof lobbying and political consulting as well as public relations. Bundling these functions was groundbreaking: they would get their clients elected and then help other clients lobby them.[1]

As oligarchs began to take over former Soviet republics, the ties between oligarchical methods and the American political system grew. Oligarchs looked to park illicit money in Western democracies, where the rule of law would protect their investments, and they favored the Republicans who championed their hierarchical view of the world. For their part, Republican politicians focused on spreading capitalism rather than democracy, arguing that the two went hand in hand.

At home, Republicans set out to vanquish the liberal consensus once and for all. As anti-tax crusader Grover Norquist wrote in *The Wall Street Journal*: "For 40 years conservatives fought a two-front battle against statism, against the Soviet empire abroad and the American left at home. Now the Soviet Union is gone and conservatives can redeploy. And this time, the other team doesn't have nuclear weapons."[2]

In the 1990s, Movement Conservatives turned their firepower on those they considered insufficiently committed to free enterprise, including traditional Republicans who agreed with Democrats that the government should regulate the economy, provide a basic social safety net, promote infrastructure, and protect civil rights.

Their first public victim was President George H. W. Bush, who had come to office from the traditional wing of the party and set out during his presidency to repair the holes cut in the country's fabric by Reagan's supply-side economics.

Bush was willing to raise taxes to address the $2.1 trillion debt Reagan had run up in his eight years in office. These tax hikes drew the fury of Movement Conservatives, who called him, and other traditional Republicans, "Republicans in name only," or RINOs, who were helping to bring "socialism" to America. Republican lawmakers moved further right, and those openly supporting the liberal consensus disappeared from party leadership.

Their primary target, though, was Democrats, who had frustrated Movement Conservatives once again in 1992 by putting former Arkansas governor Bill Clinton into the White House. James Johnson, who was from Arkansas and had stood fervently against the integration of Little Rock's Central High School in 1957, called Clinton a "queer-mongering, whore-hopping adulterer; a baby-killing, draft-dodging, dope-tolerating, lying, two-faced, treasonous activist." Surely such a man was not a legitimate president. In 1996, the Fox News Channel debuted on cable television, joining right-wing radio talk show hosts to feed the idea that their political opponents were socialists trying to destroy the country.[3]

Clinton frustrated right-wing ideologues not just with his domestic positions but also because they thought he did not push American ideology hard enough overseas in the wake of the Cold War. In 1997, political commentator William Kristol and scholar Robert Kagan brought together Dick Cheney, Donald Rumsfeld, and other neoconservatives, or "neocons," to insist that the United States should significantly increase defense spending and lead the world.

Key to their Project for the New American Century was the removal of Iraq's president Saddam Hussein from power because they believed he was destabilizing the Middle East. Iraq had allied with the USSR during the Cold War, and when in 1990 it invaded its smaller neighbor Kuwait, U.K. prime minister Margaret Thatcher had convinced President H. W. Bush to bring together an international coalition of thirty-nine countries to impose sanctions on Iraq and to stop Saddam from occupying and absorbing Kuwait.

Acting under Article 51 of the United Nations charter, which permits "collective self-defense," they did so. But after accomplishing that goal, they honored the charter and declined to topple Saddam. To the neocons' chagrin, the next president didn't seem to get the point either: the U.S. must "challenge regimes hostile to our interests and values," they said, and "promote the cause of political and economic freedom abroad."[4]

Saddam was out of reach until September 11, 2001, when nineteen al-Qaeda terrorists, inspired by Saudi exile Osama bin Laden, flew airplanes into the Twin Towers of the World Trade Center in New York City and the Pentagon outside Washington, D.C., and were on course to hit the U.S. Capitol before that plane's passengers crashed the plane into a Pennsylvania field. Neocons saw the attack as an opportunity to "hit" Saddam Hussein, although he had not been involved in the attack. Fifteen of the terrorists were from Saudi Arabia, two from the United Arab Emirates, one from Lebanon, and one from Egypt; they were operating out of Afghanistan, where the ruling extremist Islamic government—the Taliban—permitted al-Qaeda to have a foothold.[5]

President George W. Bush launched rocket attacks on the Taliban government, successfully overthrowing it before the end of the year. And then the administration undertook to reorder the Middle East in America's image. In 2002, it announced the Bush Doctrine, saying that the U.S. would preemptively strike nations suspected of planning attacks on the U.S. Then in 2003, after setting up a pro-American government in Afghanistan, the administration invaded Iraq.

But the Iraq War was not popular at home, and its unpopularity pushed the administration to equate supporting the Republicans with defending the nation against Islamic terrorists. That rhetorical strategy permitted them to strengthen the power of the president over Congress, most dramatically over the issue of "enhanced interrogation techniques," more popularly known as torture, which in 2002 the administration began using against suspected terrorists. Although the U.S. had traditionally considered torture illegal, the administration now argued that any limit to the president's authority to conduct war was unconstitutional. When news of the program broke in 2004, Congress outlawed it, only to have Bush issue a signing statement rejecting any limitation on "the unitary executive branch."[6]

Meanwhile, the shared ideas and interests among rising global elites began to create a tangled web of money laundering, influence peddling, and antidemocratic plots that festered in foreign governments and infected the United States. In 1996, Paul Manafort managed the Republican National Convention, and by 2003, he and his partner, Richard (Rick) Davis, were representing pro-Russia Ukrainian oligarch Viktor Yanukovych. In July 2004, U.S. journalist Paul Klebnikov was murdered in Moscow for exposing Russian government corruption; a year later, Manafort proposed working for Russian president Vladimir Putin's government in former Soviet republics, Europe, and the United States by influencing politics, business dealings, and news coverage. In 2008, Davis was the director of Republican presidential nominee John McCain's campaign, and McCain celebrated his seventieth birthday with Davis and Russian oligarch Oleg Deripaska on a Russian yacht at anchor in the Balkan country of Montenegro.[7]

McCain was well-known for promising to stand up to Putin, and his running mate Sarah Palin's claim that she could counter the growing power of Russia in part because "they're our next-door neighbors, and you can actually see Russia from land here in Alaska, from an island in Alaska" became a long-running joke (the comment about seeing Russia from her house came from a *Saturday Night Live* spoof). But observers noted that some of McCain's political advisors were backing the Kremlin's interests, including Russia's extension of control over Montenegro.

Steve Schmidt, a campaign advisor who was fiercely loyal to Mc-Cain, explained, "There were two factions in the campaign . . . a pro-democracy faction and . . . a pro Russia faction," led by Davis. Like Manafort, Davis had a residence in New York City's Trump Tower, owned by one of the first clients Black, Manafort, and Stone had taken on in 1980: a New York City real estate developer named Donald J. Trump.[8]

Increasingly, Republican politicians seemed to be operating on the old hierarchical idea that some people were better than others and should direct the economy, society, and politics, and they maintained that control by advancing a false narrative for their supporters that cast their opponents as enemies of the country. In 2004, having manufactured information meant to justify the invasion of Iraq, the Bush administration was deeply entrenched in that ideology, no matter what the facts showed. A senior advisor to Bush disdainfully told journalist Ron Suskind that people like him—Suskind—were in "the reality-based community": they believed people could find solutions based on their observations and careful study of discernible reality.

But, the aide continued, such a worldview was obsolete. "That's not the way the world really works anymore. . . . We are an empire now, and when we act, we create our own reality. And while you're studying that reality—judiciously, as you will—we'll act again, creating other new realities, which you can study too, and that's how things will sort out. We're history's actors . . . and you, all of you, will be left to just study what we do."[9]

CHAPTER 10

Illegitimate Democracy

n the 2008 election, Republican presidential candidate John McCain of Arizona tried to present himself as a maverick who rejected the extremes of his party, but his running mate, Sarah Palin, deliberately catered to a rising tide of populism. She accused Democratic presidential candidate Barack Obama of "palling around with terrorists," and right-wing media, especially the Fox News Channel, ran with the idea. They insisted that Obama, who was born in Hawaii to an American mother and a father of British and Kenyan citizenship, was not an American or born in the U.S.[1]

In fact, both his mother's citizenship and his birth in the U.S. made Obama a U.S. citizen, and his campaign provided a copy of his birth certificate. But the suggestion that Obama was not a legitimate president brought together racism, religion, and the Republicans' long-standing argument that Democrats were "socialists," the tag they used for anyone who supported the liberal consensus.

Although voters handily elected Obama and his vice president, Joe Biden of Delaware, the lie simmered in right-wing media, springing back to life in 2011 when Manafort client Donald Trump, considering entering the presidential race, began getting media coverage by pushing the so-called Birther conspiracy. Trump demanded to know why Obama wouldn't show his birth certificate—when in fact he had—and kept the story alive by feeding the media a series of "facts" that were, in fact, all false. Echoing the ways in which Republicans had bolstered the voter fraud narrative in the 1990s through "investigations," Trump claimed to have hired investigators to find the real story.

Republicans treated the biracial president with disdain. In September 2009, Obama addressed a joint session of Congress to discuss his plan for health care reform, a plan that later became the Affordable Care Act. When he stated, accurately, that the measure would not provide health care coverage for undocumented immigrants, South Carolina representative Joe Wilson shouted out "You lie!" in an astonishing breach of decorum that later earned him a reprimand from the House—and that he used to raise money from donors.[2]

As soon as Obama took office, Republicans channeled groups of opposition into a movement that reinvented American history. By the end of February 2009, they were calling themselves the Tea Party, after the 1773 event in which Bostonians threw tea into Boston Harbor to protest their lack of a say in their government. The name had a second meaning as well: protesters said they were Taxed Enough Already.

Leaders urged Tea Party supporters to come together to turn the country back to a mythological past based on what they interpreted to be the principles of the Constitution. Tea Partyers came from a range of Republican groups that worried about socialism, voter fraud, and what they saw as an influx of Black and Brown people. But they could agree that the Constitution was clear and easily understood and that it required a strict interpretation of the powers of the federal government. They claimed to want to return the country to the principles of the Framers. To spread that idea, Tea Party leaders quite deliberately tried to organize educational efforts, mobilize communities, and get followers to engage politically.[3]

In March 2010, Democrats passed the Affordable Care Act, popularly dubbed "Obamacare." It was the most significant overhaul of health care regulations and the largest expansion of health care coverage since Congress enacted Medicare and Medicaid in 1965. It expanded coverage through subsidies so that individuals could afford to buy health insurance in the market. The law went into effect in 2014, and by 2016 the number of uninsured Americans had been cut in half, with twenty million newly covered.

It was a Republican president, Theodore Roosevelt, who first proposed universal health care, at the beginning of the twentieth century. Republican president Dwight Eisenhower then tried to muscle such a program into being with the help of the new department created under him: the Department of Health, Education, and Welfare (HEW). In the early 1970s, President Richard Nixon—another Republican—had proposed a significant expansion of national health care, but it failed to win enough support. And when HEW became the Department of Health and Human Services in 1979, its declared mission was one of "improving the health, safety, and well-being of America."

Despite this history, right-wing media insisted that this expansion was socialism, pure and simple, and demanded the Democrats focus on the national debt, which was rising fast thanks to former president George W. Bush's unfunded military engagement in Afghanistan and Iraq as well as his dramatic expansion of Medicare drug benefits, which by 2008 cost $49.3 billion a year.

"Obamacare is a pure income redistribution play," wrote Fox News Channel personality Bill O'Reilly. "Income redistribution is a hallmark of socialism and we, in America, are now moving in that direction." Obamacare, he claimed, was "about capitalism versus socialism." Republicans opposed socialism, O'Reilly said, "but Republicans have not been able to convince the majority of Americans that income redistribution is harmful."[4]

There was another solution to that dilemma, though: flooding the zone with propaganda.

In January 2010, the Supreme Court under Chief Justice John

Roberts, whose professional career had been spent opposing the 1965 Voting Rights Act, handed down the *Citizens United v. Federal Election Commission* decision. It ruled that corporations could spend unlimited money in campaign advertising so long as they were not formally working with a candidate or a party. Corporations and billionaires promptly formed super PACs, political action committees that were allowed to take funds from "dark money" groups—nonprofits that do not have to disclose their donors. In 2006, dark money made up less than $5 million of spending in federal elections. By 2012 it was more than $300 million.[5]

Because dark money groups did not have to disclose their donors, it was not clear where that money was coming from. By January 2011, then–FBI director Robert S. Mueller III had become concerned that globalization and modern technology had changed the nature of organized crime. It had become international, fluid, and sophisticated, with multibillion-dollar stakes. Its operators did not care about ideology; they cared about money, and they were cross-pollinating across countries, religious affiliations, and political parties, sharing only their greed. Mueller warned that these criminals "may infiltrate our businesses. They may provide logistical support to hostile foreign powers. They may try to manipulate those at the highest levels of government. Indeed, these so-called 'iron triangles' of organized criminals, corrupt government officials, and business leaders pose a significant national security threat."[6]

Obama's secretary of state, Hillary Clinton, was also concerned about the rise of international oligarchy. In 2011, she took a stand against Russian president Vladimir Putin's manipulation of that country's parliamentary elections. "The Russian people, like people everywhere, deserve the right to have their voices heard and their votes counted," Clinton said. "And that means they deserve free, fair, transparent elections and leaders who are accountable to them."[7]

Elections in America were also becoming less free and fair. In 2010, Republican operatives launched Operation REDMAP, which stood for Redistricting Majority Project, a plan to take control of statehouses across the country so that Republicans would control the redistricting maps put in place after the 2010 census. Through the process of what is called gerrymandering, after Elbridge Gerry, an early governor of Massachusetts who signed off on such a scheme (even though he didn't like it), political parties could gain control of extra seats in a state by drawing districts to either "pack" or "crack" their opponents. Packing means stuffing the opposition party's voters into districts so their votes are not distributed more widely; cracking means dividing opponents' voters into multiple districts so there are too few of them in any district to have a chance of winning.

Parties have always engaged in such machinations, but new technologies enabled Republicans to shift into overdrive, hoping to hamstring Obama's ability to accomplish anything by making sure he had a hostile Congress. Party operatives raised money from corporate donors to swamp state elections with ads and campaign literature.

The plan worked. After the 2010 election, Republicans controlled the legislatures in the key states of Florida, Wisconsin, North Carolina, Ohio, and Michigan, as well as other, smaller states, and they redrew congressional maps using precise computer models. They had essentially hobbled representative democracy. In the 2012 election, Democrats won the White House decisively, the Senate easily, and a majority of 1.4 million votes for House candidates. And yet Republicans came away with a thirty-three-seat majority in the House of Representatives.[8]

Republican Mitch McConnell of Kentucky had become Senate minority leader in 2007, the year before Obama's election. He recognized that the best way to destroy Americans' faith in the federal government and return Republicans to power was to make sure the Democrats couldn't accomplish anything while Obama was in office.

On the night of Obama's inauguration, Republican leaders, including incoming House minority whip Eric Cantor, deputy whip Kevin McCarthy, and former speaker Newt Gingrich agreed over dinner to oppose anything that the new president proposed, regardless of whether they agreed with it. "For the next two years, we can't let you succeed in anything. That's our ticket to coming back," Republican senators told incoming vice president Joe Biden. In October 2010, McConnell told a reporter that "the single most important thing we want to achieve is for President Obama to be a one-term president."[9]

McConnell also deployed the Senate filibuster as a weapon. To pass an agreement to make senators stop talking and take a vote requires sixty votes, a rule that had previously been rarely used. By simply threatening a filibuster, Republicans could kill popular legislation, even a gun safety law for background checks before gun purchases that had been introduced after the massacre of twenty-six people, including twenty small children, at Sandy Hook Elementary School in Newtown, Connecticut. Although 90 percent of Americans supported the bill, forty-five senators, representing just 38 percent of the American people, killed it.[10]

Republicans made it an article of faith that their opponents could win an election only by leveraging the votes of illegitimate voters. So they were prepared to act when, in 2013, the Roberts Supreme Court handed down the *Shelby County v. Holder* decision, which gutted the 1965 Voting Rights Act. The decision declared unconstitutional the rule that states could not change voting laws without preclearance from the Department of Justice. Republican state officials immediately began to introduce voter ID laws and bills restricting voter registration, provisions that disproportionately affected minorities.

When Republicans took control of the Senate in 2014, McConnell became Senate majority leader, in position to cement the power of Republicans through the courts. This strategy had begun in the Reagan administration, when the attorney general had deliberately politicized the Department of Justice. Reagan also appointed three Supreme Court justices and one chief justice, and the rightward swing of the court continued thanks to George W. Bush, who appointed two Supreme Court justices, including a chief justice. To stop Obama from changing this trend, McConnell held up the president's judicial appointments to lower courts and finally took the unprecedented step of refusing even to consider his moderate nominee to fill a seat on the Supreme Court.

Finally, Republicans illustrated their refusal to accept Democratic governance with a dramatic rejection of the traditional U.S. principle, established in 1799 when Congress passed the Logan Act prohibiting private citizens from negotiating with foreign powers, that partisanship stops at the water's edge. In 2015, forty-seven lawmakers, including quite senior senators, signed a letter written by freshman extremist Arkansas senator Tom Cotton warning Iranian officials that they would overturn any agreement Iran made with the Obama administration as soon as they could, presumably after the 2016 election.

With Republican voters convinced that Democrats were deadly dangerous and Republican lawmakers having skewed the electoral system in their favor, the country seemed securely in Republican hands. In 2012, Republican strategist Grover Norquist had said triumphantly: "We don't need a president to tell us in what direction to go. We know what direction to go. . . . We just need a president to sign this stuff. . . . Pick a Republican with enough working digits to handle a pen to become president of the United States." But voters in that year chose Obama and Biden again.[11]

And so, in 2016, the Republicans would ride the themes of the past forty years to their logical conclusion.

Part 2

THE AUTHORITARIAN
EXPERIMENT

CHAPTER 11

A Snapshot of America

On June 16, 2015, Donald Trump came down the golden escalator at Trump Tower in New York City to announce his campaign for the U.S. presidency.

His campaign came out of reality TV, a genre of television that claimed to be unscripted but was actually heavily edited to emphasize ruthless competition among people striving for ultimate victory in a closed system. One European critic called such manufactured competition "fascist television." It fit well with America's hyperfocus on individualism.

Although there had been previous shows purporting to be "as it happened," reality TV broke new ground in the U.S. at the hands of producer Mark Burnett, whose enormously popular show *Survivor* debuted in 2000. In 2004, Burnett launched *The Apprentice*, a show that pitted aspiring businesspeople against one another for a contract to promote one of Trump's properties. Burnett split the proceeds evenly with its star: Trump himself. The former real estate investor was unprepared and erratic on set and was in deep financial trouble at the time, but the show gave the impression that he was a brilliant and very wealthy businessman elevating deserving underlings to fame and fortune.

The show's producers thought of the show as a joke, but the audience seemed to buy into Trump's image and admire him. At the same time, they appreciated that the farce they were watching showed the entire American system to be a game. The first season's finale was the nation's top program the week it aired.

By 2015, ratings for *The Apprentice* were dropping, and Trump took his show to a new stage. His descent down the Trump Tower escalator in June was a scene borrowed directly from the show. He came down to a lobby filled with paid extras, just as he had on the show (although he claimed there were thousands when there were actually dozens).

Trump seemed to embody the Republican success story: a famous self-made, self-declared billionaire real estate tycoon with multimillion-dollar properties and a beautiful former-model wife. But like that success story, Trump was more image than substance. His father had bankrolled him to the tune of $413 million in today's dollars; his companies had repeatedly declared bankruptcy; and by the 2000s he was, by his own admission, "billions of dollars in debt."[1]

But Trump was a brilliant salesman who grasped what thirty-five years of Republican rhetoric and voting distortion had made the party's base voters want far more accurately than the politicians in the Republican establishment who had created those voters.

Establishment Republicans who wanted an end to government regulation of business and taxes had courted racists, sexists, and religious zealots to stay in power but had no plans actually to give in to extremist demands, which would turn off mainstream voters. Trump stripped the cover off this sleight of hand, offering to give the extremist base a hierarchical world in which they dominated women as well as their Black and Brown neighbors.

Trump married Republican politics to authoritarianism. Speaking simply and with words that packed an emotional punch, he offered those left behind by the Republican revolution a way to recover a mythological lost world in which they called the shots. And he promised that he, and he alone, could lead the way.

America was "in serious trouble. We don't have victories any-more," he said when he announced his candidacy. "The U.S. has become a dumping ground for everybody else's problems." Claiming that U.S. unemployment was 21 percent (the real number was 5.6 percent), he attacked Mexican immigrants as criminals and rapists and warned that China was stealing American jobs while "stupid" lawmakers permitted it. He promised to make Mexico pay for a great wall between the U.S. and Mexico, and to build a trade wall between the U.S. and China. Blasting Obamacare as "amazingly destructive" and "a disaster," he promised to replace it with "something . . . much better and much less expensive."

Politicians were controlled by "special interests," he added, echoing Republican rhetoric, but he was "a truly great leader" who would bring back jobs, manufacturing, and the military, and take care of veterans. He would rebuild the country's infrastructure, make sure education stayed local, and reduce the national debt, all while backing the Second Amendment and cheering on the country. Claiming to be worth almost $9 billion and to be sitting at the heart of the American economy, he promised he would make manufacturers and foreign leaders beg for trade deals. "Sadly," he said, "the American dream is dead. . . . But . . . I will bring it back bigger and better and stronger than ever before."

Reusing Reagan's slogan, he promised to "make America great again."[2]

Years of right-wing media had prepared Trump's audience for his narcissistic vision. He was at the top of a hierarchy that sat above Black Americans, people of color, disabled Americans, and women. To this hierarchical vision, he brought authoritarianism: he was better than other people, the best businessman, the best entertainer, the best politician.

Although homegrown, his message dovetailed with rising authoritarianism around the world. In Russia, Vladimir Putin, a former agent of the Soviet state security organization, the KGB, had consolidated power among the oligarchs who rose after the fall of the Soviet Union, replacing communist leaders by monopolizing the profits of formerly publicly held industries. Putin and his allies were eager to destroy the liberal democracy that had kept Europe on an even keel since World War II, and worked to rile up old racial, ethnic, and religious hatred in order to strengthen nationalism based on the myth of a white, Christian past.

Russian political strategist Aleksandr Dugin wrote that restoring the power of the ancient Russian empire depended on destabilizing the American democracy that supported liberal democracies in Europe. He called for provoking "instability and separatism within the borders of the United States, . . . encouraging all kinds of separatism and ethnic, social and racial conflicts, . . . [and] support[ing] isolationist tendencies in American politics."[3]

Known at the time primarily as a media figure, Stephen K. Bannon, who became the Trump campaign's chief executive officer in August 2016, agreed that traditional Western civilization was fighting a war for survival. To win, current Western-style civilizations must be completely reconfigured to put a few wealthy, white, Christian male leaders in charge to direct and protect subordinates. He set out to dismantle the administrative state that was leveling the playing field among Americans, end immigration to the U.S., and isolate the nation from the other Western democratic governments he believed had taken advantage of it.

While European neofascists mythologized a fantasy medieval world, Bannon and his allies escalated the long-standing anti-liberal rhetoric of Republican talk radio hosts into hard-right paternalism. Under Bannon's direction, right-leaning Breitbart News Network had run articles attacking politically active women and Black Americans and yet could insist that Bannon was neither sexist nor racist because in their formulation, a return to a traditional society would be best for everyone.

This worldview struck a chord with disaffected white Americans who felt as if they had been left behind since the 1980s. They liked the idea of an America cut off from the rest of the world except for its dominance of trade, overseen by a hierarchy in which a few white men managed the government, the economy, and society. It was also a worldview that fit neatly into the thread of American history articulated by American enslavers in the years before the Civil War. They, too, defended a hierarchical system of paternalism as best for everyone.

A worldview that put Christianity at the center was especially appealing to evangelicals. Since the 1960s, a fundamentalist movement in the evangelical churches had clung to the Republican Party. They loved its promise to stop the secular world's recognition of the rights of minorities, women, and, more recently, LGBTQ people. Ending access to abortion had become their rallying cry, and Trump promised to end that right, even flirting with the idea of criminal punishment for women seeking abortions. Far from being disqualifying, his denigration of women and minorities personified the sort of traditional hierarchy these fundamentalists craved.

Not all Republicans were on board. For all their Democrat bashing to win voters, establishment Republicans did not actually want to dismantle the American state, which stabilized the global economy on which the modern world depended. Going into the presidential primaries, pundits had expected establishment Republican Jeb Bush, son of President George H. W. Bush and brother of President George W. Bush, to pick up the nomination, in part because the Republican contest had been front-loaded with elections in states dominated by low-information voters deemed likely to vote on the basis of name recognition, which usually helped the candidate the establishment favored.

But Trump's fame as a television star and his scorched-earth strategy of swinging viciously at Bush and his other opponents meant that his name was well enough known to voters that he won half of the delegates awarded on Super Tuesday, March 1. By the end of May he appeared to have clinched the nomination. To calm the horror of establishment Republicans, the Trump campaign brought on board former Indiana governor Mike Pence, who had deep ties to the business wing of the Republican Party, including the fantastically wealthy and politically active Charles and David Koch, whose libertarian father had backed Movement Conservatism since the 1950s.[4]

At the July Republican Convention, "never-Trump" delegates fought his nomination, only to be outraged at rules changes that gave Trump far more delegates than he had earned. Still, some could be comforted by the 2016 Republican platform, which offered Movement Conservative Republicans everything they had ever dreamed of. The platform chastised President Barack Obama for "regulating to death a free market economy that he does not like and does not understand" (which was manifestly untrue), called for originalist judges who would stop abortion and gay marriage, and insisted on returning federal power to the states.

The Trump campaign also took to new levels the party's overlap with foreign authoritarian leaders, especially those in Russia and Saudi Arabia. Not only was his program similar to Russian president Vladimir Putin's, but since 1996, Russians had invested hundreds of millions of dollars in Trump's real estate business. By 2008, one of his sons told a reporter that "Russians make up a pretty disproportionate cross-section of a lot of our assets."[5]

In 2016, Trump was in the midst of trying to get a Trump Tower in Moscow, and in June a number of his campaign advisors, including his key fundraiser and advisor, Thomas Barrack; his soon-to-be national security advisor, Michael Flynn; and his son-in-law, Jared Kushner, helped to organize a company, IP3 International (which stood for International Peace, Power, and Prosperity), to export nuclear technology to the Saudis with nuclear plants built by a joint Russian-U.S. venture.

That overlap entered new territory on June 9, when Donald Trump Jr., Kushner, and political consultant Paul Manafort, who had deep ties to Russia, met in Trump Tower with Russian operatives who offered damaging material on Democratic presidential nominee Hillary Clinton, the former secretary of state. In exchange, the Russians apparently wanted the U.S. to drop sanctions placed on Russia after its 2014 invasion of Ukraine, and support for a plan to create a Russian-allied republic out of the four eastern regions of Ukraine. The new leader would be Manafort's former boss Viktor Yanukovych.[6]

Later that month, Trump replaced his first campaign manager with Manafort, and when the Republican National Convention met in July, Trump requested a last-minute change to the platform that weakened the party's stance against Russia's 2014 invasion of Ukraine.

Once he won the Republican nomination, Trump held 232 campaign rallies, raucous affairs in which he attacked the "lying media," bashed immigrants, urged supporters to "rough up" interlopers, and mocked a disabled reporter. He promised to build a wall on the country's southern border to keep out immigrants and to make Mexico pay for it. He catered to evangelical Christians by promising a "a total and complete shutdown of Muslims entering the United States." Invoking the idea of a great leader taking charge, he promised to "drain the swamp" of Washington, surrounding himself "only with the best and most serious people."[7]

Trump's opponent turned out to be a perfect foil. Secretary of State Hillary Clinton was a highly educated, extremely well-qualified candidate who advocated protecting the rights of women and minorities and warned that Trump would pack the Supreme Court with extremists. She provided detailed policy papers. Trump, in turn, harped on an investigation into her alleged misuse of an email server. Using a method that had worked well against female politicians in Ukraine and Belarus, his supporters, led by Flynn, called for her to be arrested: "Lock her up!" became the call-and-response at his rallies.

Trump used the same media techniques Senator Joseph McCarthy had used in the 1950s when he garnered power by falsely claiming to have discovered that communists had infiltrated the U.S. government, making outrageous statements that reporters felt obliged to cover but without explaining their content or truthfulness, thus spreading his message. The media ultimately provided Trump about twice the free coverage they gave to Clinton.[8]

The Trump campaign also used social media to undermine his opponent. Bannon was a pioneer in using media to create emotional responses, and in 2014, with the help of funding from Republican mega-donors Robert and Rebekah Mercer, he launched Cambridge Analytica, a company designed to develop profiles of individuals that would enable advertisers to group them for targeted advertising. That concept had been around since 1935, when Frank Stanton—who later became the head of CBS—pioneered it, but the tools of social media, especially Facebook, enabled advertisers to address audiences with surgical precision. Before the 2016 election, the company captured information from the Facebook profiles of more than fifty million users without their permission or knowledge.[9]

Still, all bets said the election was Clinton's, until FBI director James Comey made a last-minute announcement that the agency was reopening an investigation into her emails during her time as secretary of state. Voters in swing states turned against her, and while Trump lost the popular vote by more than 2.8 million, his victories in three key swing states won him the White House by a vote of 306 to 232 in the Electoral College. Trump claimed it was a landslide victory and that he had actually won the popular vote, too, "if you deduct the millions of people who voted illegally."[10]

When the report from the email investigation found that Clinton had committed no significant wrongdoing, questions arose about whether Comey had made the announcement to appease FBI agents who disliked her.

Trump's inaugural address echoed what Republican voters had come to believe about America: it was a place of "carnage." He described a country with "mothers and children trapped in poverty in our inner cities; rusted-out factories scattered like tombstones across the landscape of our nation; an education system flush with cash, but which leaves our young and beautiful students deprived of all knowledge; and the crime and the gangs and the drugs that have stolen too many lives and robbed our country of so much unrealized potential." He insisted that other countries were "making our products, stealing our companies, and destroying our jobs." He vowed to put "America first."

He claimed that his inauguration meant that the country was "not merely transferring power from one administration to another or from one party to another, but . . . transferring power from Washington, D.C., and giving it back to you, the people. . . . The forgotten men and women of our country will be forgotten no longer. Everyone is listening to you now."

"I will fight for you with every breath in my body, and I will never, ever let you down."[11]

CHAPTER 12

A Shocking Event

T hat was some weird sh*t," former president George W. Bush remarked at the end of Trump's inaugural address.[1]

Trump's election to the White House signaled a sea change in American history. Since the 1950s, Movement Conservatives had called for destroying the active government of the liberal consensus, and since the 1980s, Republican politicians had hacked away at it but had left much of the government intact. In 2016, the nation had finally, wittingly or not, put into office a president who would use his power to destroy it.

Trump's agenda was not popular with the majority of American voters, who had backed Hillary Clinton. It was not even popular with all Republicans. While Republican leaders had spread the false narrative of "socialists" taking over the country and suppressed votes to stay in power, they were more interested in establishing the kind of oligarchy that had run the country in the 1850s, 1890s, and 1920s than in dismantling the government.

Republicans had been ramping up the rhetorical techniques of dividing the country and demonizing their opponents since the 1960s, but they did not want an apocalypse; they wanted an end to business regulation and social services and the taxes they required.

Trump had risen to the presidency thanks to their machinations, but he went far beyond them, making the leap from oligarchy to authoritarianism. He welded his followers into a movement based on the system of lies and cruelty that scholars of authoritarianism had identified after World War II. And just as they had warned, he turned previously apathetic people into ferocious partisans. They believed they were part of a heroic mission to return the nation to what he told them were its true rules and patterns, established by God and history.

Trump's drive toward authoritarianism became clear immediately, when he insisted, contrary to all evidence, that his inaugural crowd was bigger than former president Barack Obama's. This was no innocent inflation of an unimportant statistic. On the most basic level, it was an amplification of officials' critique of the "reality-based community" during the George W. Bush administration, offering a flat-out lie on its face, knowing the press would cover it.

Indeed, incredulous reporters spent significant time pushing back on the statements from Trump's White House press secretary, Sean Spicer, who issued a number of easily disprovable statements that culminated in his insistence that "this was the largest audience to ever witness an inauguration—period—both in person and around the globe." But it clearly was not.[2]

Two days later, it became clear the lie was not just about getting airtime. On NBC's *Meet the Press*, host Chuck Todd asked Trump advisor Kellyanne Conway, "What was the motive to have this ridiculous litigation of crowd size?" She answered, "Your job is not to call things ridiculous that are said by our press secretary and our president. That's not your job." When Todd pressed her to answer, she finally said, "I'll answer it this way: Think about what you just said to your viewers. That's why we feel compelled to go out and clear the air and put alternative facts out there."[3]

The idea of "alternative facts" revealed that this seemingly stupid lie about crowd size was not only a way to get media coverage but also an important demonstration of dominance. While Republicans previously had based their policy arguments, however tenuously, on some kernel of reality (as when they argued that abortion caused breast cancer because breastfeeding offers some protection against cancer but abortion means no baby to breastfeed), Trump straight-up lied, and he demanded that his loyalists parrot his lies.

This rhetorical strategy, called gaslighting, takes its name from a 1944 Ingrid Bergman film, *Gaslight*, in which a husband tries to convince his wife she's crazy by manipulating the lights in the house and insisting that what she is experiencing is not, in fact, real. As she becomes more and more disoriented, he isolates her from others with the plan of declaring her insane and gaining control of her considerable fortune.[4]

Gaslighting forces subordinates to agree that the person in charge gets to determine what reality is. Victims must surrender either their integrity or their ownership of their own perceptions; in either case, having once agreed to a deliberate lie, it becomes harder to challenge later ones because that means acknowledging the other times they caved.

When criminal enterprises use this technique, it's blackmail. Someone makes a friend, and eventually the friend asks for help with something that's a little over the line but not too far, and once the person has gone along with that first transgression, it's extraordinarily hard to get free. As Mob boss Michael Corleone put it when trying to rehabilitate his reputation, in perhaps the most memorable line from *The Godfather Part III*: "Just when I thought I was out, they pull me back in."

Even for those unconvinced by Trump's assertions, this reiteration of lies in the face of evidence did something else. It "flood[ed] the zone with sh*t," as Trump's advisor Steve Bannon put it. Keeping listeners constantly trying to defend what is real from what is not destroys their ability to make sense of the world. Many people turn to a strongman who promises to create order. Others will get so exhausted they simply give up. As scholar of totalitarianism Hannah Arendt noted, authoritarians use this technique to destabilize a population.[5]

Trump's lies demonstrated his dominance at the same time they sucked the air out of the room for Americans who were trying to produce a true picture of what was really happening. Russian-American journalist Julia Ioffe, who had chronicled Putin's takeover of Russia, noted that "the only people who were fully prepared to cover the Trump presidency properly were people who knew how authoritarian regimes worked. The Washington press corps, which treats politics as something between a baseball game and a Broadway show, was woefully unprepared."[6]

The focus on the size of the crowd also meant that Trump got to define the public conversation, just as Senator Joseph McCarthy had done during his anti-communist witch hunt in the 1950s. It was not a coincidence that McCarthy and Trump had shared a legal advisor, Roy Cohn, who designed the kind of approach they took.

While journalists were busy disputing Spicer's figures that said more people used the D.C. Metro on Trump's inauguration day than on Obama's, they had little oxygen left over for the actual numbers of people using the D.C. Metro on the day after Trump's inauguration to attend the Women's March. The largest single-day demonstration in world history, the Women's March drew Metro ridership second only to that for . . . Obama's inauguration.

Women who had watched their rights erode under the cowboy ideology of the Republicans since the 1980s not only recognized the psychological technique of gaslighting, they recognized Trump's election as deadly dangerous to their rights and to the nation. Wearing pink "pussy hats"—simple hand-knit hats with points that looked like cat ears—they turned Trump's boasting about his sexual assaults, in which he had used the vulgar word, into a symbol of empowerment. The impulse to march came from a diverse group of activists and those unaccustomed to activism, all concerned about the direction of the country under Trump.

Their concerns seemed realized just a week later, when Trump continued the process of destabilizing the government to push an authoritarian agenda. At 4:42 p.m. on January 27, the administration announced a travel ban on people coming from primarily Muslim countries. Executive Order 13769 stopped travel from Iran, Iraq, Libya, Somalia, Sudan, Syria, and Yemen for 90 days. The list of countries appeared random—Saudi Arabia, Pakistan, and Afghanistan, countries from which terrorists have sometimes come directly to the U.S., weren't on the list—and appeared to fulfill a campaign promise and assert a new view of executive power. It also stopped the admission of refugees for 120 days and suspended the Syrian refugee program.

The chief architects of the plan were Stephen Miller and Stephen Bannon. "My two Steves," Trump called them. Both were hard-line, right-wing, anti-immigrant fighters that Trump would elevate over the establishment Republicans brought on board to calm party leaders. He even put Bannon over the chairman of the Joint Chiefs of Staff and the director of national intelligence on the National Security Council. With the executive order, which Trump's advisors did not discuss with the Office of Legal Counsel, Trump indicated his intention to throw the country into chaos.[7]

Acting Attorney General Sally Yates refused to defend the ban, saying, "My responsibility is to ensure that the position of the Department of Justice is not only legally defensible, but is informed by our best view of what the law is after consideration of all the facts. . . . In addition, I am responsible for ensuring that the positions we take in court remain consistent with this institution's solemn obligation to always seek justice and stand for what is right."

Trump promptly fired her—by letter—for "refusing to enforce a legal order designed to protect the citizens of the United States." A White House statement said, falsely, that the order "was approved as to form and legality" by the Office of Legal Counsel. It called Yates "an Obama Administration appointee who is weak on borders and very weak on illegal immigration" and said, "it is time to get serious about protecting our country."[8]

Trump's sudden order created a crush of people at the airports and made it seem like Trump was right that the country was in chaos with traditional power structures breaking down—the very conditions that scholars of authoritarianism identified as ones that convinced people to turn to a strongman to provide clarity and protection.

What no one outside the government knew was that Miller and his allies within the administration were already at work on a different immigration policy: separating children of refugees at the southern border from their parents. When career officials in the government protested that such an attack on American law and fundamental human rights was outrageous, the extremists in the administration simply excluded them from planning sessions.

They also overrode the process in which staffers prepared papers based on extensive studies, then ran policies past managers who had a broader perspective in a number of areas, and finally went to political appointees to make sure the proposed policy met political goals.

Determined to enforce their vision of a hierarchical white Christian America, Miller and his allies simply worked around existing laws and officials until they found compliant ones. Increasingly, establishment Republicans who opposed Trump and his policies were excluded from his White House, leaving a vacuum filled by less talented people who would not have had much authority in a normal administration. They were willing to sign off on a policy that dehumanized the weakest members of society—immigrant children—a crucial step in the larger process of dehumanization that underlies an authoritarian's concentration of power.[9]

But for all that the Trump loyalists in the White House were creating chaos to destroy democracy, the American people were waking up to the administration's attack on American principles. Led by attorney and refugee activist Becca Heller, lawyers around the country sprang to the defense of the law and the refugees caught in the sudden ban, sometimes literally in midflight to the U.S.

At the Women's March, activist Gloria Steinem, who had been central to the women's movement in the 1970s, said: "We are here and around the world for a deep democracy that says we will not be quiet, we will not be controlled, we will work for a world in which all countries are connected. God may be in the details, but the goddess is in connections. We are at one with each other, we are looking at each other, not up. No more asking daddy."

"We are linked," she said. "We are not ranked."[10]

CHAPTER 13

Russia, Russia, Russia

E ven before Trump took office, his campaign's troubling ties to Russia showed an affinity for authoritarianism rather than for American democracy.

From the country's beginning, the Founders worried that a foreign power could take control of the nation by installing a puppet in the presidency. The Framers required that any president be native born—the only office having that condition—and in his 1796 Farewell Address, George Washington warned against political partisans turning to foreign nations for help at home, noting that the U.S. would then simply become a vassal of another power.

When someone did just that in 1798, offering to change official U.S. policy if France would help elect his preferred candidate, Congress made such interference illegal with the 1799 Logan Act. Concerned that foreign powers could use money to swing U.S. policies toward their own interests rather than that of the American people, modern Congresses established laws against asking for or accepting anything at all of value from a foreign national.

And yet, in early January 2017, Director of National Intelligence James Clapper released a report that aggregated the findings of the FBI, the CIA, and the NSA (National Security Agency, which operates under the authority of the director of national intelligence), concluding that Russia had interfered in the 2016 election to help Trump. Over the next two years, two investigations, one by Special Counsel

Robert Mueller from the Department of Justice and another by the Republican-dominated Senate Intelligence Committee, found that the Trump campaign had, at the very least, played along.[1]

The story was not just about Trump or Russia or the private dealings between the two. It was the story of authoritarianism undermining American democracy by using disinformation to manipulate voters.

Russia's interference in the 2016 U.S. election began in the decades when Republican politicians who believed that fighting socialism meant spreading free-market capitalism found common cause with global authoritarians who leveraged their anti-communism to attract U.S. funding. Then, after the fall of the Soviet Union in 1991, as oligarchs rose to power in Russia, money and influence began to flow the other way as these newly wealthy Russians invested their money in the U.S. and other democracies, where the rule of law kept it safe. Their political interests in those countries allied with those on the political right, who focused on the accumulation of wealth rather than social welfare or civil rights.

By the early 2000s, a struggle for control of resource-rich Ukraine, which sits in Eastern Europe and borders Russia, became a key battleground for the forces of democracy and autocracy. Ukraine had begun to turn toward European democracies, preferring the personal freedoms and higher standard of living they offered over Russia's rising oligarchy. Russia's leader, Vladimir Putin, wanted to regain power over Ukraine by installing a puppet government under his ally Viktor Yanukovych. To do so, in 2004 the men turned to the American political consultant who had been managing Republican campaigns since Nixon: Paul Manafort.

Using Manafort's signature methods of demonizing opponents, Yanukovych won the Ukraine presidency in 2010, but his attempts to tie the country to Russia failed. In 2014, the Ukrainian people threw him out. Putin then invaded Ukraine and claimed Crimea. Ukraine was not formally allied with the United States and the European Union, but no one who was paying attention missed that Putin's fight to control Ukraine was a threat to European democracies. The U.S. and the European Union responded with economic sanctions prohibiting certain Russian businesses and oligarchs from doing business with U.S. entities.

With Yanukovych's removal, Manafort was out of a job, and he owed about $17 million to allies of Yanukovych and Putin. His longtime friend and business partner Roger Stone was advising the floundering presidential campaign of Donald Trump, and Manafort stepped in to help. He did not take a salary, but immediately after getting the job, he did reach out to a Russian oligarch to whom he owed millions, asking him: "How do we use [this] to get whole?"[2]

Manafort began to advise the Trump campaign in March 2016, and by April, according to the Senate Intelligence Committee, Putin had launched an effort to hurt the Clinton campaign in order to boost Trump's chances. Trump campaign officials met with Russian operatives in June, apparently to discuss ending sanctions and establishing a pro-Russia republic in the regions of Ukraine Putin wanted, and that month Manafort became Trump's campaign chair.[3]

By summer, Putin ordered hacks of Democratic computer networks, and at two crucial moments, WikiLeaks, which the Senate committee concluded was allied with the Russians, dumped illegally obtained emails that were intended to hurt Clinton. The first dump, just before the Democratic National Convention in July, forced Democratic National Committee chair Debbie Wasserman Schultz to resign. The second, in October, came immediately after the release of a tape of Trump boasting about sexually assaulting women in which he said: "And when you're a star, they let you do it. You can do anything. Grab 'em by the pussy. You can do anything."[4]

Days after the first major leak from WikiLeaks, Trump openly invited Russia to hack the U.S. secretary of state's computer system, which he insisted had important information on it: "Russia, if you're listening, I hope you're able to find the 30,000 emails that are missing," he said.[5] Reporters were shocked at a political candidate openly calling for a foreign country to attack the U.S., but Trump doubled down, repeating the request.[6]

In August, Manafort officially resigned from the campaign, but he continued to advise it unofficially, passing secret campaign polling data to his Ukrainian business partner, Konstantin Kilimnik, whom the Senate Intelligence Committee called "a Russian intelligence officer." At the same time, he "continued to coordinate with Russian persons . . . to undertake activities on their behalf."[7]

Meanwhile, Russian operatives were mirroring Bannon's Cambridge Analytica, flooding social media with disinformation. Their fake stories did not necessarily explicitly endorse Trump, but rather spread lies about Clinton in order to depress Democratic turnout, or riled up those on the right by falsely claiming that Democrats intended to ban the Pledge of Allegiance, for example. This sort of disinformation was an old Republican tactic, but social media made it more pervasive than before.

The goal of the propaganda was not simply to elect Trump. It was to pit the far ends of the political spectrum against the middle, tearing the nation apart. Fake accounts drove wedges between Americans over issues of race, immigration, and gun rights. A study by the National Bureau of Economic Research later found that in the last three months of the election, users shared false content on Facebook thirty-eight million times.

It worked. Trump's supporters did not object to his open attack on American democracy by calling for Putin's help. Instead, they began to wear T-shirts that said things like: "I'd Rather Be Russian Than a Democrat." They also began to put slogans on Facebook pages and elsewhere that offered "free helicopter rides" to their opponents, a chilling reference to the Chilean dictator Nixon had helped bring to power, Augusto Pinochet, whose goons murdered dissidents by tossing them from helicopters.

Government officials were aware that something was up between the Trump campaign and Russia and that it could be compromising national security. In July, Trump operative George Papadopoulos told an Australian official that the Russians were giving the campaign dirt on Clinton, and the Australian government shared the information with the U.S. By the end of July, FBI director James Comey opened a counterintelligence investigation into Russian interference in the 2016 election.

President Barack Obama directly confronted Putin over the issue, warning him not to attack election infrastructure, and in August began briefing congressional leaders. He asked the four top politicians in Congress—the majority and minority leaders of each house—to issue a joint statement warning that Russia was interfering with the election.

But according to Obama's White House chief of staff, Denis McDonough, it took three weeks to get Senate majority leader Mitch McConnell on board to release any statement at all, and the one that emerged played down the crisis. Finally, on October 7, the secretary of Homeland Security and the director of national intelligence issued a joint statement warning that Russia was interfering with the U.S. election.

And on November 8, Trump won.

Immediately after the election, the FBI caught Trump national security advisor Lieutenant General Michael Flynn assuring Russian ambassador Sergey Kislyak that the new administration would change

U.S. policy toward Russia. Then it turned out that Trump's attorney general, Jeff Sessions, had also had contact with Kislyak during the campaign despite having told senators during his confirmation hearing that he had not.

Soon after taking office, Trump asked Comey to drop the investigation of Flynn, and when Comey refused, Trump fired him. The next day he told a Russian delegation he was hosting in the Oval Office: "I just fired the head of the F.B.I. He was crazy, a real nut job. . . . I faced great pressure because of Russia. That's taken off."[8]

In the midst of public outcry over Comey's firing, Deputy Attorney General Rod J. Rosenstein in May appointed former FBI director Robert Mueller as special counsel to oversee the FBI investigation into Russian efforts to influence the 2016 presidential election.

The Russia investigation became the defining event for the Trump presidency. Trump fought back in part because it was important for him to distance himself from the potentially illegal behavior being exposed by investigators. There was more to his counterattack than that, though. If he could get Americans to reject the truth and accept his lies about what had happened, they would be psychologically committed to him.

Reversing reality, Trump and his allies insisted that he was an innocent victim and that the investigators were the ones who had broken the law. They claimed the investigation was a Democratic "witch hunt," despite the fact that Comey, Rosenstein, and Mueller were all Republicans and Trump had appointed Rosenstein himself. They began to attack the Obama administration for investigating Russian attacks on the election and to call Obama and his vice president, Joe Biden, along with the career intelligence and justice officials who tried to defend the country against foreign interference, part of a "deep state" conspiracy to injure the president. Trump saturated Twitter and the media with attacks on the FBI and hounded its agents from office, making a special effort against those agents who specialized in money laundering.[9]

Trump purged officials who accepted the findings of the Intelligence Community from his administration. He replaced Director of National Intelligence Dan Coates, a well-regarded former Republican senator who maintained that Russia had interfered in the 2016 election. Trump also fired Attorney General Jeff Sessions, replacing him first with Sessions's loyalist chief of staff, Matthew Whitaker, who became acting attorney general without Senate confirmation, and then with William Barr, who had been President George H. W. Bush's attorney general when Bush pardoned those involved in the Iran-Contra scandal. Barr took office on February 14, 2019, just as Mueller was finishing his report. Before letting anyone else see it, Barr spun the document as a complete exoneration of the president. The media repeated his misstatement.

In fact, Mueller's report established that Russia had illegally intervened in the election to benefit Trump and that the campaign "expected it would benefit electorally from information stolen and released through Russian efforts." Mueller publicly complained to Barr about the spin he had put on the report, but it was too late: Trump crowed that he was exonerated, and his supporters not only bought it, they accepted it as proof that the institutions of government were persecuting their president. Barr then appointed his own investigator, John Durham, to prove that it was Ukraine, not Russia, that had hacked the election (the investigation closed in 2022 without any proof of those allegations).[10]

Republican lawmakers helped Trump's disinformation campaign, using their positions to mislead the public and legitimize his lies. House Republicans, especially those in the right-wing Freedom Caucus, along with a bloc of right-wing senators, backed the president. Since the Republicans controlled the Senate, their chairing of key committees helped them legitimize his allegations. Senators Ron Johnson of Wisconsin, Charles E. Grassley of Iowa, and Rand Paul of Kentucky echoed Trump in calling for investigations of Democrats.

Trump was consolidating his power. Even those Republicans who disliked his tactics liked his ability to get support from voters, and so they stayed silent even as Trump began to swing U.S. policy toward Russia, notably by undermining the North Atlantic Treaty Organization (NATO). Formed in 1947 to stand against the USSR, NATO had shifted to countering an aggressive Russia. Trump's actions weakened U.S. ties to traditional European allies, and he threatened to withdraw support for Ukraine in its defensive war against the Russian invaders. Republican senators appeared to have faith that their control over sanctions—which the Treasury Department continued to use over Russian cyberattacks, for example—and over funding for Ukraine would keep pressure on Russia.

In the end, thirty-four people and three companies were indicted or pleaded guilty in the attack on the 2016 election or its cover-up, including Papadopoulos, Manafort, Manafort's partner Rick Gates, Flynn, Kilimnik, Trump lawyer Michael Cohen, Roger Stone, twelve Russian intelligence operatives, thirteen Russian nationals, and three Russian companies. Before he left office, Trump pardoned those who had refused to cooperate with the Department of Justice: Flynn, Stone, Manafort, and Papadopoulos. In 2022, a jury found the single person indicted after Durham's investigation—a lawyer associated with Hillary Clinton—not guilty.

But Trump loyalists believed Trump, not the investigators. Republicans who might have turned the tide stayed silent, while others backed their president, and his base agreed that he had been attacked by a deep state run by leftist Democrats. He had successfully sold his own narrative over the truth, and his supporters would continue to believe him rather than those calling him out. Even after the dust had settled, Trump dumped complaints about "Russia, Russia, Russia" and "the Russian hoax" into the news to undercut any attempts to stop him. He and his allies portrayed anyone who protested either as operatives of the deep state or as victims of "Trump Derangement Syndrome"—tinfoil-hat-wearing conspiracy theorists.

CHAPTER 14

The Streets of Charlottesville

Trump's attempt to exert control over his supporters might have begun as a way to protect himself from potential legal repercussions for his behavior, but it quickly became part of an effort to create a movement. Trump's anti-immigrant policies and language of dominance heartened right-wing gangs that had previously operated on society's margins. Six months into Trump's presidency, they launched a coming-out party.

On August 11, 2017, racists, antisemites, white nationalists, Ku Klux Klan members, neo-Nazis, and members of other "alt-right" groups met in Charlottesville, Virginia, to "Unite the Right." The man who organized the rally, Jason Kessler, claimed he wanted to bring people together to protest the removal of a statue of Confederate general Robert E. Lee from a local park. But the rioters turned immediately to chanting slogans from the German Nazis of the 1930s: "You will not replace us," "Jews will not replace us," and "Blood and soil." They gave Nazi salutes and carried Nazi insignia; many had brought battle gear and went looking for fights. By the end of the next day, they had killed counterprotester Heather Heyer and injured nineteen others. After the governor of Virginia declared a state of emergency, the rioters went home.

The United States has always had violent street mobs, from anti-Catholic gangs in the 1830s to Ku Klux Klan chapters in the 1860s to anti-union thugs in the Depression. In the 1930s, anti–New Deal businessmen determined to overthrow FDR's presidency deliberately tried to tap into the passions of the nation's traditional anti-immigrant, anti-Black, anti-union, and anti-Jewish brawlers. They hoped to create the same sort of violent right-wing gangs in the U.S. that had helped overturn governments and install right-wing dictators in Europe.

In 1934, they sent Wall Street broker Gerald MacGuire to Europe to see how fascist leaders had mobilized veterans to enable them to seize power. When MacGuire returned, he tried to recruit retired U.S. Marine major general Smedley Butler to lead a similar paramilitary coup against FDR. MacGuire claimed to represent U.S. financial interests and to have $6 million to put behind the effort.

Butler alerted the authorities and the attempt failed, but fascism had shown anti–New Dealers a way to marry their ideology to popular political activism. Get people fighting first and they can be led toward right-wing politics next. In America the hallmark of budding fascism was not intellectuals discussing how to take power; it was populist violence.[1]

There was a straight line from the anti–New Deal violence of the 1930s to the street brawlers at Charlottesville. Since the 1950s, opponents of the liberal consensus had urged supporters to think of themselves as heroic, individualistic cowboys who had not only the right but also the duty to protect their families from the alleged socialism of the government. That narrative initially helped to spark extraordinary violence against Black Americans and other minorities, but by 1992, right-wing violence had begun to shift toward violence against the government itself.

In August of that year, the idea erupted at Ruby Ridge, Idaho. Randy Weaver, a former factory worker who had moved his family to northern Idaho to escape what he saw as the corruption of American society, failed to show up for trial on a firearms charge. When federal marshals tried to arrest him, a firefight left Weaver's fourteen-year-old son and a deputy marshal dead. Federal and local officers then laid an eleven-day siege to the Weavers' cabin, during which a sniper wounded Weaver and killed his wife, Vicki.

Right-wing activists and neo-Nazis from a nearby Aryan Nations compound swarmed to Ruby Ridge to protest the government's attack on what right-wing media insisted was simply a man protecting his family. Negotiators eventually brought Weaver out, but the standoff at Ruby Ridge convinced western men they had to arm themselves to fight off the government.[2]

The next February, the same theme played out in Waco, Texas, when officers stormed the compound of a religious cult whose former members reported that their leader, David Koresh, was stockpiling weapons. A gun battle and a fire ended the fifty-one-day siege on April 19, 1993. Seventy-six people died.[3]

While a Republican investigation cited "overwhelming evidence" that exonerated the government of wrongdoing, talk radio hosts nonetheless railed against the administration, especially Attorney General Janet Reno, for the events at Waco.[4]

Talk radio host Rush Limbaugh stoked his listeners' anger with reports of the "Waco invasion" and talked of the government's "murder" of citizens, making much of the idea that a group of Christians had been killed by a female government official who was single and—as opponents made much of—unfeminine. Reactionary rocker Ted Nugent featured an obscene caricature of Reno for years in his stage version of "Kiss My Glock."[5]

Alex Jones, who in 1999 would go on to start the right-wing conspiracy site InfoWars—with the tagline "There's a War on For Your Mind!"—claimed to be horrified by the government's attempt to break into the cult's compound. He dropped out of community college to start a talk show on which he alleged that Reno had "murdered" the people at Waco and warned that the government was about to impose martial law. The modern militia movement took off.

The combination of political rhetoric and violence radicalized a former army gunner, Timothy McVeigh, who decided to bring the war home to the government. "Taxes are a joke," he wrote to a newspaper in 1992. "More taxes are always the answer to government mismanagement. . . . Is a civil war imminent? Do we have to shed blood to reform the current system? I hope it doesn't come to that! But it might."[6]

On April 19, 1995, a date chosen to honor the Waco standoff, McVeigh set off a bomb at the Alfred P. Murrah Federal Building in Oklahoma City. The blast killed 168 people, including 19 children younger than six, and wounded more than 800. When the police captured McVeigh, he was wearing a T-shirt with a picture of Abraham Lincoln and the words "Sic Semper Tyrannis." The same words John Wilkes Booth shouted after he assassinated Lincoln, they mean "Thus always to tyrants" and are the words attributed to Brutus after he and his supporters murdered Caesar. By 1995, right-wing terrorists envisioned themselves as protectors of American individualism in the face not of a tyrant but of a socialist government.

In 2009, Elmer Stewart Rhodes, a lawyer and former paratrooper who had been a staffer for Republican congressman Ron Paul of Texas, started a right-wing gang called the Oath Keepers. Claiming to take their inspiration from the patriots who stood against the British regulars on Lexington Green in 1775, they pledged to stand against what they considered a tyrannical government.[7]

The Oath Keepers showed up in 2014 when Nevada cattle rancher Cliven Bundy announced that he did not recognize the government's power over the federal land on which he had been grazing his cattle for more than twenty years. Bundy owed the government more than $1 million in grazing fees for running his cattle on public land, even as he disparaged the "Negro" who lived in government housing and "didn't have nothing to do," and wondered whether Black people "are . . . better off as slaves, picking cotton and having a family life and doing things, or are they better off under government subsidy?" Officials from the Bureau of Land Management set out to impound Bundy's cattle but backed down when he and his supporters showed up armed.[8]

By then, the antigovernment movement was deep in Republican Party leadership. Senator Dean Heller of Nevada called Bundy and his supporters "patriots," and he and other Republicans openly supported Bundy until his racist comments finally prompted them to turn away. From the outset of the standoff, Democrat Harry Reid, also of Nevada and Senate majority leader at the time, called Bundy and his supporters "domestic terrorists" and warned, "It's not over. We can't have an American people that violate the law and then just walk away from it. So it's not over."

It wasn't. Two years later, Bundy's son Ammon was at the forefront of the right-wing takeover of Oregon's Malheur National Wildlife Refuge, arguing that the federal government must turn over all public lands to the states to open them to private development. The occupiers called themselves Citizens for Constitutional Freedom.[9]

When antigovernment gangs marched on Charlottesville at the 2017 Unite the Right rally, they were the logical outcome of the right-wing militancy that the anti–New Dealers had tried to cultivate in 1934 to bring down FDR. The ensuing decades of violence were nurtured by bullies who justified their actions with a right-wing political ideology.

In Charlottesville, leaders brought together different groups, dressed similarly and carrying the emblem of tiki torches, to organize and attack the government. This time, though, the president stepped up to lead them. Trump refused to condemn the rioters, telling a reporter that there were "very fine people, on both sides."[10]

The president's defenders denied that he had meant to encourage the alt-right, but the reality was there for anyone willing to see.

The Unite the Right rally drew a clear political line in America. Former vice president Joe Biden watched the events at Charlottesville and concluded that the soul of the nation was at stake. Trump's praise for the "very fine people" aligned with the rioters horrified him. "With those words, the president of the United States assigned a moral equivalence between those spreading hate and those with the courage to stand against it," Biden said, "and in that moment, I knew the threat to this nation was unlike any I'd ever seen in my lifetime." He committed to running for president to defeat the man he believed threatened our democracy.[11]

Trump was building a right-wing populist army. But Republicans still did not speak out.

CHAPTER 15

The First Impeachment

Republican lawmakers stayed behind Trump so long as he was delivering their wish list. And he was doing that, for sure. In addition to the 2017 tax cut, which slashed the corporate tax rate from 35 percent to 21 percent, Trump's presidency enabled Senate majority leader Mitch McConnell to complete the judicial project begun by President Ronald Reagan's attorney general, Edwin Meese: decimating the judiciary that stood behind the liberal consensus. During Trump's term, McConnell churned through judicial nominees, putting in place more than one out of every four federal judges and, crucially, three Supreme Court justices.

But would Republicans back Trump after news broke in September 2019 that he had undermined national security to use the power of the government to steal the 2020 election? Republicans had turned against President Richard Nixon for far less when they learned that his operatives had bugged the headquarters of the Democratic National Committee in Washington's Watergate Hotel and it became clear the president had covered up the scandal. Back then, they agreed with Democrats that Nixon had "acted in a manner contrary to his trust as President and subversive of constitutional government, to the great prejudice of the cause of law and justice and to the manifest injury of the people of the United States."[1]

Trump's 2019 subversion of constitutional government made Watergate look quaint. The story broke on Friday, September 13, 2019, when the chair of the House Select Committee on Intelligence, Democrat Adam Schiff of California, sent an astonishing letter to Trump's acting director of national intelligence, Joseph Maguire. It said that members of the Intelligence Committee knew Maguire was illegally withholding a whistleblower complaint about classified information. By law, Maguire had to turn it over to Congress. Instead, he had taken it to Trump loyalist Attorney General William Barr.

"The Committee can only conclude," Schiff wrote in bold type, "that the serious misconduct at issue involves the President of the United States and/or other senior White House or Administration officials."[2]

Within days, Trump admitted that on July 25 he had called the new president of Ukraine, Volodymyr Zelensky, to enlist his help against former vice president Joe Biden, who was beating Trump in most polls going into the 2020 election season. Zelensky was desperate for the money Congress had approved to help his country fight Russian-backed separatists in the regions Russia had occupied after the 2014 invasion, but Trump indicated he would release the money only after Zelensky announced an investigation into the actions of Biden's son Hunter during his time on the board of Ukrainian energy company Burisma.

There were some old themes in this story. Trump was, once again, using an investigation to prod the media into spreading lies about an opponent, as his 2016 campaign had done with the investigation of Hillary Clinton's emails. Significantly, he had not asked Zelensky for an actual investigation, only for an announcement of one. He could trust the American media to pick up the story and, as media reports of the investigation into Hillary Clinton's emails had done to her campaign, seriously weaken Biden's candidacy.

Once news of the call became public, Trump defended it with his usual strongman hyperbole: it was "a beautiful phone call," "a very friendly and totally appropriate call" in which he made no demands of Zelensky—"NO quid pro quo!" He reminded people that they had backed him during the Russia investigation, maintaining that complaints about the phone call were "a continuation of the Greatest and most Destructive Witch Hunt of all time!" by "the Radical Left Democrats and their Fake News Media partners." And then, when the story heated up, he promised to release "the complete, fully declassified and unredacted transcript" of the phone call, kicking the can down the road as he had done over calls for him to release his taxes or his wife's immigration records.[3]

But there was something ominously new, too. No longer a candidate, Trump was now the president of the United States, and he was using the power of the government to force a foreign government to take part in a campaign to hurt his political enemies.

Like the autocrats he admired, Trump was not simply breaking a law: he was rejecting the idea that ordinary people had a right to govern themselves. By ignoring the rule of law, he was trying to establish that powerful men can—and should—stack the deck to hold on to power.

How would Americans react?

A week after Schiff sent his letter, Democratic House speaker Nancy Pelosi of California began a formal impeachment inquiry, and the following day, apparently to head off the investigation, Trump released a "readout"—notes taken by others who had been on the phone call with Zelensky. Although incomplete, it was still bad enough: it proved that Trump asked Zelensky to "do us a favor" in connection with the release of the promised aid. That afternoon, the White House finally gave the whistleblower complaint to the House and Senate Intelligence Committees.[4]

The next day, September 26, the House Intelligence Committee released the complaint to the public, and people could read for themselves the whistleblower's concern that Trump was soliciting foreign interference in the 2020 election and that both Trump's personal lawyer Rudy Giuliani and Attorney General William Barr were implicated in the scheme. The complaint laid out how Trump tried to strongarm Zelensky into smearing the Bidens and how White House officials had buried the tape of the call on a secret server.[5]

In October, three House committees—Intelligence, Oversight, and Foreign Affairs—began to collect testimony from current and former officials in the State Department. Trump promptly accused Schiff, the Intelligence Committee chair, of treason and said there was a "coup" under way. Secretary of State Mike Pompeo, a Trump loyalist, said that State Department officials would not appear before Congress, and White House counsel Pat Cipollone said the White House would not cooperate with the inquiry.[6]

But a number of officials were willing to testify voluntarily, and the story they told reached far beyond the problematic phone call. Trump and his allies were running a shadow foreign policy to advance the president's interests. Their plans directly opposed the interests of the United States.

After Russia invaded Ukraine in 2014, the U.S. had prioritized supporting democratic Ukraine. State Department officials had put one of the nation's very top diplomats, Marie Yovanovitch, in Ukraine, where she stood firm against the nation's corrupt leaders. Eager to get rid of her, those men told Trump's team, led by his ally and sometime lawyer Rudy Giuliani, that if Trump would fire Yovanovitch, they would announce an investigation into Hunter Biden and would say that Ukraine, rather than Russia, had interfered in the 2016 U.S. election.

Trump's team and the corrupt Ukrainians were reaching an agreement when, on April 21, Zelensky's victory ruined their plans. Apparently out of patience, Giuliani simply announced on Twitter that

Ukraine was investigating Hillary Clinton's campaign and the DNC for conspiring with "Ukrainians and others to affect [the] 2016 election." The next day, Yovanovitch was recalled, clearing the way for Trump's team to get to Zelensky.

In May, acting White House chief of staff Mick Mulvaney arranged for "three amigos"—Gordon Sondland, a wealthy hotel owner Trump had made the U.S. ambassador to the European Union; Kurt Volker, then a volunteer special envoy to Ukraine; and energy secretary Rick Perry—to work around the State Department and to pressure Zelensky. Giuliani, too, continued to badger the Ukrainian president to announce an investigation, telling him that Trump was his client. On July 25, Trump called Zelensky to squeeze him personally, and in August, Volker and Sondland drafted a statement for Zelensky to read on television. It would announce an investigation into Burisma and allege that Ukraine, not Russia, had intervened in the 2016 election.[7]

But a U.S. official on Trump's July 25 call threw sand in the gears by filing a whistleblower complaint.

The story was clear: Trump and his cronies were undermining U.S. interests and using the power of the government to keep him in the presidency. In the public impeachment hearings that began in November, Trump loyalists in the House of Representatives made no effort to disprove the overwhelming evidence against the president. Instead, led by Representatives Doug Collins of Georgia, Jim Jordan of Ohio, and John Ratcliffe of Texas, they supported the president's attempt to create an alternative reality. They badgered witnesses, compared Democrats to Nazis, and insisted that those investigating the scandal were elitists who hated Trump's regular-guy supporters. They manufactured sound bites for right-wing media, which used them to create a false narrative that would skew not only the past but also the future.

But something else emerged from the hearings: a powerful defense of American values. Ambassador Marie Yovanovitch, NSC official Dr. Fiona Hill, and Lieutenant Colonel Alexander Vindman, all naturalized U.S. citizens, championed the principles they believed America stood for. All three had either lived in or studied the Soviet Union, and their testimony and presence contrasted the authoritarianism of Russian president Vladimir Putin with what they believed to be the democratic values of the United States.[8]

While Yovanovitch testified before Congress, Trump personally attacked her by tweet, giving a real-time demonstration of the dangers of an autocratic leader. As he had told Zelensky: "She's going to go through some things."[9]

A top-level intelligence analyst before becoming the top expert in Russia and European affairs on the National Security Council under Trump, Hill hammered home that those smearing Ukraine—including those congresspeople questioning her—were parroting Russian disinformation and that Putin was flooding the country with such disinformation to destabilize democracy.

Most effective, perhaps, was Vindman, who had come to America with his father and two brothers from Ukraine when it was a Soviet republic. Along with both of his brothers, Vindman joined the U.S. military, where he was wounded serving in Iraq. "I have a deep appreciation for American values and ideals and the power of freedom," he said in an opening statement. "I am a patriot, and it is my sacred duty and honor to advance and defend OUR country, irrespective of party or politics."[10]

Vindman echoed the language of World War II America when he spoke of the "all-volunteer" army, "made up of a patchwork of people from all ethnicities, religions, and socio-economic backgrounds who come together under a common oath to protect and defend the Constitution of the United States of America." Then he assured his father that, unlike in an authoritarian country like Russia, he and his family would be safe despite his testimony against the president.

He would be okay, he said, because he was in America. "Here," he said, "right matters."

Democrats in the House of Representatives voted on December 18, 2019, to impeach the president for abuse of power and obstruction of Congress. On January 21, 2020, the Senate trial of Donald Trump began.

In the Senate trial, Trump's lawyers and allies ignored all the evidence and simply echoed the talking points of right-wing media outlets. Trump had done "absolutely nothing wrong." His phone call with Zelensky was "a perfect phone call" and the Democrats had been out to get Trump since the early days of the Russia scandal.

Their defense of the president was so inept that Senate Republicans took on the job of defending him themselves. Although Ted Cruz of Texas noted, "Out of one hundred senators, you have zero who believe you that there was no quid pro quo. None. There's not a single one," Republican senators stood behind Trump. "This is not about this president. It's not about anything he's been accused of doing," McConnell told his colleagues. "It has always been about November 3, 2020. It's about flipping the Senate."[11]

Schiff, the leading House manager of the Senate impeachment trial, made a final stand on American principles. He recounted the facts of the case and laid out the dangers of an unchecked president. "Can we be confident that he will not continue to try to cheat in [this] very election? Can we be confident that Americans and not foreign powers will get to decide, and that the president will shun any further foreign interference in our Democratic affairs?" Schiff asked. "The short, plain, sad, incontestable answer is no, you can't. You can't trust this president to do the right thing. Not for one minute, not for one election, not for the sake of our country. You just can't. He will not change and you know it."

"He has betrayed our national security, and he will do so again. He has compromised our elections, and he will do so again. You will not change him. You cannot constrain him. Truth matters little to him. What's right matters even less. And decency not at all."

Schiff begged the Republicans to say "enough." "If right doesn't matter, it doesn't matter how good the Constitution is. It doesn't matter how brilliant the Framers were. . . . If right doesn't matter, we're lost. If the truth doesn't matter, we're lost. The Framers couldn't protect us from ourselves if right and truth don't matter."[12]

Against overwhelming evidence that Trump had used the power of the presidency to try to steal an election, on February 5, 2020, Senate Republicans acquitted him of abuse of power, by a vote of 48 for conviction to 52 for acquittal. Utah senator Mitt Romney crossed the aisle to vote with the Democratic minority, thus robbing Trump of a pure party-line vote that would enable him to insist that impeachment was a partisan witch hunt. (Trump surrogates found a way around that problem quickly: they simply said that Romney wasn't a Republican.) On the second article, obstruction of Congress, the vote was 47 for conviction to 53 for acquittal.[13]

Republican senators had sacrificed democracy for power. The Republican Party was now the Trump Party. Convinced by right-wing media that used House Republicans' sound bites to create a false narrative, and without any Republican leaders contradicting them, his loyalists believed that the Ukraine scandal was a "hoax" just as they had bought his claim that the Russia scandal was.[14]

And yet the forty-eight senators who voted to convict Trump represented eighteen million more Americans than the fifty-two Republicans who voted to acquit. It was increasingly obvious that a minority was gaming the system against a majority and that their only hope for retaining power was to repress that majority.

But the Ukraine scandal and Republican leaders' protection of a president who was weaponizing the presidency also galvanized those opposed to Trumpism. The day after the Senate vote, Bill Kristol, former leader of the neoconservative movement and previously a Republican in word and deed, tweeted: "Not presumably forever; not perhaps for a day after Nov. 3, 2020; not on every issue or in every way until then. But for the time being one has to say: We are all Democrats now."[15]

CHAPTER 16

Destabilizing the Government

E ven before the Senate acquitted him, Republicans in Washington told reporters that Trump was planning revenge against those who crossed him in the impeachment trial. "It's payback time," one Republican said. "He has an enemies list that is growing by the day."[1]

The day after his acquittal, Trump fired two key impeachment witnesses: U.S. ambassador to the European Union Gordon Sondland and Lieutenant Colonel Alexander Vindman, the top expert on Ukraine at the National Security Council, who had reassured his father that he would not face retaliation for his congressional testimony. Trump also fired Vindman's twin brother, Yevgeny, from the National Security Council. Yevgeny had reported Trump's phone call to superiors but had not publicly testified against him.[2]

Days later, Trump put fierce loyalist John McEntee in charge of the White House office of personnel, urging him to ferret out anyone insufficiently loyal and to make sure the White House hired only true believers. McEntee had no experience in personnel or significant government work, but he and Trump set out to get rid of the fifty thousand nonpartisan civil servants who are hired for their skills, rather than their politics.[3]

Since 1883 those federal workers have been protected from exactly the sort of political purge Trump and McEntee wanted to execute. But the administration got around this safeguard by reclassifying certain federal workers covered by civil service protections as employees who work in "a confidential, policy-determining, policy-making or policy-advocating" job. Those sorts of employees can be exempted from civil service protections. One Trump loyalist at the Office of Management and Budget identified 88 percent of his agency as movable to this new "Schedule F."[4]

And yet Republican leaders remained steadfastly silent, some apparently interested in getting the judges they wanted in place, others apparently afraid of Trump's increasingly vocal, and potentially violent, base.

When he originally campaigned for the presidency, Trump had not seemed that different from his Republican predecessors. He complained about federal bureaucracy, embracing the idea that federal officeholders simply sucked tax dollars. He promised his supporters he would "drain the swamp" of Washington, D.C., and when he began to fill the four thousand or so political appointments presidents have to make when they take office, he chose cabinet secretaries who were wealthy and well-connected businesspeople or evangelicals—or both.[5]

But Trump quickly went further. He began by elevating his son-in-law and daughter, Jared Kushner and Ivanka Trump, to positions within the administration. As unpaid senior advisors, neither faced Senate confirmation hearings, and they got around laws against hiring family members by declaring they would not take salaries. Kushner's ludicrous portfolio demonstrated Trump's faith that the right people could do anything: his brief eventually included ending the conflict between Israelis and Palestinians, solving the opioid crisis, and so on, despite his lack of experience in any of the areas assigned to him.

Trump's daughter Ivanka was similarly unelected and unqualified, but by March 2017 she had her own office in the West Wing. The following month she represented the U.S. at a meeting in Berlin of the Group of 20, or G20, an international forum designed to address global economic issues and made up of nineteen countries with most of the world's largest economies, as well as the European Union.

Replacing career professionals with family members and friends eroded one of the key pillars of democratic government: a bureaucracy loyal not to a leader but to the state itself.

Trump also cut swaths through nonpartisan career officials. As soon as he took office, he asked for the State Department and the U.S. Agency for International Development (USAID) to cut their budgets by 37 percent and refused to fill positions there and elsewhere. When Congress would not cut funding for the Department of Agriculture, Secretary of Agriculture Sonny Perdue announced he was moving two of his department's research agencies from Washington, D.C., to Kansas City. He said that the move was to save money, but critics warned that as career officials declined to move, it would gut the agencies. In the end, more than half of their employees quit.[6]

Once in office, Trump grew increasingly angry at the civil servants who continued to investigate his campaign's ties to Russia, insisting that they were all Democrats who wanted to hound him from office. He took advantage of his ability to fill positions temporarily while waiting for Senate confirmations. Saying he liked the flexibility to move people in and out of office quickly, he relied on "acting" officials (who needed no confirmation) rather than nominating permanent appointees.

In April and May 2020, Trump slashed oversight of his administration. He fired the inspectors general of the Departments of Defense, Health and Human Services, and Transportation—all of whom were "acting"—and of the State Department and the Intelligence Community. That last one was Michael Atkinson, who had told the House

Intelligence Committee that Acting Director of National Intelligence Joseph Maguire was withholding the whistleblower complaint, launching the Ukraine scandal; in his letter to Maguire, committee chair Adam Schiff had explicitly demanded that the administration not retaliate against Atkinson. In their place, Trump appointed inspectors he believed would be more compliant.[7]

Appointing unqualified figures is a key tactic of authoritarians, who turn to staffers who are fiercely loyal because they are not qualified or talented enough to rise to power in a nonpartisan system. They recognize that without the leader who elevated them, they will never again be in power—and sometimes will be in prison—so they will cleave to him to the end.

Trump's preference for acting advisors meant that he put into office those who would not be able to withstand scrutiny. At least two of them were in office illegally: the acting secretary of the Department of Homeland Security, Chad Wolf, and his acting deputy, Ken Cuccinelli. In spring 2020, Trump threatened to adjourn Congress and just appoint a whole slew of "acting" officials.[8]

On February 4, 2020, the night before Senate Republicans acquitted him of the charges of abuse of power and obstruction of Congress in his first impeachment trial, Trump delivered the State of the Union address. The speech was a compellingly crafted narrative, with Trump as the all-powerful fictional hero. He once again presented a portrait of a nation that had been on the verge of catastrophe before he swept in to save it. It repeated a theme that ties into the American mythology of the cowboy who saves the villagers from destruction.

Trump began by touting the successes of his administration, but it was all lies. He talked of how he had turned the economy around from the devastation of his predecessor, President Barack Obama, when in fact he had inherited a growing economy that had since slowed. And he talked of how Republicans were determined to protect health care and coverage for preexisting conditions, even while his administration was, at that very moment, in court trying to destroy that access.

He did not stop with the general myth, but went on to play the game show host turned autocratic ruler. In the course of the speech, he demonstrated that he, the president, could raise hurting individuals up to glory. He promoted an older African American veteran to general. He awarded a scholarship to a child who had previously been unable to get one. He had his wife, Melania, award the Presidential Medal of Freedom to talk show host Rush Limbaugh, a man ill with terminal cancer (who obligingly pretended to be surprised and overwhelmed, although he had done interviews before the speech in which he indicated he was aware of what was about to happen). He reunited a military family. Contrived though all these scenarios were, they made him the catalyst for improving the lives of individuals in ways to which we all can relate. It was reality TV: false, scripted, and effective.[9]

More than that, it was designed to demonstrate Trump's power. As communications scholar Michael Socolow pointed out on Twitter, it mirrored the performances of Hitler, who worked similar transformations on individuals during his speeches to demonstrate that he had an almost magical power to change lives.[10]

The 2020 State of the Union was a fire-and-brimstone speech, with the good guys, who were pure good, lining up against the bad guys, who were pure evil. Trump warned of the danger of "others"— undocumented individuals, for example. In his telling, they became vicious criminals, although studies overwhelmingly show that immigrants commit crimes far more rarely than native-born Americans.

Republican congresspeople, who surely knew that what they were hearing was completely divorced from reality, repeatedly jumped to their feet to applaud it. The president had made it clear he controlled the reliably Republican voters in his base, and no Republican could cross him. It was clearly Trump's party, to do with as he wished.

CHAPTER 17

Embracing Authoritarianism

What Trump wanted was to be reelected, possibly to take advantage of the Department of Justice policy that a sitting president should not be charged with a crime, possibly to consolidate his power and become one of the autocrats he admired. It did not appear that he was particularly interested in the job itself. From February 2020 onward, his entire focus would be on reelection.

But in March the U.S. outbreak of the novel coronavirus pandemic threw a monkey wrench into Trump's plans.

The administration had ignored the pandemic-preparedness measures the Obama administration had put in place, and when a wave of desperately ill coronavirus patients hit U.S. hospitals, a lack of personal protective equipment (PPE) had medical personnel wearing garbage bags to care for them.

To manage the crisis, the administration sidestepped professionals from the Federal Emergency Management Agency (FEMA) and gave Kushner yet more responsibility, putting him in charge of a coronavirus response team to create a so-called public-private partnership that would get the private sector on board to fight the pandemic. Kushner gathered a team from consulting and private equity firms to find the personal protective equipment and other supplies the country lacked.

Kushner outlined his approach for reporters on April 3: "This is a time of crisis, and you're seeing certain people are better managers than others. . . . The president also wanted us to make sure we think outside the box, make sure we're finding all the best thinkers in the country, making sure we're getting all the best ideas." He instructed members of the team to pay special attention to tips from "VIPs," including right-wing journalists.[1]

But Kushner's team didn't know hospital specifications, have connections with suppliers, or know the laws surrounding equipment. Their response was inadequate and incoherent. Faced with that chaos, the administration blamed the World Health Organization for working with China and formally withdrew from the organization in July. Then it embraced a strategy of mass infection and replaced information from medical professionals with political messaging.

Eventually, it settled on demonizing Dr. Anthony Fauci, who had directed the National Institute of Allergy and Infectious Diseases for four decades and had received the Presidential Medal of Freedom from President George W. Bush. They blamed him for a range of offenses, from not identifying the origin of the disease, to blocking quack cures, to imposing mask mandates. Meanwhile, U.S. rates of infections and deaths were among the worst in the world.

Finally, Trump openly rejected the idea that the federal government had any responsibility for managing the pandemic. He insisted that governors should be the ones to issue stay-at-home orders, and he refused to use the Defense Production Act (DPA) to speed up production of PPE, although he did use it to enable meatpacking industry leaders to continue production without addressing the health and safety of their workers. He told states they were on their own for testing and masks.

The administration's full-blown embrace of the long-standing attempt to destroy the active federal government of the liberal consensus did more than that. It re-created exactly the conditions the liberal consensus was designed to end: it enabled a few well-connected individuals to turn a public need into a private fortune. When other countries sent masks, gowns, and so on, they went not to the states or to FEMA but to the private sector to sell at up to fifteen times their usual cost. The official in charge of distributing the materials said this was because the private sector already had efficient distribution systems in place and, he told reporters, "I'm not here to disrupt a supply chain."[2]

In April, Senate minority leader Chuck Schumer of New York begged Trump to fill the "federal void" and appoint a "senior military officer" as a "czar" to coordinate a federal response to the crisis and to use the DPA to increase production, procurement, and distribution of medical devices and equipment. He called for "a data-driven, organized and robust plan from the federal government." Trump responded: "If you spent less time on your ridiculous impeachment hoax, which went haplessly on forever and ended up going nowhere (except increasing my poll numbers), and instead focused on helping the people of New York, then New York would not have been so completely unprepared for the 'invisible enemy.'" (Schumer had, in fact, called for a declaration of a public health emergency on January 26.)[3]

By mid-April, Trump appeared desperate. The pandemic had crashed the economy, a key factor for reelection. The administration was botching its response to the crisis, and significant pushback was coming from those terrified of infection, worried about shortages of the most basic supplies, and suddenly laid off. When, in the absence of federal policy, governors shut down their states to combat the spread of the deadly virus, Trump made an extraordinary announcement. He had "absolute authority" to force states to reopen, he said: "When somebody is President of the United States, the authority is total. . . . The federal government has absolute power," and he had the "absolute right" to use that power if he wanted to.[4]

In some ways, this profound misunderstanding of the power of the presidency was simply the logical outcome of Trump's belief in hierarchical ranks. He had always denigrated those he perceived as weak or inferior; his campaign rallies were orgies of dominance displays. Once he was in office, his advisors had sought to enforce that hierarchy by using the power of the government against society's weakest members. They had, for example, violated both U.S. and international law to deter immigration by separating children from their parents at the southern border between the U.S. and Mexico. It was an astonishing assertion that their policies trumped both rights and the law. Officers kept no records to enable the reunion of the traumatized families of more than five thousand separated children.[5]

By 2020, Trump was stronger than he had been in 2017. He had consolidated his supporters through disinformation about the Russia investigation. The Ukraine scandal brought the entire Republican Party to his defense. He had removed professionals from government positions and installed cronies in their place. And most of all, he had turned more and more consistently to his base, including their violent gangs, for support, intimidating party members who might challenge him.

In 2019, Trump had tried to use the power of the federal government in foreign affairs to rig the election. In 2020, he set out to rig the election by using the power of the federal government at home.

Trump brought all of his tools to the effort. He assured his supporters that they were in the majority, that he would win, and that if he lost it would be because the system was "rigged." Then, as Republicans openly acknowledged that high voter participation would "be extremely devastating to Republicans," Trump and his allies worked to keep his opponents from voting. Put in charge of the United States Postal Service, Trump loyalist Louis DeJoy dramatically rearranged service hours, trashed mail-sorting machines, and raised the cost of posting mail-in ballots, all at a time when the pandemic meant in-person voting could be deadly.

Meanwhile, Trump and his allies weaponized the pandemic, ignoring health concerns and complaining that Democrats were deliberately sabotaging the economy. Although polls showed that two thirds of Americans were worried that lockdown rules would be lifted too early, the Fox News Channel advertised rallies to reopen businesses and schools and then showed protests in Colorado, Illinois, Florida, Tennessee, Wisconsin, and Washington, organized by some of the same Republican operatives who had organized the Tea Party movement in 2009.

Trump whipped up the violence he had endorsed in 2017 at Charlottesville against the state governors trying to manage the horror in their states. "LIBERATE MINNESOTA!" "LIBERATE MICHIGAN!" "LIBERATE VIRGINIA, and save your great 2nd Amendment. It is under siege!"[6] Trump tweeted on April 17. In Michigan, gangs waving Trump signs and flying Confederate flags claimed that lockdown orders violated their liberty and shouted "Lock her up!" at Democratic Governor Gretchen Whitmer. On April 30, armed protesters calling themselves "American Patriots" rallied at the Michigan statehouse to threaten the legislators, and the lack of response by law enforcement cheered others on.

Then, on May 25, 2020, Minneapolis police officer Derek Chauvin killed George Floyd by kneeling on his neck for nearly nine minutes. A bystander captured a video of Floyd's death on her phone, and the visual demonstration of a white government officer casually murdering a Black American brought protesters in Minneapolis and then Los Angeles, Denver, Chicago, and New York City to the streets, insisting that "Black Lives Matter." Protests spread to Phoenix, Arizona, as well as Louisville, Kentucky, where twenty-six-year-old Breonna Taylor had been killed in her home on March 13 by plainclothes police officers executing a warrant to search for drugs they believed a man with whom Taylor had previously had a relationship might have sent her (he had not).[7]

The protests gave Trump the excuse he needed to use troops against Americans. "When the looting starts, the shooting starts," Trump tweeted on May 29. He insisted the protesters were "organized and driven by anarchic and left extremist groups, far-left extremist groups, using antifa-like tactics, many of whom travel from outside the state to promote the violence." Attorney General William Barr backed him up, noting: "It is a federal crime to cross state lines or to use interstate facilities to incite or participate in violent rioting, and we will enforce those laws."[8]

On June 1, after a call with Russian president Vladimir Putin, Trump told state governors on a phone call: "You have to dominate, if you don't dominate, you're wasting your time. . . . You've got to arrest people, you have to track people, you have to put them in jail for 10 years and you'll never see this stuff again." Later that day, a massive police presence, including officers from Customs and Border Protection (CBP), cleared peaceful protesters from Lafayette Square, across from the White House, using tear gas, rubber bullets, and flash-bang explosives to prepare for an appearance by the president.

Then, accompanied by senior officials representing the Department of Justice, the National Security Council, the military, and family members—including Kushner and Ivanka—Trump crossed the square and walked to historic St. John's Episcopal Church. Surrounded by cameras, he held up a Bible and said: "We have a great country . . . the greatest country in the world. We will make it even greater, it won't take long. . . . It's coming back, it's coming back strong, it will be greater than ever before."[9]

That day was a turning point. The Black Lives Matter movement was a popular protest against rising authoritarianism, and two thirds of adult Americans supported it. But while Republican lawmakers remained silent, the events of June 1 made former political leaders (including all four living presidents), more than 1,250 former members of the Department of Justice, Democratic lawmakers, and, crucially, military leaders take a stand against Trump.

It was virtually unheard of for military officers to comment on politics, but a wave of leaders from the U.S. Air Force, Army, and Navy spoke up to call for justice for Black Americans and to reiterate that their loyalty was to the U.S. Constitution. Because their cooperation would be imperative for Trump to pull off an authoritarian takeover, their warning that June 1, 2020, might well "signal the beginning of the end of the American experiment" grabbed headlines. Implicitly and sometimes explicitly, they condemned the president. The Pentagon disarmed the National Guard troops stationed in Washington, D.C., and sent the regular troops that had been moved to the city back to their home bases.[10]

Far from ending the crisis, the military's resistance drove Trump to try to create his own army. With the help of Attorney General William Barr, he took control of the law enforcement teams from the FBI; the Bureau of Alcohol, Tobacco, Firearms, and Explosives; the Secret Service; the Drug Enforcement Agency; the CBP; and eighty other, smaller forces that make up about 132,000 federal law enforcement officers. On July 20 the Trump administration announced it would send federal officers into cities run by Democrats, ostensibly to fight crime there. Acting director of Homeland Security Chad Wolf dismissed the objections to federal intervention in Chicago and elsewhere, saying: "I don't need invitations by the state, state mayors, or state governors to do our job. We're going to do that, whether they like us there or not."[11]

Two days later, the Trump campaign released an ad suggesting that the choice in 2020 was between "PUBLIC SAFETY" and "CHAOS AND VIOLENCE." But observers quickly noted that the image of street violence in the ad was not from the United States; it was from Ukraine in 2014. And the image was not of police officers defending the rule of law; it was the opposite. It was a picture of democratic pro-testers being attacked by the forces of corrupt oligarch Viktor Yanu-kovych, who had won Ukraine's presidency thanks to the help of Paul Manafort.[12]

It was hard not to see the error as intentional.

CHAPTER 18

Rewriting American History

Trump went beyond this attempt to build his own army. To win his cause, he told his followers that they were fighting a war for the soul of America, giving them a perverted version of American history. "We will never cave to the left wing and the left-wing intolerance," he told a crowd. "They hate our history, they hate our values, and they hate everything we prize as Americans."

He rejected the multicultural society that democracy promised, telling them: "Our country didn't grow great with them. It grew great with you and your thought process and your ideology." And he echoed fascists who promised to return their country to divinely inspired rules that, if ignored, would create disaster. At a rally, Trump said: "The left-wing mob is trying to demolish our heritage, so they can replace it with a new oppressive regime that they alone control. This is a battle to save the Heritage, History, and Greatness of our Country!"[1]

In his rewriting of history, the ideological threads of global authoritarianism came together with America's peculiar history to overturn American democracy.

Russia's Vladimir Putin and Hungary's Viktor Orbán had defended replacing self-government in their own countries because, they said, liberal democracy was obsolete. Because democracy welcomes minorities, immigrants, women, and LGBTQ people as equals, they argue, it undermines the virtue necessary for society to function.

Orbán was open about his determination to overthrow the concept of Western democracy, replacing it with what, on different occasions, he called "illiberal democracy" or "Christian democracy." He wanted to replace the multiculturalism at the heart of democracy with what he called "Christian culture," stop the immigration that he believed undermines Hungarian culture, and reject "adaptable family models" in favor of "the Christian family model." What he wanted, in short, was to destroy the equality before the law on which democracy depends and restore a traditional, patriarchal society dominated by white men.

During Trump's term, the American right openly embraced this ideology. In 2019, Fox News Channel personality Tucker Carlson endorsed Hungary's antiabortion and anti-immigration policies. The next year, Trump's vice president, Mike Pence, spoke at a forum in Budapest, where he denounced immigration and urged traditional social values. He told the audience he hoped that the U.S. Supreme Court would outlaw abortion thanks to the three justices Trump had put on the court.

Those attacking democracy insisted they were defending traditional America. They focused relentlessly on immigration and insisted that traditional families were under attack: "real" America was being destroyed by multiculturalism and secular values.

That idea thrilled the evangelical voters who had flocked to Trump, believing he would overturn abortion rights and restore a world in which they felt important. Getting rid of secular values meant insisting that the United States was founded as a Christian nation and that anyone trying to embrace secular values was attacking those foundations.

In 2019, Trump's attorney general, William Barr, attempted to use the Framers' words to justify this radical reworking of the nation's founding principles. He told an audience that by "self-government," the Framers did not mean the ability of people to vote for representatives of their choice. Rather, he said, they meant individual morality:

the ability to govern oneself. And because people are inherently wicked, that self-government requires the authority of a religion: Christianity.

This sleight of hand directly contradicted the actual work of the Framers. James Madison stood passionately against the establishment of any religion by the government, explaining that what was at stake was not just religion but also representative government itself.

The establishment of religion attacked a fundamental human right—an unalienable right—of conscience, Madison said. If lawmakers could destroy the right of freedom of conscience, they could destroy all other unalienable rights. Madison warned specifically that they could control the press, abolish trial by jury, take over the executive and judicial powers, take away the right to vote, and set themselves up in power forever.

The idea of using government power to establish a "traditional" form of society relied not on the nation's founding principles but on its dark history of inequality. In mid-July 2020, under the guise of supporting human rights, a report from the State Department's Commission on Unalienable Rights reworked American history into a vision of white Christian nationalism that looked much like the worldview of the southern enslavers before the Civil War.

The report, written under evangelical secretary of state Mike Pompeo, began by stating that the primary tradition "that formed the American spirit" was "Protestant Christianity . . . infused with the beautiful Biblical teachings that every human being is imbued with dignity and bears responsibilities toward fellow human beings, because each is made in the image of God." It claimed that the Founders established the United States to secure property rights and religious liberty and that the Constitution imposed strict limits on the government in order to protect that liberty.[2]

In the 1850s, southern enslavers used a similar argument to try to take over the United States government, keep it from doing anything but protect property, and throw the power in the country to the states, where a minority could enforce its will unchecked by a popular majority. The stunted version of history embraced by Trump and his allies translated this old ideology into an authoritarian argument for the future. It erased the victory of democracy in the Civil War, the ongoing struggle for equal rights that followed and that lasted until the 1970s, and the liberal consensus that finally tried to make those rights real.

In August, Trump finally recognized that the Republican National Convention would have to bow to the pandemic and be virtual. He announced he would hold a three-night television event from the White House, a plan that deliberately bound his leadership and authoritarian ideology to the historical symbols of the nation. Vice President Mike Pence spoke at Fort McHenry, where Francis Scott Key wrote "The Star-Spangled Banner"; First Lady Melania Trump spoke from the newly renovated Rose Garden; and Secretary of State Mike Pompeo spoke from Jerusalem in front of sites important to Christian evangelicals while on an official taxpayer-funded trip to the Middle East, although Senate-confirmed State Department appointees are not allowed even to attend a political party convention, let alone speak at one.

Even before the convention, the Trump campaign had been quietly incorporating Nazi imagery into its messaging, as both a dog whistle for right-wing supporters and a way to get free press from outraged observers, and the White House convention drew on imagery from dictatorships. A parade of family members described Trump as wonderful, subordinates offered generic over-the-top praise, and every speaker demonized anyone who didn't support Trump's continued rule. The convention included demonstrations of mercy from the president as he pardoned a criminal and granted citizenship to five immigrants (who were apparently not told they would be part of the convention).

And the convention had the trappings of dictators, from the First Lady's dress that evoked a Nazi uniform—almost certainly to provoke a response while appealing to the alt-right—to carefully chosen cathedral ceilings and impressive architecture, to the wall of flags, all evoking tradition, majesty, and might. The televised spectacle concentrated all that power not in our democratic government, but in one man.

Trump turned the White House, the people's house, into the background for a political rally, emblazoned with flags and sporting jumbotrons that spelled out "Trump/Pence." It looked like a futuristic movie dystopia as Trump tried to sell the classic alternative reality of authoritarians who have little actual good news to report. In his now-familiar refrain, he claimed that the country was in chaos caused by his lawless opponents and that he alone could solve the problem. He would return his supporters to the positions of authority they felt they had lost, ushering back in the good old days when the country was great.

The Republican Party, which had formed to stand against the enslavers who had all but taken over the nation's government and restore democracy, was now on board with Trump's dictatorship. Party leaders wrote no campaign platform to outline policies and goals for the future. Instead, they passed a resolution saying that "the Republican Party has and will continue to enthusiastically support the President's America-first agenda."[3]

In September, just before the 2020 election, Trump made American history central to his reelection effort. He attacked the 1619 Project, a historical initiative by *The New York Times* that centered human enslavement and the racial patterns it set at the heart of American history. In response, Trump established the 1776 Commission, saying it would end the "radicalized view of American history" that vilified the nation's Founders and taught a "twisted web of lies" that he called "a form of child abuse." He claimed—without evidence—that "students are now taught in school to hate their own country, and to believe that the men and women who built it were not heroes, but rather villains." Calling studies that emphasize American racism "one-sided and divisive," he opposed their view of "America as an irredeemably and systemically racist country."[4]

Trump's handpicked 1776 Commission was made up not of historians but of right-wing activists and politicians. Although the federal government does not determine school curriculum, he placed the commission inside the Department of Education and charged it with promoting "patriotic education" in the nation's schools, national parks, and museums.

Meanwhile, Democratic nominee Joe Biden recalled the nation's greatest achievements with much greater perception. In October, in Gettysburg, Pennsylvania, a town hallowed by history, he called for the nation to put aside division and come together. He talked about race: "Think about what it takes for a Black person to love America. That is a deep love for this country that for far too long we have never fully recognized." He talked about disparities of wealth: "Working people and their kids deserve an opportunity."

And he talked about Lincoln and how at Gettysburg, he called for Americans to dedicate themselves to a "new birth of freedom" so that the men who had died for that cause "shall not have died in vain." "Today we are engaged once again in a battle for the soul of the nation," Biden said. "After all that America has accomplished, after all the years we have stood as a beacon of light to the world, it cannot be that here and now, in 2020, we will allow government of the people, by the people, and for the people to perish from this earth."[5]

But Trump had done his work too well. His propaganda, cruelty, and demonstrations of dominance had empowered his followers and made his leadership central to their identity. At a debate in early

October he snarled, spat, lied, bullied, badgered, and apparently tried to infect Biden with Covid-19, for it later turned out he had tested positive for coronavirus before the debate. Determined not to admit he had been wrong about a deadly virus, he attempted to demonstrate his strength over it, but his illness turned the final days of the campaign into chaos. Nonetheless, his supporters stayed with him. By late October, when Trump supporters in Texas organized to drive a Biden campaign bus off the road and Donald Trump Jr. cheered them on, it was clear: they had turned against democracy.

CHAPTER 19

January 6

As early as 2019, Trump had "joked" about staying in power regardless of the election results, and in summer 2020, as his numbers plummeted, he floated the idea of delaying the election. Republican lawmakers still didn't make a stand against him. But in a sign that he had little faith that Trump would pull off a win, Mitch McConnell pushed through the confirmation of a third right-wing Trump appointee to the Supreme Court, Amy Coney Barrett, on October 31, when balloting was already under way for the November 3 election.

On that same day, Trump's ally Steve Bannon told a private audience that Trump was going to declare that he had won the 2020 election no matter what. Trump knew that Democratic mail-in ballots would show up in the vote totals later than Republican votes cast on Election Day, creating a "red mirage" that would be overtaken later by Democratic votes. "Trump's going to take advantage of it," Bannon said, by calling the election early and saying that the later votes were somehow illegitimate. "That's our strategy. He's gonna declare himself a winner." Bannon continued: "Here's the thing. After then, Trump never has to go to a voter again. . . . He's gonna say 'F*ck you. How about that?' Because . . . he's done his last election."[1]

That's almost how it played out.

Early returns on the evening of Election Day 2020, November 3, showed Trump with leads. But, more quickly than anyone expected,

Democratic votes turned the key state of Arizona blue, and the Fox News Channel called the race for Biden. Furious, Trump took to the airwaves at about two-thirty the next morning and declared he had won, although ballots were still being counted and several battleground states had no clear winner. "We won't stand for this," he told supporters, assuring them he had won. "We'll be going to the U.S. Supreme Court. We want all voting to stop."[2]

But it didn't, and by the time all the ballots were counted, the election was not close: Biden beat Trump by more than 7 million votes and by 306 to 232 in the Electoral College, the exact same Electoral College margin Trump had declared a landslide when it favored him in 2016.

Trump publicly insisted the election had been rigged, although his own attorney general, William Barr, who had been a steadfast defender, said the election was legitimate and the conspiracy theories his team was advancing were "ridiculous." But Trump refused to let go of the lie that he had won and, crucially, was able to find allies in Republican leadership willing to help him overturn American democracy, either by actively helping or by staying silent.

Over the next few months, the Trump campaign challenged the election by demanding recounts—all of which confirmed that Biden had won. Trump or his surrogates filed and lost at least sixty-three lawsuits over the 2020 election, most of which were dismissed for lack of evidence. And yet right-wing media continued to hype the idea that the election was stolen, and election officials and ballot counters received death threats.

Trump and his allies also held informational sessions with state legislators to convince them they had the power to disregard the will of the voters and choose their own electors. Notably, Trump's allies pressured officials in Georgia to throw out the votes from Democratic-leaning Fulton County. When they failed to do so, Trump himself got on the phone with Georgia secretary of state Brad Raffensperger and told him: "I just want to find 11,780 votes, which is one more than we have."[3]

As legal challenges failed, Trump's allies turned to a plan advanced by right-wing lawyer Kenneth Chesebro and turned into a memo by lawyer John Eastman, a professor at Chapman University's Fowler School of Law in California. It called for Trump supporters in seven battleground states to meet secretly and submit a false slate of electors for Trump to Congress and the National Archives. Then, on January 6, when it came time for Vice President Mike Pence to count the electoral votes from the 2020 election, making Democrat Joe Biden president, he could refuse to count the electors from the apparently contested states.

That would mean either that Trump would be elected outright or that Democrats would put up such a fight that Pence could say there was no clear winner and send the election to the House of Representatives, where each state gets one vote. Since there were more Republican delegations than Democratic ones, Trump would be president.

This was an extraordinary rejection of the theory of democracy—that voters have a right to choose their leaders—but Trump loyalists believed they were in the right. "This is a fight of good versus evil," Trump's evangelical chief of staff, Mark Meadows, wrote on November 24, 2020, to Supreme Court justice Clarence Thomas's wife, Ginni, who urged state legislators to sign on to the false elector scheme. Meadows continued: "Evil always looks like the victor until the King of Kings triumphs. Do not grow weary in well doing. The fight continues."[4]

When Pence refused to participate in the plan—likely knowing that if the coup failed, he'd be the one left holding the bag—Trump fell back on the old tactic of spreading a false narrative through an investigation. He plotted to name Jeffrey Clark, a lawyer for the environmental division of the Justice Department, as attorney general. Clark planned to announce to the battleground state legislatures that the Department of Justice was "investigating various irregularities" in the election—this was a lie—and that they should choose a new set of electors. Only the threat that the entire leadership of the Department of Justice would resign made Trump back down.

Republicans had gone along with the charade that the election had been stolen, seemingly hoping to pick up Trump's supporters for their own political ambitions. In the House, especially, Trump's allies began to echo his accusations and to say they would question the counts from certain states. Such challenges required a paired vote with a senator, and McConnell tried hard to hold his conference from joining the radicals in the House. It didn't work. Josh Hawley of Missouri, who saw himself as a top 2024 presidential contender, and Ted Cruz of Texas, who didn't want to be undercut, led eleven other senators in a revolt to challenge the ballots. McConnell had lost control of his conference; Trump now called the shots.

On January 3, all ten living former defense secretaries signed an op-ed in *The Washington Post* warning that any "efforts to involve the U.S. armed forces in resolving election disputes would take us into dangerous, unlawful and unconstitutional territory." They also seemed to put colleagues on notice: "Civilian and military officials who direct or carry out such measures would be accountable, including potentially facing criminal penalties, for the grave consequences of their actions on our republic."[5]

But Trump was still not out of cards to play. He had been courting right-wing mobs since August 2017 and had openly turned to them during the campaign, telling the Proud Boys in September, for example, to "stand back and stand by." Then, on December 19, frustrated by his inability to get the election overturned, Trump tweeted to his supporters that it was "statistically impossible to have lost the 2020 Election. Big protest in D.C. on January 6th. Be there, will be wild!"[6]

At the "Stop the Steal" rally on January 6, held at the Ellipse near the White House, Trump and his surrogates told the crowd that they had won the election, and he warned: "We are going to have to fight much harder." He claimed that Chinese-driven socialists were taking over the country and assured the crowd: "We're gathered together in the heart of our nation's capital for one very, very basic and simple reason: To save our democracy." He told them, "You'll never take back our country with weakness. You have to show strength and you have to be strong. We have come to demand that Congress do the right thing and only count the electors who have been lawfully slated. Lawfully slated. . . . And we fight, we fight like hell, and if you don't fight like hell you're not going to have a country anymore."[7]

And, knowing they were armed, he told them to march to the Capitol.

The violent attack on the United States government that followed brought to life the mythological history that the Republicans had come to celebrate, tying Trump's authoritarianism to the Republicans' embrace of America's unequal past. Trading "1776" slogans, the Trump Republicans who attacked the Capitol believed they were writing a new history of the United States, one that finally embraced the hierarchical version of American history claimed by the Confederates before them. After decades of feeding hungry voters ideas and images straight out of the nation's white supremacist past, Republican politicians and pundits had created a mob determined to end American democracy. One of the rioters accomplished what the southern troops of the 1860s had never been able to: he carried the Confederate battle flag into the United States Capitol.

From their hiding spots, lawmakers begged the president to call off his supporters, but he did nothing for more than three hours. After 5:40 p.m., when the National Guard had been deployed without his orders, thus making it clear the rioters would be overpowered before either taking over the government themselves or giving him an excuse to declare martial law, Trump issued a video statement.

"I know you're hurt," he said. "We had an election that was stolen from us. It was a landslide election, and everyone knows it, especially the other side, but you have to go home now. . . . We love you. You're very special."[8] He tweeted: "Remember this day forever!"[9]

CHAPTER 20

The Big Lie

I n the wake of the attack on the U.S. Capitol, it initially seemed as if Trump had become so toxic that the Republicans would veer away from him and back toward the safer ground of politics before 2016. While pro-Trump media tried to blame the attack on left-wing antifa, all four of the country's living ex-presidents—Democrats Jimmy Carter, Bill Clinton, and Barack Obama, and Republican George W. Bush—called out Trump and his party for inciting the rioters.[1]

Trump immediately lost his access to Facebook, Instagram, and his beloved Twitter, and people across the country called for his removal through the Twenty-Fifth Amendment, impeachment, or resignation. Cabinet members and White House staff resigned, and finally a handful of Republican politicians spoke out against the president.[2]

But Trump refused to back down. Although aides warned him there was talk of removing him, he nonetheless spoke to supporters in a video on January 7: "I know you are disappointed," he said, "but I also want you to know that our incredible journey is only just beginning." At the time, he seemed delusional, but it was actually true, at least for a growing group of people who came to be known as election deniers.[3]

When the House of Representatives voted to impeach Trump for a second time on January 13, 2021, for incitement of insurrection, only 10 Republicans voted in favor, while 197 voted no (4 did not vote). In the Senate, 7 Republican senators joined the Democrats to convict, while 43 continued to back Trump.[4]

Having suffered no consequences for his actions inciting his followers to attack our democracy, like the Confederates in 1865, Trump continued his behavior, falsely telling his supporters that he had been cheated out of a landslide victory by thieving Democrats.

Far from retreating, Trump had moved to the stage that scholars of authoritarianism call a "Big Lie," a key propaganda tool associated with Nazi Germany. This is a lie so huge that no one can believe it is false. If leaders repeat it enough times, refusing to admit that it is a lie, people come to think it is the truth because surely no one would make up anything so outrageous.

In his autobiography, *Mein Kampf*, Adolf Hitler wrote that people were more likely to believe a giant lie than a little one, because they were willing to tell small lies in their own lives but "would be ashamed to resort to large-scale falsehoods." Since they could not conceive of telling "colossal untruths, they would not believe that others could have the impudence to distort the truth so infamously." He went on: "Even though the facts which prove this to be so may be brought clearly to their minds, they will still doubt and waver and will continue to think that there may be some other explanation."[5]

The U.S. Office of Strategic Services had picked up on Hitler's manipulation of his followers when it described Hitler's psychological profile. It said, "His primary rules were: never allow the public to cool off; never admit a fault or wrong; never concede that there may be some good in your enemy; never leave room for alternatives; never accept blame; concentrate on one enemy at a time and blame him for everything that goes wrong; people will believe a big lie sooner than a little one; and if you repeat it frequently enough people will sooner or later believe it." Parroting the lie becomes a loyalty pledge, even if—especially if—you don't actually believe it.[6]

Big lies are springboards for authoritarians. They enable a leader to convince followers that they were unfairly cheated of power by those the leader demonizes. In the U.S., the power of Trump's Big Lie to rally supporters meant that the Republican Party gradually purged those members who continued to stand against him, and leaders consistently refused to acknowledge that Biden had won the election. "Election denier" became a political identity, and going into Biden's presidency, most Republicans simply affirmed that he was the current president.

The belief that Democrats cheated in the election translated into an insistence that the electoral system must be strengthened to keep Democratic voters—especially Black voters—from the polls. In 2021, nineteen Republican-dominated states changed their election laws to make it harder to vote. Some of them also took the ability to certify the votes away from nonpartisan officers and gave it to partisan boards.[7]

The Big Lie permitted the final destruction of the liberal consensus, focusing first on the right to vote itself. As Senate minority leader, Mitch McConnell had used the filibuster to guarantee that the Democrats couldn't protect voting rights, end the partisan gerrymander, stop dark money from pouring into elections, or restore the 1965 Voting Rights Act.

But the Big Lie meant the Republicans could skew the mechanics of the electoral system even further: Trump supporters began to talk up a fringe constitutional theory called the independent state legislature doctrine, arguing that state legislatures alone could choose presidential electors without regard to state constitutions, courts, or governors. This doctrine would enable a Republican legislature to write whatever rules for voting it wished, cutting Democrats out of the vote altogether. Had this doctrine been in place for the 2020 election, Trump would have won.

Indeed, Republicans called for exactly what those backing the destruction of the liberal consensus had advocated since 1937. They wanted to destroy the power of the national government and throw government back to the states. Furious at federal government organizations that thwarted Trump, including the FBI and the Centers for Disease Control and Prevention (CDC), Trump Republicans called for disbanding them. In 2022, extremist chair of the Arizona state Republican Party Kari Lake announced: "We're gonna push back with our state's rights. We're sovereign states. We are not serfs of the federal government."[8]

The Supreme Court, stacked with "originalists" after years of Republican appointments, turned hard right during the Trump years with McConnell's help. It bolstered the states' rights advocates. Rather than preserving established law, as American courts had always prioritized, it repeatedly threw out precedent and emphasized that the states, rather than the federal government, should determine the laws under which we live.

That restriction on federal authority had immediate consequences for equal rights. Refusing to "intrude on state sovereignty," on June 24, 2022, the six radicals on the court overturned the 1973 *Roe v. Wade* decision that had legalized abortion. They argued that the right to determine abortion rights must be returned "to the people's elected representatives" at the state level, even as states were restricting the right to vote. For the first time in our history, the court explicitly refused to recognize an established constitutional right.

In the *Dobbs v. Jackson Women's Health Organization* decision, the court took the position that the Fourteenth Amendment did not give the federal government the power to protect certain civil rights. This brought into question the right to use contraception and the rights to interracial and gay marriage, all protected under the same legal argument as abortion. So Democrats set out to protect those rights through federal legislation. But Republicans in Congress overwhelmingly voted to oppose such laws. Although 62 percent of Americans supported reproductive rights, 99 percent of House Republicans voted against them. Although more than 90 percent of Americans supported the right to use birth control, 96 percent of House Republicans voted against it. Although 70 percent of Americans supported gay marriage, 77 percent of House Republicans voted against it. In the Senate, Republicans filibustered the measures altogether.[9]

The destruction of federal power also signaled an end to federal regulation of business. On June 30, 2022, the Supreme Court overturned a legal concept that had been in place since the 1930s. In *West Virginia v. Environmental Protection Agency* it embraced what became known as the major questions theory of the non-delegation doctrine. This theory said that Congress cannot delegate "major questions" to the executive branch. Because most of the agencies that enforce business regulations are housed in that branch—and have been since George Washington's term—the decision suggested that the government regulation at the heart of the liberal consensus could become virtually impossible.

Trump's right-wing extremists threw power to the states, where gerrymandering had put extremists in control. State houses passed draconian abortion laws, passed extreme gun laws, and wrote laws prohibiting public school teachers from teaching "divisive concepts."

But this state-based system did not mean that voters in the states could do as they wished. Instead, the right-wing mythological reading of history created a loophole that permitted the federal government to act, so long as Supreme Court justices believed those actions reflected the early history of the country. The Constitution does not protect the right to abortion because it does not mention that right, Justice Samuel Alito wrote in the *Dobbs* decision, but the court actually can protect rights not mentioned in the Constitution so long as they are "deeply rooted in this Nation's history and tradition" and "implicit in the concept of ordered liberty."[10]

The court then struck down a New York state law restricting the concealed carrying of guns on the grounds that history suggested such a restriction was unconstitutional. But, in fact, in both the *Dobbs* decision and *New York State Rifle & Pistol Association, Inc. v. Bruen*, the court used stunningly bad history, if it could be called history at all. Abortion was, in fact, deeply rooted in this nation's history not only in the far past but also in the past forty-nine years, and individual gun rights were not part of our early history.

Thus, the court imposed on the nation a so-called originalism that returned power to the states, leaving the door open for state lawmakers to get rid of business regulation and gut civil rights, but its originalism also left the door open for the federal government to impose laws on the states that are popular only with an extremist minority, exactly contrary to what the Framers tried to write into our Constitution.

In its imposition of minority rule first by insisting on states' rights and then by demanding federal protection of laws it wanted, the Republican Party echoed the southern Democrats before the Civil War. Like today's Republicans, as southern enslavers lost support, they entrenched themselves in the states, then took over the machinery of the federal government and then the Supreme Court. The court then agreed that the center of democracy was in the states, no matter how undemocratic state legislation was.

Regardless of who was in the White House, and with the help of the language of authoritarianism and the use of mythological history, the MAGA Republicans appeared to be on track to accomplish what the Confederates could not: the rejection of the Declaration of Independence and its replacement with the hierarchical vision of the Confederates.

Part 3

RECLAIMING AMERICA

CHAPTER 21

What Is America?

Today's crisis in democracy has brought us back to the same question that haunted the Founders: Are the principles on which this nation was founded viable? Is it really possible to create a country in which everyone is equal before the law and entitled to have a say in their government, or are some people better than others and thus have the right—and the duty—to rule?

In 1776, the Founders threw off the European tradition dictating that some men were better than others. They declared as "self-evident" the truths that "all men are created equal" and that governments are legitimate only if they rely not on dynasty or religion, but on the consent of the governed. The Founders were so sure of these propositions that they gave them the form of a mathematical constant. They were rebelling against not just one king, but against all kings, and standing firm on the idea that men had a right to determine their own fates.

For all that the congressmen meeting in Philadelphia got around the sticky little problem of Black and Indigenous enslavement by defining "men" as "white men," and for all that it never crossed their minds that women might also have rights, the Declaration of Independence was an astonishingly radical document. In a world that had been dominated by a small class of rich men for so long that most people simply accepted that they should be forever tied to their status at birth, a group of upstart legislators on the edge of a continent declared that no man was born better than any other, and that every man had a right to choose the government under which he lived.

It is impossible to overstate the intellectual daring required to institute a new form of government. The Founders' courage was physical, too: they were not exaggerating when they pledged to one another "our lives, our fortunes, and our sacred honor." If their bid to win independence failed, their names at the foot of the Declaration of Independence were the signatures to their own death warrants. Benjamin Franklin meant it when he said that if they did not hang together, they would hang separately.

And yet . . .

The same men who put their lives on the line to establish that all men are created equal literally owned other human beings. They considered Indigenous people "savages" and women subordinate to men by definition. Neither Black men nor Indians nor women fell into their definition of people who were "equal" or who needed to consent to the government under which they lived.

Indeed, it was by removing those people from their definition of the body politic that the Founders were able to imagine political equality. If all but a small number of white men were excluded from participating in government, then it wasn't much of a stretch to see "all men" as having similar interests and as being able to work together to govern themselves.

Equality, then, depended on inequality.

So was the whole concept of American democracy a sham from the start?

In August 2019, *The New York Times Magazine* launched a project that suggested it was. Spearheaded by journalist Nikole Hannah-Jones, the project discarded the date of 1776 for the nation's founding and replaced it with 1619, the date of the first landing of twenty to thirty enslaved Africans at the English colony of Virginia. It placed race, Black Americans, and enslavement "at the very center of the story we tell ourselves about who we are as a country."[1]

Its authors argued that the landing of the Black slaves, traded for supplies by the pirates who had stolen them from another ship, marked "the country's very origin" because it "inaugurated a barbaric system of chattel slavery that would last for the next 250 years." From slavery "and the anti-black racism it required," the editors claimed, grew "nearly everything that has truly made America exceptional: its economic might, its industrial power, its electoral system, its diet and popular music, the inequities of its public health and education, its astonishing penchant for violence, its income inequality, the example it sets for the world as a land of freedom and equality, its slang, its legal system and the endemic racial fears and hatreds that continue to plague it to this day."

In response, Trump organized his own project, the 1776 Commission. Its members released their report on the federal holiday that celebrates the birthday of the civil rights icon Reverend Martin Luther King Jr., and just days before Democratic president Joe Biden's inauguration. They presented a version of America based in the uplifting pronouncements of the Founders alone, suggesting American democracy was established as soon as the lawmakers of the Second Continental Congress articulated it.

The report highlighted the nation's founding documents from the Revolutionary Era, especially the Declaration of Independence, saying that the principles written in the Declaration "show how the American people have ever pursued freedom and justice." It glided over the reality of the glaring inequalities in our history, offering up the historical myth that authoritarians require: that the nation had been founded on divinely inspired and timeless principles that were pure in our past and were now being challenged by enemies. No other nation, it said, had worked harder or done more to bring to life "the universal truths of equality, liberty, justice, and government by consent."[2]

The 1776 Report demonstrated in real time how leaders seeking to undermine democracy have tied American history to their cause. The historical inequality embedded in our founding—that "all men are created equal"—depends on the subordination of minorities and women. Whenever members of marginalized groups seem to approach equality, antidemocratic leaders can drum up supporters by insisting that they are attacking national principles and reducing white men to subservience. Those leaders reject the idea of equality, but, paradoxically, they root that rejection in our founding. Their version of America depends on keeping political power and economic opportunity away from Black and Brown Americans and keeping women in roles as wives, mothers, or sexual objects, as they were in the founding era. To justify that exclusion, it also requires defining the powerless as inferiors, either criminals or weak-minded people unable to think and act for themselves.

When Trump's followers attacked the U.S. Capitol on January 6, 2021, they were embracing this strand of American history, one that stretches beyond 1619 to the enslavement of Indigenous Americans that began as soon as European sailors dropped anchor off the American continents. That version of history was articulated clearly by the Confederates whose battle flag Trump Republicans carried into the U.S. Capitol on January 6. "I repudiate, as ridiculously absurd, that much lauded but nowhere accredited dogma of Mr. Jefferson, that 'all men are born equal,'" South Carolina senator James Henry Hammond wrote before the Civil War. In his view, voters had no right to determine policy; their role was simply to choose one set of leaders or another.[3]

The U.S. history that emphasized the inequality the Founders practiced rather than the equality they preached gave us the Jim Crow and Juan Crow laws of the late-nineteenth and twentieth centuries. It also gave us the policies that crowded Indigenous Americans onto reservations where disease and malnutrition, as well as lack of opportunity, killed many of them and pushed the rest into poverty. It gave us the 1924 Immigration Act, which ranked immigrants according to their country of origin.

The intersection of that hierarchical theme in U.S. history and authoritarianism came together quite explicitly in the German fascism of the 1930s, when Nazi lawyers and judges turned to America's Jim Crow laws for inspiration. Hitler looked to America's Indigenous reservations as a way to rid a country of "unwanted" people. He called the Ukrainians, Poles, and Jews whom he intended to massacre "Indians."[4]

Antidemocratic leaders in the U.S. have convinced their followers not only that they are losing significance but also that by joining a movement to put their leaders in power they are defending the nation's traditions. Those they convince willingly abandon the principle of equality and replace it with a conviction that some people are better than others and should be in control. In the twenty-first century, Trump used the classic tools of authoritarian leaders to assure his followers that this was America's true history and that they would return to relevance and power as they recovered it. That promise to own both the past and the future was a heady mix, and it came close to ending American democracy.

But this is not the only story of the United States of America.

Over three centuries, Americans who believed in the principles of democracy, those ideals articulated by the Founders, however imperfectly they lived them, have asserted the principles of equality and government by consent even in the face of such repression, even as they died for their beliefs. More often than not, those articulating the nation's true principles have been marginalized Americans who demanded the nation honor its founding promises. Their struggles have constantly renewed the country's dedication to the principles articulated in the Declaration of Independence. Their fight for equality reveals the true nature of American democracy: it is, and has always been, a work in progress.

The fundamental story of America is the constant struggle of all Americans, from all races, ethnicities, genders, and abilities, to make the belief that we are all created equal and have a right to have a say in our democracy come true. We are always in the process of creating "a more perfect union."

It is enslaver Thomas Jefferson articulating those principles, and it is also Abraham Lincoln deciding to leave his lucrative law practice to stop the spread of human enslavement into the American West.

But, just as powerfully, it is ordinary Americans like Harriet Beecher Stowe turning her grief for her dead eighteen-month-old son into the story of why no mother's child should be sold away from her; Rose Herera suing her former enslaver for custody of her own children; Julia Ward Howe demanding the right to vote so her abusive husband could not control her life any longer; Sitting Bull defending the right of the Lakota to practice their own new religion, even if he did not believe in it; Saum Song Bo telling *The New York Sun* that he was insulted by their request for money to build a pedestal for the Statue of Liberty when, three years before, the country had excluded people like him; Dr. Héctor García realizing that Mexican Americans needed to be able to vote in order to protect themselves; Edward Roberts claiming the right to get an education despite his physical paralysis; Stormé DeLarverie, the drag king who was identified with the first punch at the Stonewall riot that jump-started the gay rights movement.

Our history is former sharecropper Fannie Lou Hamer continuing to organize Black Mississippi voters to have a say in our democracy even after Mississippi police officers beat her nearly to death because, as she said, "The only thing they could do was kill me."[5]

And like all Americans before her setting out to change the country, Hamer did not work alone. She came from a community, and she brought a community together. While Republicans since the 1980s have insisted the symbol of the United States is the whitewashed American cowboy who dominated the West with manly individualism, in fact the key to survival in the American West was family and friends: kinship networks, trading partners, neighbors who would show up for a barn raising. Working together, across racial lines, ethnic lines, gender lines, and age lines, was what enabled people to defend their rights against a small group of elites determined to keep control of the country.

So, is it possible to create a nation in which every person, from all our many backgrounds, is truly equal before the law and entitled to a voice in our government?

Writing from Jim Crow America in the midst of the Depression, Black poet Langston Hughes thought it was. "O, let America be America again," he wrote in 1935. "The Land that never has been yet—And yet must be—the land where *every* man is free." He called for those who made America, "Whose sweat and blood, whose faith and pain, Whose hand at the foundry, whose plow in the rain" to "bring back our mighty dream again."[6]

CHAPTER 22

Declaring Independence

F ar from being part of a divine plan, the idea of American democracy emerged from the peculiar circumstances of thirteen
of the eighteen British-governed colonies in North America in
the years between 1763 and 1776. The desperate attempts of the British government to raise money to pay for the Seven Years' War convinced a motley group of colonists that they could create a new nation
based on an idea: that men were entitled to have a say in their government.

It was not an easy sell.

In 1763, in the aftermath of what was known in the colonies as the
French and Indian War, British colonists were quite content with their
position in the British empire. They liked the steady hand of the king's
officials. It brought order to the colonies, which were governed by
England but were neither English nor orderly.[1]

The population of the British North American colonies came from
Ireland, Scotland, Germany, Switzerland, Sweden, Spain, the conti-
nent of Africa, the Caribbean, and of course North America itself.
The people were split by language, culture, and religion: in addition to
Protestants, not only did Jews and Catholics put down roots in early
America, but Muslims, hailing from Africa, were among the earliest
settlers, and Indigenous Americans practiced their own religions.

Colonists were divided by legal status, too. By 1763, most—though
not all—Black Americans were enslaved to their white neighbors, and

while Indigenous Americans lived throughout the colonies, they usually did not share the same legal protections as whites. Women and children were legally considered the property of their husbands or fathers. And yet the colonial economy depended on Black, Indigenous, and women's labor.

Even colonists who shared racial or ethnic identities didn't much trust one another. Those wealthier folks who lived in settled communities on the coastline thought the poorer folks who had moved west to find land on the frontier were lawless, profane, uncultured, uneducated, and overly religious; westerners returned the favor by thinking easterners were snooty money-grubbers who deliberately left their western countrymen to the mercies of violent gangs and the Indigenous Americans who wanted no part of those moving onto their lands.

Neither did those in the rural areas trust those in the bigger towns, which clustered around seaports and contained newcomers from all over the globe, with their new ideas, new economies, new pastimes . . . and new diseases. Cities were places of great excitement, ferment, and possibility, but they were also places of great danger, as well as places of social stratification, where wealthy men jostled against sailors and sex workers.

In 1763, it seemed the only thing holding this mess of humanity together was the strength of the British crown, and colonials were happy to rely on it.

Immediately after the Seven Years' War, that reliance on British power seemed to be a good call. British authorities had turned the war in Europe over to mercenaries and focused on the North American colonies. They had supplied the armies locally, creating an economic boom, while colonists fought in every major engagement, strengthening their ties to the Crown. When the war ended, British subjects in North America had reason to believe they were the equals of their cousins in England. The economy had thrived during the war, and they foresaw a bright future as they moved into the land on the western side of the Appalachian Mountains.

That euphoria was short-lived.

The king's ministers and Parliament set out to guard against another expensive war between colonists and Indigenous Americans and to pay for the recent war that had badly stretched the treasury. They prohibited colonists from crossing the Appalachian Mountains and enacted a number of revenue measures, including the 1765 Stamp Act. This law hit virtually everyone by taxing printed material from newspapers and legal documents to playing cards.[2]

What Parliament saw as a way to raise money to pay for an expensive war—one that had benefited the colonists, after all—colonial leaders saw as an abuse of power. At stake was not just money. The fight over taxes tapped into a struggle that had been going on in England for more than a century: Could the king be checked by the people?[3]

Over the course of the next dozen years, colonists would come to answer this in the most radical way possible: they concluded that the people had the right to govern themselves. But getting a majority of the dissimilar and disorderly colonists to be willing to risk their lives and their livelihoods for that principle would require leaders to explain to ordinary colonists the intellectual arguments underlying complicated laws. Between 1765 and 1776, they mobilized people in the streets and used an extensive media network that emphasized community. American fascists used a similar strategy later, but the colonists used it for democracy rather than autocracy.

With the imposition of the Stamp Act, men in Boston took to the streets to warn that their rights as Englishmen were under attack. In August 1765, rioters attacked the homes of colonial officials. They hacked open stamp collector Thomas Hutchinson's front door with an axe and looted the house. Groups of dockhands, sailors, and workers would call themselves the Sons of Liberty, and similar gangs would spring up across the colonies, organizing for their right to consent to their own government.[4]

While the Sons of Liberty was generally a catchall title for those causing trouble over the new taxes, enabling people to remain anonymous, prominent colonists joined them and at least partly directed their actions. Lawyer John Adams recognized the importance of the gang activity for changing the political equation, writing in his diary that gatherings of the Sons of Liberty "tinge the Minds of the People, they impregnate them with the sentiments of Liberty. They render the People fond of their Leaders in the Cause, and averse and bitter against all opposers."[5]

Meanwhile, John Adams's cousin Samuel Adams, who was deeply involved with the Sons of Liberty, recognized that building a coalition in defense of liberty within the British system required conversation and cooperation. Voters elected him to the Massachusetts legislature, where his colleagues promptly made him clerk of the House, responsible for corresponding with other colonial legislatures. Across the colonies, the Sons of Liberty began writing to like-minded friends, informing them about local events, asking after their circumstances, organizing.

By 1766, the Stamp Act was costing more to enforce than it was producing in revenue. Parliament agreed to end it but claimed "full power and authority to make laws and statutes . . . to bind the colonies and people of America . . . in all cases whatsoever." It imposed new revenue laws.[6]

News of the new taxes reached Boston in late 1767, prompting the Massachusetts legislature to circulate a letter to the other colonies opposing taxation without representation and standing firm on the colonists' right to equality in the British empire. Meanwhile, the Sons of

Liberty and their associates called for boycotts on taxed goods and broke into the warehouses of those they suspected weren't complying. Women demonstrated their sympathy for the rights of colonists by weaving their own cloth and drinking coffee rather than relying on tea.

When British officials sent troops to Boston in October 1768 to kill the revolt in its cradle, colonial leaders turned to the printed word to draw on the Massachusetts commonwealth's long history of community cooperation to urge unity against the growing threat of tyranny. In March 1770, British soldiers shot into a crowd of angry men and boys harassing them, killing five and wounding six others. Engraver Paul Revere turned the altercation into the Boston Massacre. His instantly famous engraving, which circulated almost like a poster, showed soldiers in red coats smiling as they shot at colonists, including Black man Crispus Attucks, "Like fierce Barbarians grinning o'er their Prey; Approve the Carnage, and enjoy the Day."[7]

News of the repeal of all but one of the revenue duties—the one on tea—and the removal of the troops to an island in the harbor calmed tensions in Boston, leading Samuel Adams and his colleagues to worry that their campaign for the right to self-government would be lost. Building on their success in using the power of the written word to transmit information during the Stamp Act crisis, Adams and his colleagues Dr. Joseph Warren and Mercy Otis Warren in 1772 began to organize committees of correspondence to write to other colonists sharing information about their rights.

Then, in May 1773, Parliament gave the East India Company a monopoly on tea sales in the colonies. This move was intended to help the failing company financially and, by lowering the cost of tea in the colonies, convince people to buy it, thus establishing Parliament's right to impose a tax. In Boston, the committee of correspondence posted a guard on Griffin's Wharf at the harbor to make sure the tea could not be unloaded. On December 16, 1773, men dressed as Indigenous Americans boarded the trading vessel *Dartmouth*. They broke open 342 chests of tea and dumped the valuable leaves overboard.[8]

Parliament responded by closing the Port of Boston, moving the seat of government to Salem, stripping the colony of its charter, requiring colonists to pay for the quartering of soldiers in the town, and demanding payment for the tea.[9]

By fall 1774, concerned delegates from the colonies met for six weeks at Carpenters' Hall in Philadelphia to figure out how to respond to the government actions and also how to work together to advance a constitutional opposition to tyranny, as Samuel Adams put it. This First Continental Congress reflected that the weight of government had begun to shift from Britain to the colonies. Massachusetts took advantage of that shift, organizing the Massachusetts Provincial Congress to take control of the governance of the colony. It stockpiled supplies and weapons in Concord, and called for towns to create companies of "Minute Men," ready to fight on short notice.

Finally, determined to end the rebellion, British officials ordered General Thomas Gage to arrest Samuel Adams and Boston merchant John Hancock, who were rumored to be in the Lexington area. On the night of April 18, 1775, Gage sent out about seven hundred British troops to arrest the men and seize the supplies in Concord. Sons of Liberty William Dawes and Paul Revere rode out ahead of them, warning the locals that the British regulars were coming. At about four o'clock the next morning, the British soldiers found several dozen minutemen waiting for them in the darkness before dawn on the Lexington town green. When ordered to go home, the men began to leave.

But then a gun went off. The soldiers opened fire. Eight locals were killed, and another dozen wounded. The regulars marched on to Concord to destroy the guns and powder still there after the patriots had removed most of it, but they found their return to Boston cut off by minutemen firing from behind trees, houses, and the glacial boulders littered along the road.[10]

Still, the colonists were not quite ready to declare independence. The First Continental Congress had disbanded the year before with plans to meet again if tensions had not ceased, and under the circumstances, delegates regrouped on May 10 in Philadelphia as the Second Continental Congress. They elected John Hancock president of the body. Delegates made plans for raising an army, but, still hoping to avoid war, they sent a petition to the king reiterating their loyalty and suggesting that the problems between the colonies and the British government could be laid at the feet of corrupt officials, not the king himself. Even before it reached him, the king declared the American colonies to be in rebellion.

There was still one last step to take before the colonies would declare independence: they had to be ready to separate from the king. In January 1776, a newly arrived immigrant from England provided that spark with his pamphlet *Common Sense*. In it, Thomas Paine rejected the idea that any man could be born to rule others and thought it ridiculous for an island to rule a continent. He called for independence. Paine's spark set to flame more than a decade of accumulating tinder. The forty-seven-page pamphlet sold more copies per capita than any other book in American history and reached even more than those who bought it, as advocates of independence read it aloud in taverns and meetinghouses.[11]

By April, state and local governments across the colonies began to write declarations of independence, and a convention in Virginia asked Congress to consider declaring "the United Colonies free and independent States, absolved from all allegiance to, or dependence upon, the Crown or Parliament of Great Britain."[12]

Congress postponed debate for three weeks while a committee prepared a document announcing independence and explaining why it was imperative. Congress appointed John Adams of Massachusetts, Benjamin Franklin of Pennsylvania, Thomas Jefferson of Virginia, Robert R. Livingston of New York, and Roger Sherman of Connecticut to write the draft, but after generally agreeing what should be in the document, the members turned the project over to Jefferson. He, in turn, cribbed from other declarations to produce a draft, which Congress then cut by a quarter.[13]

The final document, adopted by Congress on July 4, 1776, explained to other nations that the people of the colonies needed to dissolve their ties to Britain and "assume among the powers of the earth, the separate and equal station to which the Laws of Nature and of Nature's God entitle them," because not just Parliament but also the king had repeatedly tried to establish a tyranny over them.

And with that, the men who signed the Declaration of Independence on July 4, 1776, pledged their "Lives, [their] Fortunes and [their] sacred Honor" to defend truths that twelve years of mob action, committees of correspondence, political debates, newspapers, and broadsides had convinced them were "self-evident": "that all men are created equal, that they are endowed by their Creator with certain unalienable Rights, that among these are Life, Liberty and the pursuit of Happiness.—That to secure these rights, Governments are instituted among Men, deriving their just powers from the consent of the governed."

In 1815, after their retirement from the crush of public business, John Adams and Thomas Jefferson chewed over the events of forty years before. "What do We mean by the Revolution?" Adams mused. "The War? That was no part of the Revolution. It was only an Effect and Consequence of it. The Revolution was in the Minds of the People, and this was effected, from 1760 to 1775, in the course of fifteen Years before a drop of blood was drawn at Lexington."[14]

CHAPTER 23

The Constitution

The Declaration of Independence had asserted the colonists' new country would be based on the ideas of equality and self-government, rather than on social hierarchies, religion, or ethnicity, but it said nothing about how such a government might actually work. Because the white men who drafted the Declaration saw it primarily as an assertion of their own right to be equal to other white men in England, they did not immediately take on the larger implications of their principled stand. Instead, they focused on the nuts and bolts of building a government. And after a false—but very instructive—start, they came up with a complicated plan to enable the states to work effectively together while also tripping up tyranny: the Constitution.

That false start was the Articles of Confederation, hammered out by the Second Continental Congress during the Revolutionary War, when fears of government tyranny were still uppermost in lawmakers' minds.

The Articles of Confederation centered power in the states rather than in a national government. They declared a "firm league of friendship" among the thirteen new states, overseen by a congress of men chosen by the state legislatures and in which each state had one vote. In the document's first substantive paragraph, the authors wrote: "Each state retains its sovereignty, freedom and independence, and every Power, Jurisdiction and right, which is not by this confederation expressly delegated to the United States, in Congress assembled." The new pact gave the federal government few duties and even fewer ways to meet them.[1]

Bringing the states together into a loose confederation of friendship was a disaster. Within a decade, states refused to contribute money to the new government and were starting to contemplate their own trade agreements with other countries. An economic recession in 1786 threatened farmers in western Massachusetts with the loss of their farms when the state government in the eastern part of the state refused to relieve debtors; in turn, when farmers organized under Revolutionary War captain Daniel Shays and marched on Boston, propertied men were so terrified their own holdings would be seized that they raised their own army for protection. The new system clearly could not protect property of either the poor or the rich and thus faced the threat of landless mobs.[2]

The nation seemed on the verge of tearing itself apart, and the new Americans were all too aware that both England and Spain were standing by, ready to make the most of the opportunities such chaos would create.

And so, in 1786, leaders called for a reworking of the new government. The result of their effort, the United States Constitution, became the fundamental framework for a government based not in men or religion, but in law. It explicitly declared that "no religious Test shall ever be required as a Qualification to any Office or public Trust under the United States."

Crucially, unlike the Articles of Confederation, the U.S. Constitution was based on the idea that the federal government, rather than the states, was the heart of the new system. It asserted that power to govern derived from the people of the nation, and it created a national government to represent them. The document began: "We the people of the United States, in order to form a more perfect Union. . . ."

The Constitution established a representative democracy, a republic, in which voters would elect lawmakers who would represent the people. That legislative branch would be a balance to a single leader at the head of the executive branch; each would prevent the rise of a tyrant from the other side. Congress would write all "necessary and proper" laws, levy taxes, borrow money, pay the nation's debts, establish a postal service, establish courts, declare war, support an army and navy, and organize and call forth "the militia to execute the Laws of the Union" and "provide for the common Defence and general Welfare of the United States."

The president would execute the laws, but if Congress overstepped, the president could veto proposed legislation. In turn, Congress could override a presidential veto. Congress could declare war, but the president was the commander in chief of the army and had the power to make treaties with foreign powers. It was quite an elegant system of paths and trip wires, really.

How to enact representation in the new republic was harder to figure out. How could the people have a say in their government without leaving them prey to demagogues who would tear the new nation apart? It was not an easy question, especially with the uneven demographics of the country: small states were jealous of larger states' population numbers, while northern leaders had no intention of letting southern leaders inflate their power by counting their enslaved neighbors as part of their population base.

So the Framers divided Congress into two houses: the House of Representatives, in which states were represented according to their population, and the Senate, in which every state had two votes.

To guarantee that individual states wouldn't grab too much power in the House by creating dozens and dozens of congressional districts, the Framers specified that a district could not be smaller than thirty thousand people. Then they required a census every ten years to make sure there was an accurate sense of who was where. To avoid "rotten boroughs" in which politicians inflated their power by counting people who could not vote, the Framers counted enslaved Americans not as a full person but as three fifths of a person.

The system was designed to adapt to new circumstances, but slowly. To ensure that the House could respond to changes in society, the Framers established that it would turn over entirely every two years. The Senate should be slower, they thought, and so they gave senators a six-year term, allowing only a third of the Senate to turn over every two years (in 1789 a special committee wrote three lists of senators and then a senator drew the lists out of a small wooden box to assign their terms; senators from states added later drew straws to determine their terms). Senators would not be elected directly by the people but would be chosen by the state legislatures.

The Framers placed the executive midway between the rapid turnover of representatives and the slower turnover of senators. Presidents would serve for four years, making them more responsive to the people than senators but not tied to popular political whims like representatives.

But how could voters from far-flung colonies have any idea who would be the best candidate for such an important role as chief executive? In those days before mass media, unless they were seamen, most men rarely traveled far from their homes, and it was entirely possible that the different states would cast ballots only for favorite sons, for how could a man in Massachusetts know who was a great thinker in Georgia?

With this in mind, the Framers came up with a representative system for presidential elections. Voters would cast ballots for "electors," made up of as many prominent men in their states as the state had senators and representatives. Those men would meet as a body—the Electoral College—and settle on a man or, more likely, a few men who would be a decent president. If the electors could not agree on a president, the choice would go to the House of Representatives, where every state would have a single vote.[3]

Finally, the Framers authorized a third branch of government, the judicial branch, with a Supreme Court to settle disputes between inhabitants of the different states. They also guaranteed that every defendant had the right to a jury trial but said little else about the judiciary.

What they were clear about was that the new national government overshadowed the states. They provided that "the Times, Places and Manner of holding Elections for Senators and Representatives, shall be prescribed in each State by the Legislature thereof," but went on to stipulate that "the Congress may at any time by Law make or alter such Regulations, except as to the Places of chusing Senators." The federal government had the final word.

The Constitution provided that "the Citizens of each State shall be entitled to all Privileges and Immunities of Citizens in the several States" and promised that "the United States shall guarantee to every State in this Union a Republican Form of Government, and shall protect each of them against Invasion. . . ."

Finally, it declared: "This Constitution, and the Laws of the United States which shall be made in Pursuance thereof; and all Treaties made, or which shall be made, under the Authority of the United States, shall be the supreme Law of the Land; and the Judges in every State shall be bound thereby, any Thing in the Constitution or Laws of any State to the Contrary notwithstanding."

The Framers fought over different provisions of the document they had produced, prompting eighty-one-year-old Benjamin Franklin to remind them that "States are on the point of separation, only to meet hereafter for the purpose of cutting one another's throats." He added, "I can not help expressing a wish that every member of the

Convention who may still have objections to it, would with me, on this occasion doubt a little of his own infallibility, and to make manifest our unanimity, put his name to this instrument."[4]

They did, and popular ratifying conventions put the Constitution into effect on June 21, 1788.

But the Framers weren't quite done. Those still nervous about government tyranny had refused to sign on to the Constitution without a promise to amend it immediately with a list of rights that would be free from interference by the national government. The First Congress of the United States passed the Bill of Rights—the first ten amendments to the Constitution—to put fences around the federal government, saying it could not establish any specific religion, silence the press, police speech, stop the people from assembling peacefully, take away the right of the people to bear arms, deny trials by jury, arbitrarily seize property, and so on. These rights were not rights given to individuals, as the modern Supreme Court has interpreted them, but rather were designed to hold back the government if it began to overreach.

States ratified the Bill of Rights on December 15, 1791, and the framework for the United States of America was in place. The principles behind it were democratic—that every citizen should have an equal say in the government and that every citizen would be equal before the law—although its practice was almost exclusively limited to white men.

It was a "great experiment," as first president George Washington called it shortly after he took the oath of office, but it had a crucial flaw: the Framers did not foresee the rise of political parties. They figured that, having thrown off monarchy, Americans would all agree on their form of government. To the degree that they disagreed, Framer James Madison argued in the famous essay "Federalist No. 10," they would break into small factions and so cancel each other out, much as the presence of many religious sects in the country ensured that none gained the upper hand over the others.[5]

But partisanship appeared almost immediately. Southern leaders opposed Washington's policies, conceived by Treasury secretary Alexander Hamilton, that strengthened the hand of northern businessmen in the national government. Virginians like Madison and Thomas Jefferson maintained that their opposition to such national power made them the true defenders of the Constitution.

Partisanship turned out to be an important innovation. It engaged ordinary voters and provided oversight of lawmakers, but it also weakened the nation's framework, hampering representation and many of the checks the Framers had built into the system.

The first thing to go was fair representation. By 1796, political leaders had divided into two camps, and Jefferson saw that he would have won the presidency if only Virginia's electors had all voted as a bloc in the Electoral College rather than splitting their votes between him and John Adams of Massachusetts. Jefferson urged Virginia to adopt a winner-take-all system that would give all of the state's electoral votes to whichever candidate got a simple majority. It was a stunning change and one that appalled Madison, who wanted to amend the Constitution to prevent it. He died before he could get such an amendment ratified, and other states quickly followed Virginia, manipulating the new system to give their own top candidates a leg up. Today, only Maine and Nebraska still split their electoral votes, with the result that candidates campaign almost exclusively in states with large electoral vote counts.[6]

The Framers also did not foresee—although this, perhaps, they should have—that eventually, politicians desperate to keep their party in power would add new, sparsely populated states to the Union, as the Republican Party did when it brought six new states into the country between 1889 and 1890. They were quite open that their goal was to make sure they controlled the Senate in order to stop legislation they didn't like, even if the American people wanted it.[7]

The Framers also did not foresee the growth of vast cities, possible thanks to modern industry—including steel—and transportation. They could never have imagined the astounding size differences that would develop in the modern era between states like California, which according to the 2020 census has almost forty million people, and Wyoming, which has fewer than six hundred thousand.[8]

Living in small, largely rural states, the Framers put a lower limit but no upper limit on representation. When the 1920 census revealed that urban Americans outnumbered rural Americans for the first time, the House in 1929 capped its numbers at 438 to keep power away from those urban dwellers, including immigrants, whom lawmakers considered dangerous, thus skewing the Electoral College in favor of rural America. Today, the average congressional district is 761,169 individuals, which both makes representation less effective and reduces the power of states with more people.[9]

The government that the Framers designed, hammered out by fifty-five young white men sweltering in Philadelphia in summer 1787 to permit individuals to have an equal say in their government without succumbing to tyranny, was an astonishing feat, but it was not perfect.

Fortunately, the Framers recognized that their work would need adjustment. They wrote into the Constitution that future generations could amend it.

CHAPTER 24

Expanding Democracy

Frfrom the beginning, Indigenous Americans, Black Americans, and women noted that the principles articulated in the Declaration of Independence ought to apply to them as well as to propertied white men.

In 1774, the year after her enslavers relinquished their claim on her, Boston poet Phillis Wheatley wrote to Mohegan cleric Samson Occom about the hypocrisy of leaders who rallied for freedom while practicing enslavement. "In every human Breast, God has implanted a Principle, which we call Love of Freedom; it is impatient of Oppression, and pants for Deliverance," she wrote, adding, "I will assert, that the same Principle lives in us." She noted "the strange Absurdity of their Conduct whose Words and Actions are so diametrically, opposite. How well the Cry for Liberty, and the reverse Disposition for the exercise of oppressive Power over others agree,—I humbly think it does not require the Penetration of a Philosopher to determine."[1]

John Adams's wife, Abigail, agreed and sought to prescribe a solution to the "strange Absurdity" that Wheatley identified. "I long to hear that you have declared an independency," she wrote to John in March 1776, "and by the way in the new Code of Laws which I suppose it will be necessary for you to make I desire you would Remember the Ladies, and be more generous and favourable to them than your ancestors. . . . Remember all Men would be tyrants if they could."[2]

The Framers did not include rights for women in the new code of laws. But the principles outlined in the Declaration of Independence gave those excluded from those principles by the Constitution both the language and the right to challenge their exclusion. Famously, in 1852, formerly enslaved maritime worker Frederick Douglass asked, "What to the Slave is the Fourth of July?" He honored the Founders as "great men" but asked: "Are the great principles of political freedom and of natural justice, embodied in that Declaration of Independence, extended to us?"[3]

In that question, Douglass drew attention to a theme that excluded Americans had emphasized since the nation's founding. In 1791, Black mathematician and naturalist Benjamin Banneker directly called out then–secretary of state Thomas Jefferson for praising the "proper ideas of the great valuation of liberty, and the free possession of those blessings to which you were entitled by nature," while at the same time "detaining by fraud and violence so numerous a part of my brethren under groaning captivity and cruel oppression. . . ."[4]

In 1848, Douglass had been present at the Seneca Falls Convention in upstate New York when reformers insisting that women should have equal rights wrote a Declaration of Sentiments. Following the format of the Declaration of Independence, they asserted that "all men and women are created equal" and that "the history of mankind is a history of repeated injuries and usurpations on the part of man toward woman, having in direct object the establishment of an absolute tyranny over her."[5]

As proof they listed the facts that men refused to let women vote and compelled their obedience to laws they had no say in creating, including ones that took all their property and gave all power—including that of owning their children—to husbands. Men limited the educational opportunities available to women, shut them out of most professions, and worked to destroy women's confidence in their own strength to trick them into dependency. The reformers at Seneca Falls demanded "immediate admission to all the rights and privileges which belong to them as citizens of these United States."

The Declaration of Independence gave marginalized Americans not just the language but also the grounds to challenge the laws that made them unequal. While the Revolutionary War was still raging, Elizabeth Freeman, an enslaved woman living in Sheffield, Massachusetts, heard the language of her new state constitution's declaration that "all men are born free and equal," echoing the Declaration of Independence. She sued for her freedom. Her lawyers argued that the principles in the constitution meant that the state could not defend enslavement, and a jury agreed, awarding Freeman and an associated plaintiff thirty shillings in damages and the costs of the trial.[6]

Quock Walker, suing around the same time for freedom and damages, also won his case in a Massachusetts courtroom. The judge concluded that enslavement had been a "usage" in the colony but that "the Idea of Slavery is inconsistent with our own conduct & Constitution & there can be no such thing as perpetual servitude of a rational Creature."[7]

Not every bid for equality was as successful as those of Freeman and Walker. In the early Republic, judges grappled with the idea that the concept of liberty and independence should include women. The 1805 case of *Martin v. Massachusetts* explored whether women could make their own political decisions. The presiding judge concluded that the idea of liberty could not possibly mean the destruction of men's patriarchal authority. Instead, men included women in the new order by redefining them as "Republican mothers," whose role in the new society was not to vote and hold office, but rather to rear their sons to be good citizens and patriots.[8]

Indigenous Americans also turned to the courts to protect their rights. The Cherokees in Georgia had adjusted to the influx of Euro-Americans by adopting a plantation economy, including slavery;

developing their own written language and newspaper; and, in 1827, establishing their own constitution based on the U.S. Constitution.

When Congress passed the 1830 Indian Removal Act, Chief John Ross and his advisors, acting under the advice of Senators Daniel Webster of New Hampshire and Theodore Frelinghuysen of New Jersey, hired former attorney general William Wirt to defend their rights under the U.S. Constitution. They lost their first suit, but in 1832, in *Worcester v. Georgia*, the Supreme Court declared that the Cherokees were a sovereign nation and could make their own laws, settling "for ever" the question "as to who is right and who is wrong," as one Cherokee put it.[9]

But the Cherokees' victory ran up against another group clamoring for inclusion in the new system: poor white men.

The Constitution created a framework for democracy but didn't really make it clear how ordinary people—ordinary men in those days—would engage with their government aside from those few who had the right to vote for leaders. The Framers expected that governmental affairs would continue to be run by folks like them, and since they did not expect that their new country would develop political parties, they hoped they could harness a man's self-interest to create a government that would not become tyrannical.

This abstract system broke down fast. By the 1820s, southern leaders worried that northern merchants and bankers would take over the new nation. When congressmen threw their votes to the Massachusetts-born son of a former president, John Quincy Adams, for the presidency in 1824 over the southern Indian-fighter Andrew Jackson, their fears seemed to have come true. Jackson promptly began to characterize the federal government as a distant tyranny run by elites that was trampling the rights of ordinary white men.

Southern white men began to argue that true democracy was

located not in the federal government but in the states. The federal government was distant, they argued, and its leaders were trying to impose their unwelcome values on people whose needs and cultures were different than the leaders acknowledged. One such intrusion was the decision in *Worcester v. Georgia* recognizing the Cherokees' sovereignty. Andrew Jackson, who defeated Adams to become president in 1829 and thus was in office when the decision came down, made it clear he would not enforce it. One man recalled that "he sportively said in private conversation that if . . . called on to support the decree of the Court he will call on those who have brought about the decision to enforce it[;] that he will call on the Militia of Massachusetts."[10]

Jackson's supporters, members of the new Democratic Party, began to articulate a new language of democracy, based in ordinary men rather than in the traditional ruling class. Poet Walt Whitman in 1855 juxtaposed "The President, holding a cabinet council . . . surrounded by the Great Secretaries" with "three matrons stately and friendly . . . the crew of the fish-smack . . . the Missourian . . . toting his wares and his cattle . . . the indescribable crowd is gather'd—it is the Fourth of Seventh-month—(What salutes of cannon and small arms!)"[11]

But for all of Whitman's celebration of the many peoples in the United States, the demand of poorer white men for inclusion in the government was based on the idea of keeping other marginalized people out. States' rights democracy kept white men in charge, for they were the voters who determined the shape of the state governments. Those white men advanced their own interests at the expense of their Brown and Black neighbors, declaring it the nation's "Manifest Destiny" to push Indigenous Americans off their lands and take over parts of Mexico to establish plantations and plantation slavery there. Above all, they protected and extended the practice of human enslavement that people like Elizabeth Freeman had successfully challenged seventy years before.

The triumph of this populist "democracy" took Indigenous American lands in the Southeast, enabling the southern system of enslavement to spread into the rich "Black Belt," so called for the color of its soil. Those white enslavers for whom the booming economy worked best defended states' rights, which allowed a minority to impose its will over the wishes of a national majority, as the heart of American democracy.

They silenced their opponents, took away the right to petition the government to end human enslavement, closed off access to opposing opinions, and in 1837 murdered Elijah P. Lovejoy, who had moved to Alton, Illinois, from Albion, Maine, to begin a newspaper dedicated to the abolition of human enslavement. Elijah's younger brother, Owen, saw Elijah shot and swore his allegiance to the cause of abolition. "I shall never forsake the cause that has been sprinkled with my brother's blood," he declared.[12]

By the 1850s, these defenders of human enslavement made up only a small minority of the country. Realizing that the vast majority of Americans objected to their ideology, they rewrote American history, claiming that the Framers had deliberately established a nation based in states' rights and white supremacy.

The nation was a collection of states, President Franklin Pierce insisted in 1855, and the Framers had deliberately established only "a Federal Republic of the free white men of the colonies."[13]

The Democrats set out to shape the nation according to their new version of history. They advanced the idea that the question of human enslavement should be decided not by the national majority, but by "popular sovereignty" in which local voters got to decide the fate of the institution. But they quickly hedged that idea of voters' choice by making it impossible for voters to choose to build states without enslavement. Under their system, southern enslavers could pick up the extra states they needed to overawe the free states in the national government and spread enslavement across the country. Then they prohibited the federal government from interfering with slavery.

This popular sovereignty, politicians said, was the true meaning of American democracy. And it meant that the nation would throw out the self-evident truths of the Declaration of Independence that all men were created equal and had a right to a say in their government, and become one based instead on racial hierarchies in which some people were better than others and had the right to rule.

But not everyone agreed. In 1858, rising politician Abraham Lincoln told an audience: "I ask you in all soberness, if all these things, if indulged in, if ratified, if confirmed and endorsed, if taught to our children, and repeated to them, do not tend to rub out the sentiment of liberty in the country, and to transform this Government into a government of some other form. Those arguments . . . are the arguments that kings have made for enslaving the people in all ages of the world. . . . Whether it come from the mouth of a King, an excuse for enslaving the people of his country, or from the mouth of men of one race as a reason for enslaving the men of another race, it is all the same old serpent."[14]

CHAPTER 25

Mudsills or Men

By 1860, the American South was producing more than two billion pounds of cotton annually, grown and processed by enslaved Americans and their poor white neighbors. The wealthiest southerners were the nation's richest people, drinking French wine under European masterpieces in one of their several gracious homes while their wives wore imported silk gowns.

The elite southerners, those who enslaved more than twenty of their Black neighbors, insisted that theirs was the perfect economic, political, and social system. They explained that the nation's Founders had made a terrible error in their assertion that all men were created equal. In place of that "fundamentally wrong" idea, they proposed "the great truth" that white men were a "superior race." And within that superior race, some men were better than others.[1]

In 1858, South Carolina senator James Henry Hammond explained that society was made up of two groups. Most people were "mudsills," named for the timbers driven into the ground to support gracious homes above. They performed "menial duties" and had "a low order of intellect and but little skill." A few people made up "that other class which leads progress, civilization, and refinement." They oversaw the mudsills' lives and labor. Mudsills produced capital that accumulated in the hands of society's leaders, who used that great wealth to invest in business and culture to move the country forward.[2]

Southern elites saw themselves not as brutal exploiters, but as a modern-day incarnation of genteel British aristocrats. In their view, southern leaders were not money-grubbers like northern merchants and men on the make, but chivalrous men with fine manners and unparalleled courage and great skill on horseback. They protected their dependents—enslaved people, women, and their poor white neighbors—and defended their own honor. Meanwhile, their "civilized" and "Christian" oversight elevated their "inferiors"; removing them from that protection would be cruel.

But those wealthy southerners were only too aware that they were a tiny minority of the U.S. population. By 1860, the North had 22 million of the nation's 31 million people. Only 9 million lived in the South, and 4 million of them were enslaved Black Americans. White elites made up only about 4 percent of the southern white population: about 0.6 percent of the nation's people.[3]

To maintain their power, southern leaders made common cause with southern men who defended local government, and for whom opposition to the federal government had become the core of their political identity. In the 1840s, when northern leaders began to try to stop the expansion of slavery through federal law, southern white leaders insisted that such action was an attack on democracy, which they were coming to define as states' rights.

By the 1850s, southern leaders had narrowed that definition of democracy even further. They insisted that the Framers had never intended for democracy to mean that voters got to influence policy; they could merely vote to change their leaders. Indeed, they argued, the Framers had set up the system so that it could never come under the sway of a mob. Federal lawmakers could do nothing that was not explicitly enumerated in the Constitution; the Framers had limited the government so it could do nothing but protect property. Even if an overwhelming majority of Americans wanted the government to do something more expansive, it could not.

In their eyes, anyone questioning this definition of democracy was trying to destroy the country by starting a race war. White men must stick together, or Black Americans would take over their region and, once freed from oversight, would steal white men's property and rape white women and children (the mirror of what enslavers themselves were doing to Black people). Leaders outlawed possession of books and pamphlets that questioned the slave system—those that urged solidarity among poor white men as well as those challenging enslavement—and they provoked violence against those they called agitators. By closing off access to factual information, enslavers could use the media, churches, society, and politics to spread their worldview first in the South and then nationally.

Their worldview was taking over the country.

In the 1850s, Southern elites who controlled the government of their states took over first the Democratic Party and then, through it, the Senate—where each state had two seats regardless of population—and the White House. Control of those two institutions meant they also took control of the Supreme Court.

With that power, they removed established limits on the slave system. In 1854, Congress passed the Kansas-Nebraska Act repealing the 1820 Missouri Compromise that had limited slavery to the East. Two years later, a southern representative beat Massachusetts senator Charles Sumner almost to death on the Senate floor for complaining about it.

In 1857, the Supreme Court, whose chief justice hailed from a slave state, said explicitly in *Dred Scott v. Sandford* that the Founders had not intended to include Black Americans in the Declaration of Independence, regarding them as "beings of an inferior order, and altogether unfit to associate with the white race, either in social or political relations; and so far inferior, that they had no rights which the white man was bound to respect; and that the negro might justly and lawfully be reduced to slavery for his benefit."[4]

In that same decision, the court also ruled that Congress had no power to stop slavery from spreading into the territories. Popular sovereignty became the rule of the West, with a stunning implication: slavery would become national. The Constitution required states to protect property of all kinds, which in turn meant that if a single enslaver brought enslaved Americans into a territory, the eventual state would have to protect enslavement there. Slave states would quickly outnumber free states, and their representatives would work to make enslavement national, sweeping the free North into their system.

But just as southern elites seemed about to turn their radical revision of the country into the law of the land, their opponents woke up.

White men from poor backgrounds found outrageous the idea of a hierarchical world in which men were stuck forever either rich or poor. The 1825 opening of the Erie Canal had siphoned men to the West while new factories back East had upended the economy and established cities, creating a way for young men from the backwoods to rise to prosperity. Hammond, who preached about mudsills, had bought his way to prominence with his wife's money, and his Senate seat was handed to him by his friend the governor after Hammond had been exposed for raping his nieces. To northern men on the make, someone like Hammond couldn't hold a candle to hardworking, principled people like themselves.[5]

When Congress opened the West for slavery and Democratic president Franklin Pierce claimed the Founders had intended the United States to be a white man's republic in which "free white men" ruled over "the subject races . . . Indian and African," northern men abandoned their previous political affiliations and joined together to oppose the "Slave Power." Newspapermen like Joseph Medill of the *Chicago Tribune* called out as "false all through" the idea that the Founders had not meant "all men are created equal" when they put that sentiment into the Declaration of Independence, and people all across the North agreed.

Most white northerners didn't much care about Black rights. But enslavement had turned the South into an oligarchy, reducing poor white men to landless destitution, and they worried the same would happen in the West and North if enslavers were permitted to take over. They held meetings and rallies across the North just as the revolutionary generation had done, warning that America was falling under the sway of an oligarchy. They launched such widespread attacks on Illinois senator Stephen Douglas, who had pushed through the Kansas-Nebraska Act, that he joked he could travel across the country by the light of his own burning effigies. And they began to coalesce into a new political party: the Republicans.

Douglas and the Democrats stood firm on popular sovereignty, courting racists by insisting that white supremacy was true Americanism and that anyone opposing it was a "n****r lover." But in 1858, Illinois lawyer Abraham Lincoln ran for the U.S. Senate against Douglas, facing the racist crowds with humor and insisting that the idea that "all men are created equal" must prevail. "I should like to know," Lincoln said in July 1858, "if taking this old Declaration of Independence, which declares that all men are equal upon principle and making exceptions to it where will it stop. . . . If that declaration is not the truth, let us get the Statute book, in which we find it and tear it out! Who is so bold as to do it!"[6]

Lincoln rejected the idea that the nation should be based on white supremacy. He tied his political position—equality before the law—to the real history of the nation's founding. White male voters began to listen.

Douglas won reelection, but Lincoln's insistence on equality before the law evolved into a political ideology that would challenge that of the southern enslavers. He rejected the idea that society moved forward thanks to the efforts of a few rich men, and denied that most people belonged to a lower, menial class into which they were, as he said, "fatally fixed" for life.

Instead, Lincoln argued that society progressed thanks to the hard work and innovation of ordinary people. While rich men had no incentive to think up new ideas, he said, ordinary Americans worked and innovated so they could provide for themselves. As they did, they made more money than they and their families needed, so they would use the surplus to buy goods that would support merchants, shoemakers, and so on. In turn, those people would work hard and accumulate capital, which would support a few financiers and industrialists, who would use their own accumulated capital to hire men just starting out, and the cycle would begin again. The heart of the system was not wealthy men, but hardworking ordinary ones.

The key to making this system work was the government's guarantee that all men—not just rich white men—were equal before the law and had equal access to resources, including education. Lincoln had grown up poor and, as a young man trying to establish himself, had watched his town of New Salem, Illinois, die because settlers didn't have the resources to dredge the Sangamon River to increase their river trade. Had the government simply been willing to invest in economic development, the men could have brought prosperity to the town. Without that investment, workingmen failed. If only the government would step in to do what individuals couldn't, Lincoln believed, it would keep the economic playing field between rich and poor level, dramatically expand opportunity, and develop the economy.

This was a profound innovation: Lincoln adjusted the liberalism of the Founders, which focused on protecting individual rights from an overreaching government, to acknowledge that maintaining those rights required government action.

Lincoln's vision made sense to men like him, who had worked their way up from hardscrabble backgrounds to respectability. When the Republicans nominated Lincoln for president in 1860, they set his vision up against that of enslavers. To build enthusiasm for their candidates, Republicans established local clubs where young men could throw parties and invite young women. They also enlisted the help of the enthusiasts who flocked behind the western "rail splitter," encouraging local quasi-military marching groups to spread their message. "Wide Awakes" wore capes and black hats and carried torches in their long parades to escort Republican politicians to political events. There they protected the speaker and filled up the venue. By 1860 there were as many as half a million Wide Awakes, who then brought their friends to join the movement.[7]

Their tactics worked. Republicans tied equality before the law to the principles of the Founders. They emphasized the danger of giving up democracy to an elite that based its power on a white supremacist reading of U.S. history. They promised to use the federal government for everyone. In 1860, voters chose Lincoln's vision of equality before the law and elected him to the White House.

Thwarted from taking control of the United States, the leaders of seven southern states, claiming to uphold democracy, took the radical step necessary to keep themselves in charge. They railroaded their states out of the Union even before Lincoln took office in March 1861, setting out to create their own nation based on the "great truth" that "the negro is not equal to the white man; that slavery subordination to the superior race is his natural and normal condition." They believed that "this, our new government, is the first, in the history of the world, based upon this great physical, philosophical, and moral truth," and that they would lead the rest of the world to new economic prosperity, based on their new form of government.[8]

CHAPTER 26

Of the People, by the
People, for the People

L incoln's vision gave the fledgling Republican Party a set of principles to reorganize the government into one that actively worked for ordinary men. Rather than simply protecting the property of wealthy slaveholders, the government would allow all men equal access to resources, including education, so they could be economically secure.

Such a plan was not in the works when Republicans took power in March 1861, but a month later, the new government of the seven seceding southern states fired on Fort Sumter, the federal fort in South Carolina's Charleston Harbor, formally launching the Civil War. The Republicans would have to innovate, and fast.

Enlisting more than two million soldiers and sailors into the war effort, moving them, equipping them, and arming them would eventually cost the United States more than $5 billion. To raise the necessary funds, the Republican Congress invented national taxation. Lawmakers deliberately constructed revenue laws to shift ownership of the American government away from the bankers, who had previously provided Treasury funds, to the American people. Then, worried that taxes high enough to raise the necessary income would crush poor men, the Republicans invented the nation's first income tax, graduating it into two different brackets of 3 percent and 5 percent.

"The weight must be distributed equally," said Vermont Republican representative Justin Smith Morrill, "not upon each man an equal amount, but a tax proportionate to his ability to pay."

Republicans deliberately used tax policy to reinforce national interests over state power. They gave the federal government authority to collect the tax directly, to demonstrate that people were supporting the United States of America and not individual states. The federal government had a right to "demand" 99 percent of a man's property for an urgent necessity, Morrill said. When the nation required it, "the property of the people . . . belongs to the Government."[1]

As war costs mounted, far from objecting to taxes, Americans asked their congressmen to raise them, out of concern about the growing national debt. Republican senator John P. Hale of New Hampshire told his colleagues: "The condition of the country is singular . . . I venture to say it is an anomaly in the history of the world. What do the people of the United States ask of this Congress? To take off taxes? No, sir, they ask you to put them on. The universal cry of this people is to be taxed."[2]

Having imposed taxes, lawmakers set out to enable men to pay them by using the government to give ordinary men access to resources. In 1862, they passed the Homestead Act, giving western land to anyone willing to settle it; the Land-Grant College Act, providing funds to establish state universities; the act establishing the Department of Agriculture, to provide scientific information and good seeds to farmers; and the Pacific Railway Act, providing for the construction of a railroad across the continent to get men to the fields and the mines of the West.

Still, in 1863, after two years of battlefield losses that had disheartened democracy's defenders, it was not at all clear that the United States would survive. In November of that year, Lincoln spoke at the dedication of a national cemetery for the soldiers killed in the July

1863 Battle of Gettysburg. He urged Americans to uphold their history. Dating the establishment of the country from the Declaration of Independence, which protected equality, rather than from the Constitution, which protected property, he warned them that the principles the Founders had declared self-evident were now at risk.

"Four score and seven years ago our fathers brought forth on this continent, a new nation, conceived in Liberty, and dedicated to the proposition that all men are created equal," he told them. "Now we are engaged in a great civil war, testing whether that nation, or any nation so conceived and so dedicated, can long endure." Lincoln urged Americans to rededicate themselves "to the great task remaining before us," asking them to "here highly resolve . . . that this nation, under God, shall have a new birth of freedom—and that government of the people, by the people, for the people, shall not perish from the earth."[3]

The Gettysburg Address marked the birth of a new nation, one that would not include human enslavement except as punishment for crime. In 1865, Congress passed the Thirteenth Amendment to the Constitution, abolishing slavery, and sent it off to the states for ratification. But that amendment was not just about Black freedom. For the first time in history, a constitutional amendment increased, rather than decreased, the power of the federal government. It provided that "Congress shall have power to enforce this article by appropriate legislation."

Lincoln's Republicans had reenvisioned liberalism. They reworked the Founders' initial national government, held back by the Framers through the Bill of Rights, into an active government designed to protect individuals by guaranteeing equal access to resources and equality before the law for white men and Black men alike. They had enlisted the power of the federal government to turn the ideas of the Declaration of Independence into reality.

When the armies of the United States defeated those of the Confederacy, it seemed that with the help of a newly active government, the ideology of the Declaration of Independence had triumphed once and for all.

Northern leaders were convinced that white southerners would cheer the end of the Slave Power and welcome the new government. They were so sure of that outcome that when General Robert E. Lee surrendered the Army of Northern Virginia at Appomattox Court House on April 9, 1865, General U. S. Grant required only that the officers promise that neither they nor their men would ever again fight against the United States. After turning over their military weapons and ammunition, they were allowed to keep their sidearms and horses. Grant wanted them "to be able to put in a crop to carry themselves and their families through the next winter."[4]

But that leniency did not buy peace. Believing that "something decisive and great must be done" to save white supremacy and the states' rights on which it depended, the mentally unstable actor John Wilkes Booth shot President Lincoln on April 15 while he was at the theater. Even war could not shake some southerners' devotion to their worldview.[5]

That included Lincoln's vice president, Democrat Andrew Johnson, who took over the presidency after Lincoln's death. Johnson wanted to end slavery for economic reasons: he believed it concentrated wealth and thus squeezed poor white men. But he had no intention of reordering the racial hierarchies of the South, or of the nation. He readmitted to the body politic not the southern Black men who had fought to save the United States, but rather the southern white men whose attempt to create a nation based in human enslavement had led to the deaths of more than six hundred thousand Americans and cost the United States more than $5 billion.

Johnson offered blanket amnesty to all former Confederates who took an oath of loyalty to the United States, except for a few high-ranking officers and those worth more than twenty thousand dollars. To them he promised generosity that he promptly delivered. He pardoned all but about fifteen hundred of them over the summer of 1865.

That lack of accountability immediately undermined the rule of law in the southern states. Southern state legislatures tried to circumscribe the lives of Black Americans with Black Codes that prohibited Black people from owning firearms, for example, or congregating. They had to treat their white neighbors with deference and were required to sign yearlong work contracts every January or be judged vagrants, punishable by arrest and imprisonment. White employers could get them out of jail by paying their fines, but then they would have to work off their debt in a system that was not technically racial slavery but was not much different. With Johnson urging them on, racist white southerners attacked their Black neighbors and in 1866 launched race riots in Memphis and New Orleans that killed dozens of people.[6]

Violence against Black Americans did not make Johnson rethink his plans to put former Confederates back in power. So long as southern states abolished enslavement, repudiated Confederate debts, and nullified the ordinances of secession, Johnson was happy to readmit them to full standing in the Union.

There was no way northern Republican lawmakers were going to rebuild southern society on the same blueprint that had existed before the Civil War, especially since the upcoming 1870 census would count Black Americans as whole persons for the first time in the nation's history, giving southern states more power in Congress and the Electoral College after the war than they had had before it. Having just fought a war to destroy the South's ideology, northern lawmakers were not about to let it regrow in peacetime.

Congress rejected Johnson's plan for Reconstruction.

After months of hearings and debate, Congress proposed its own plan. It called for amending the Constitution to protect the rights of Black Americans in states where they could neither vote nor testify in court or sit on a jury to protect their own interests.

Congress's solution was the Fourteenth Amendment. It nullified the *Dred Scott* decision that said Black Americans were inferior to white Americans, saying: "All persons born or naturalized in the United States and subject to the jurisdiction thereof, are citizens of the United States and of the State wherein they reside."

The amendment also addressed the *Dred Scott* decision in another profound way. It gave the federal government power to protect individuals even if their state legislatures had passed discriminatory laws. It said: "No State shall make or enforce any law which shall abridge the privileges or immunities of citizens of the United States; nor shall any State deprive any person of life, liberty, or property, without due process of law; nor deny to any person within its jurisdiction the equal protection of the laws."

That's quite a sentence. While the Constitution guaranteed that citizens everywhere were entitled to the "Privileges and Immunities of Citizens," the Fourteenth Amendment affirmatively guaranteed that no state could discriminate against anyone. It went on to say that "Congress shall have power to enforce, by appropriate legislation, the provisions of this article."

On July 9, 1868, Americans changed the U.S. Constitution for the fourteenth time, adapting it to construct a new nation in which the federal government would guarantee that citizens of every state would be equal before the law. In 1870, Congress put teeth behind that guarantee, creating the Department of Justice, whose first job was to bring down the Ku Klux Klan terrorists in the South.

Ideally, of course, states would write fair laws and treat citizens equally without federal interference, and when it turned out that the

Fourteenth Amendment didn't protect Black voting, Congress passed and sent off to the states for ratification the Fifteenth Amendment to the Constitution, guaranteeing Black men the right to vote. When the Fifteenth Amendment was added to the Constitution in 1870, most American men believed that the system had been fixed: the right to vote should protect all interests in the states.[7]

The Civil War and its aftermath were America's second attempt at creating a nation based on the Declaration of Independence, establishing once and for all the supremacy of the federal government, and using it to guarantee equality before the law and equal access to resources.

CHAPTER 27

America Renewed

When General Robert E. Lee surrendered his Army of Northern Virginia to General U. S. Grant on April 9, 1865, in the parlor of Wilmer McLean's home in Appomattox Court House, Virginia, he was taken aback by the sight of Lieutenant Colonel Ely Parker, an engineer on Grant's staff. Then Lee realized that Parker was an Indigenous American, a member of the Seneca Nation. "I am glad to see one real American here," Lee allegedly said. Parker responded: "We are all Americans."[1]

Parker's reply, even if—maybe especially if—it was apocryphal, captured an important truth. Many Americans thought the bloodshed of the battlefields had paid for the blood drawn by the lash, freeing the nation to realize its full potential. For a few years it seemed they might be right: the nation might protect civil rights in the states and make sure people had access to the vote to guarantee that laws reflected the will of the majority.

Although elite white men fell back into believing that they alone should have power, the Fourteenth and Fifteenth amendments had created the possibility that the United States could become a multicultural and even perhaps multigendered democracy. For the next several generations, those excluded from an equal seat at the table would redefine what it meant to be an American, keeping a dream of human equality alive.

The Fourteenth Amendment had expanded citizenship to "all

persons born or naturalized in the United States, and subject to the jurisdiction thereof," but it introduced the word *male* into the Constitution for the first time. While it left the states to determine who could vote, that insertion suggested that members of Congress were not inclined to end the nation's patriarchal system.

Women had just backed the U.S. government with their money, buying bonds and paying taxes; with their loved ones, sending their sons and husbands and fathers off to war; with their labor, working in factories and fields and taking over from men in the nursing and teaching professions; and even with their lives, spying and fighting for the U.S. government. Women like Boston abolitionist Julia Ward Howe, the author of the "Battle Hymn of the Republic," claimed the right to have a say in the postwar nation.

When Congress did not explicitly include women in the Fifteenth Amendment in 1870, suffragists decided simply to assert their right to vote. According to the Fourteenth Amendment, anyone born in the U.S. was a citizen. If so, women were certainly citizens and thus should be able to vote. In 1872, they held a vote-in across the nation, and in New York state, suffragist Susan B. Anthony successfully cast a ballot. She was later tried and convicted—in an all-male courtroom in which she did not have the right to testify—for the crime of voting.[2]

Meanwhile, in Missouri, a voting registrar named Reese Happersett refused to permit suffragist Virginia Minor to register. Minor sued him, and the case worked its way up to the Supreme Court. In 1875, the justices handed down the unanimous *Minor v. Happersett* decision agreeing that women were indeed citizens . . . but saying that citizenship did not necessarily convey the right to vote.[3]

Minor v. Happersett was a profound blow to the idea of equality. In the South, it paved the way for white supremacists to keep Black Americans from the polls in 1876, returning white supremacists to power that would not be broken until after the passage of the 1965

Voting Rights Act, eighty-nine years later. In the West, it justified the practice of excluding nonwhite people from voting by using naturalization laws from the early nineteenth century that limited naturalization to "free white" immigrants.

Soon the nation's lawmaking was back in the hands of elite white men. In 1882, Congress passed the Chinese Exclusion Act, prohibiting the immigration of workers from China, and in 1884, the Supreme Court ruled that unassimilated Indians were not U.S. citizens. In 1889, an attempt to protect Black voting made lynching spike, and in 1890, Mississippi wrote a new constitution preventing Black men from voting, on grounds other than race. All but one state in the country, Massachusetts, followed suit, adding poll taxes, literacy clauses, and so on to limit participation in government by immigrants as well as by Black and Brown Americans.[4]

The attempt to disenfranchise Black, Brown, poor, and female Americans was, in part, a response to their demonstration that they embraced the characteristics of the American dream as the Republicans had set it out during the war. Indeed, in the late nineteenth century marginalized people increasingly defined that dream for white Americans. When Black southerners began to move to the West after the "redemption" of the South by white supremacists, they explained to the Senate that they wanted not only physical safety but also education, fair wages, property, and the right to have a say in the government under which they lived. Excluded from rights by their states, the Exodusters, as they were called, publicly articulated a national identity based in the old vision of the Lincoln Republicans.

After the war, Americans who could not vote deliberately wrote themselves into a worldview that called for education, hard work, and prosperity. Books like Horatio Alger's 1868 bestselling *Ragged Dick*, the rags-to-riches story of a bootblack who studies and works hard to become a prosperous businessman, presented these characteristics as a model for rising white boys. Those seeking a foothold in the postwar world used their mastery of those same characteristics to demonstrate how much they, too, belonged.[5]

Key to this belonging was education. Before the war, educating enslaved people had been a crime in southern states. After emancipation, formerly enslaved Americans recognized that their inability to read and write placed them at the mercy of men who could, and they made education a priority. Indigenous Americans eager to adapt to the white man's world did the same, a drive that had tragic consequences when government officials insisted on educating children away from their parents.

Those claiming a stake in the new country centered their personal histories around education. Booker T. Washington's 1901 autobiography, *Up from Slavery*, famously told of how he worked in a salt mine and a coal mine before enrolling at Hampton Normal and Agricultural Institute, where he worked as a janitor to pay for his room and board. Ohiyesa, a Santee Dakota, and Yankton Dakota Zitkála-Šá also highlighted their education in their writings. Ohiyesa worked his way up through medical school at Boston University, from which he got his degree in 1890, the first Indigenous American certified in Western medicine. Zitkála-Šá became a well-known writer and musician.[6]

When formerly enslaved minister George Washington Williams published his groundbreaking two-volume *The History of the Negro Race in America from 1619 to 1880* in 1882, he devoted two chapters to the attempts of white Americans to keep Black Americans uneducated. He concluded with a section extolling the Black population's "Wonderful Achievements as a Laborer, Soldier, and Student." "This remarkable people have now 14,889 schools, with an attendance of 720,853 pupils! And this does not include the children of color who attend the white schools of the Northern States," he added.[7]

Women, too, pushed for the right to attend school. Postwar prosperity gave more families the resources to educate their daughters, and quiet girls like Laura Jane Addams of Rockford, Illinois, the motherless daughter of a prominent businessman and politician, set off to class with their books. Mary Church of Memphis, who went by "Mollie," did the same. Three years younger than Addams, Church was the daughter of a prosperous businessman father and an entrepreneurial mother, both of whom had formerly been enslaved.

By the end of the nineteenth century, women made up more than half the country's high school graduates. This steady stream of newly educated young women headed to newly opened women's colleges, where previously isolated young women like Addams and Church learned higher mathematics, history, theory, and law and, crucially, made lifelong friendships.

Education represented a commitment to work hard. Black leaders constantly emphasized the hard work of Black Americans, sometimes noting that they had, after all, produced the extraordinary wealth of the Old South. Black newspapers made much of a rising Black middle class in border states and the West, downplaying the grinding poverty that characterized much of the late-nineteenth-century South. And businesspeople like hair-care product mogul Madam C. J. Walker and Wall Street broker Jeremiah Hamilton rose to prosperous heights. Among Indigenous Americans, Comanche cattle rancher Quanah Parker did the same.

Once people were educated and prosperous, the next stage of the Lincolnian vision was for them to take part in the cultural and scientific advancement of the nation. There, too, formerly excluded Americans shone. Hundreds of vibrant Black newspapers under the direction of people like George Ruby, T. Thomas Fortune, and Ida B. Wells explored the country from the perspective of its Black citizens. Asian and Mexican immigrants told their own stories, and new histories of women and of Black America by Elizabeth Cady Stanton and George Washington Williams made it clear that the country had never been exclusively white and male. Memoirs by labor leaders Terence V. Powderly and Samuel Gompers confirmed that it had never been exclusively wealthy, either.

Fine art by people like Edmonia Lewis, a sculptor of Black and Indigenous heritage, who carved into marble images of abolitionists and Indigenous Americans, and painter Henry Ossawa Tanner drew international attention. Scientists like George Washington Carver, who popularized southern crop rotation and experimented extensively with peanut crops, helped to address the problems of the new age.

Visibly disproving white supremacists' racist and sexist characterizations of them, people who were unable to vote claimed their place in American society by publicly celebrating the characteristics of the American dream. But they never celebrated the individualism white politicians preached.

Instead, they repeatedly held up the nation's promise of equality to demonstrate its failings. Indigenous Americans went to battle against a government whose ideology depended on the theft of their lands. When forced onto reservations, they published books and articles explaining their traditions and noting that so-called Christians seemed far less Christian than those practicing traditional religions. When government officials broke treaties, Indigenous men like Hunkpapa Lakota Sitting Bull and Comanche leader Quanah Parker visited Washington to demand the government honor them.

They sued for their rights. In Tennessee, for example, after the Supreme Court struck down civil rights legislation in 1883, Ida B. Wells tested the court's decision by riding in a first-class railroad car. When the conductor physically dragged her out of her seat, Wells not only bit him—a potentially deadly act in an era before antibiotics—she sued. Initially, she won, but the Tennessee supreme court ultimately reversed the decision, claiming Wells was not acting in good faith. Shut out from the law, she turned to journalism to publicize the attacks on Black people.[8]

Twelve years later, in 1895, Wong Kim Ark, an American-born child of Chinese immigrants, was denied reentry to the U.S. after a visit to China. He sued, arguing that the Fourteenth Amendment established birthright citizenship, and he won. In the 1898 *United States v. Wong Kim Ark* decision, the Supreme Court determined that the children of immigrants to the U.S.—no matter how unpopular immigration was at the time—were U.S. citizens, entitled to all the rights and immunities of citizenship, and that no act of Congress could overrule a constitutional amendment.[9]

Those excluded from political power leveraged their networks and communities to change society. Mollie Church, who was now known by her married name of Mary Church Terrell, had become an educator. She worked with Black journalist Josephine St. Pierre Ruffin, publisher of the newspaper *The Woman's Era*, to bring together suffrage and civil rights. Along with Ida B. Wells and others, they fought lynching. Jane Addams and others established "settlement houses" in the immigrant areas of big cities that brought new and old Americans together to begin to clean up urban streets and tenements. These activists used their educations to document the lives of working women and men. They gathered information, looking at everything from factory conditions and pay to health and work-related injuries, and used it to pressure lawmakers to address those poor conditions, especially for women and children.[10]

Women were also coming to realize their power as consumers. In 1891, Florence Kelley (the daughter of a Civil War congressman) and Josephine Shaw Lowell (the sister of Union officer and abolitionist leader Robert Gould Shaw) organized the National Consumers League to pressure industrialists to treat their workers better. "To live means to buy, to buy means to have power, to have power means to have responsibility," Kelley said.[11]

Workingmen helped to reinforce the idea that the American system depended on those working their way up rather than on wealthy elites. When it turned out that wartime contracting and financial policy had privileged the wealthy, workers in 1866 organized the first national labor union. They called for the government to establish an eight-hour day, higher wages, and better working conditions.

In 1882, they organized the first Labor Day parade in New York City, carrying banners that read "Labor Built This Republic and Labor Shall Rule It," "Labor Creates All Wealth," "No Land Monopoly," "No Money Monopoly," "Labor Pays All Taxes," "The Laborer Must Receive and Enjoy the Full Fruit of His Labor," and "The True Remedy Is Organization and the Ballot." In 1894, President Grover Cleveland made Labor Day a national holiday.

Workingmen forged connections that bridged the old world of rural communities and the new world of urban industry. Keeping alive the camaraderie of the war, they organized into fraternal organizations that established the idea of mutual aid and stability in an unstable era that championed individualism. The Grand Army of the Republic, the Knights of Pythias, the Patrons of Husbandry (also known as the Grange), and the Odd Fellows provided life insurance policies for their members and made sure that the widows and children of their unfortunate "brothers" didn't starve. Members mixed together across class lines and sometimes even across racial lines.[12]

Even as white men limited suffrage, and murdered some of those who claimed their right to have a say in their government, Black Americans, people of color, women, and workers had never lost sight of the Declaration of Independence. At the turn of the twentieth century, Black cowboy Nat Love, who had become a Pullman porter, wrote the tale of his journey from enslavement to prosperity. In it he described a world in which even the racism and structural inequalities of the late nineteenth century could not hold him back: "This grand country of ours is the peer of any in the world, and . . . volumes cannot begin to tell of the wonders of it. . . . I have seen a large part of America, and am still seeing it, but the life of a hundred years would be all too short to see our country. . . . America, I love thee, Sweet land of Liberty, home of the brave and the free."[13]

In an era of pervasive and violent repression, people who were legally excluded from equality kept the idea of American democracy alive for everyone. They also suggested a way forward.

CHAPTER 28

A Progressive America

I n the late nineteenth century, plenty of white reactionaries had abandoned the ideals of the Declaration of Independence, if indeed they ever accepted them. And they were not going to be stopped by the Fourteenth and Fifteenth amendments, or Congress's 1870 establishment of the Department of Justice to stop white southerners from terrorizing their Black neighbors. When racial discrimination became illegal, opponents of Black rights simply took a new tack. They began to argue that Black voters were trying to redistribute wealth from hardworking white taxpayers to public works projects to benefit the states' poorer inhabitants.

They warned that letting poorer men vote was "socialism" and would destroy the individualism that lay at the heart of American liberty.

Republicans who were enjoying the benefits of an expanding economy were quite open to the idea that poor voters endangered the country. Enormous advances in technology had brought new products and services to the country—bananas, for example, as well as national railroads—and by the 1880s, upwardly mobile Americans had enough leisure time and money to celebrate weddings with special dresses and cakes and to give their children toys on their birthdays. Massive factories like industrialist Andrew Carnegie's plant in Homestead, Pennsylvania, churned out steel to make buildings like Chicago's Home Insurance Building, completed in 1885, its ten stories making it so astonishingly high it could only be called a "skyscraper."[1]

This innovation was possible, Republicans insisted, because they used the government to protect the ability of men like Carnegie to run their businesses as they saw fit. Tariff laws guaranteed that domestic industries would not have to compete with foreign products, so businessmen could innovate, bringing new products and new profits that would enable them to develop their businesses further. That development paid the country in jobs, permitting all Americans to enjoy a rising standard of living.

That vision was a reworking of the worldview of elite enslavers, updated for the era of industrialization. Carnegie explained in 1889: "Individualism, Private Property, the Law of Accumulation of Wealth, and the Law of Competition" were the very height of human achievement. While the new economy created great disparities of wealth, he thought those differences were inevitable and a good thing. The money flowing up to the top enabled the country's wealthiest men to build libraries and concert halls and universities and art collections that raised the cultural standards of the whole country. If it were diverted into the pockets of workers, he argued, it would simply be used for housing, food, and leisure that would benefit no one but the workers themselves.[2]

Newspapers celebrated leading industrialists as the nation's heroes, and Republicans took credit for creating the environment for them to work their magic. Across the country, men served by the new economy cheered on its leaders. By the 1880s, it was common knowledge that industrialists controlled Congress. Even the staunchly Republican *Chicago Tribune* complained: "Behind every one of half of the portly and well-dressed members of the Senate can be seen the outlines of some corporation interested in getting or preventing legislation." The Senate, *Harper's Weekly* noted, was "a club of rich men."[3]

Even casual observers could see that the nation was not in the rosy shape Republicans claimed. On shop floors in eastern factories, workers shoveled coal or worked looms for fourteen to sixteen hours a day for pennies, and if their health broke down or they lost a limb, they were out of both work and luck. In the West, rains had failed for five years, and the hot winds baked crops dry in two days. "This would be a fine country if only it had water," a hopeful farmer said over a western joke. "Yes, and so would hell" was the punch line. Farmers were saddled with high-interest mortgages, middlemen skimmed the profits when crops went to market, and freight charges from railroad monopolies took the rest.

Yet Republicans insisted that those asking the government to address the needs of workers and farmers were un-American. As Carnegie said: "The Socialist or Anarchist who seeks to overturn present conditions is to be regarded as attacking the foundation upon which civilization itself rests." Men of wealth had to stand against workers who tried to control politics.[4]

Hoping to level the playing field, Democrats promised to lower the tariff that enabled industrialists to collude to raise prices. Republican reformers joined them to elect Democrat Grover Cleveland to the White House in 1884. But their hopes fell apart fast as horrified business Republicans stopped tariff reform in the Senate and then pulled out every stop they could to make sure their candidate, Benjamin Harrison, won in 1888. Harrison lost the popular vote by about a hundred thousand votes but finagled a win in the Electoral College. Cleveland, moving out of the White House despite having won the popular vote, warned: "The gulf between employers and the employed is constantly widening, and classes are rapidly forming, one comprising the very rich and powerful, while in another are found the toiling poor. . . . Corporations, which should be the carefully restrained creatures of the law and the servants of the people, are fast becoming the people's masters."[5]

The vision of a nation in which a few wealthy men ruled seemed to be hardening into place. Harrison's men promised "This is A BUSI-NESS MAN'S ADMINISTRATION . . . [and] before the close of the present Administration business men will be thoroughly well content with it." Lest there be any doubt about that permanent control, over twelve months in 1889 and 1890, the Republicans added six new states to the Union in the largest acquisition of states since the original thirteen. North Dakota, South Dakota, Idaho, Wyoming, Montana, and Washington had so few people their addition would not change the makeup of the House much, but the Republicans expected they would add twelve new Republican senators and eighteen Republican presidential electors. They openly boasted they would control the government for the foreseeable future.[6]

But in the summer of 1890, a new political movement began, quietly, to take shape. In western towns, workers and poor farmers and entrepreneurs shut out of opportunities by monopolies began to talk to one another. They discovered a shared dismay over a government that seemed to work only for the rich industrialists, and anger that they seemed to be working themselves to the bone only to have the fruits of their labor taken by the rich. "Wall Street owns the country," western organizer Mary Elizabeth Lease told audiences. "It is no longer a government of the people, by the people, and for the people, but a government of Wall Street, by Wall Street, and for Wall Street."[7]

Westerners suffering in the new economy began to come together. Reviving older social organizations, they distributed literature across the country explaining how tariffs worked and how railroad monopolies jacked up prices. Newspapers began to echo their arguments, and where there weren't local newspapers, members of the growing political movement, the Farmers' Alliance, began to print them.

Their vision of the country's political economy defended the idea that the government should treat everyone equally. Alliances declared that farmers and entrepreneurs shared the same interests as workers, and called for "the reform of unjust systems and the repeal of laws that bear unequally upon the people."[8]

The new western movement also reflected the community focus of marginalized Americans, redefining what it meant to be a success in America. Rather than the cutthroat individualism of those like Carnegie, they called for reviving an older tradition, one in which "manliness" meant honesty, generosity, community-mindedness, and dignity. They called for "a manly, honest defense of popular rights, a clear cut expression of principles, a bold demand for the restoration of that of which they have been despoiled under the deceitful forms and names of law." They rejected the era's political fights for dominance, and so there was room in their political coalition for women and often, despite the era's Jim Crow walls, for Black farmers.[9]

Supporters of the Alliance movement wanted the nation to honor its Civil War promise of equality before the law and equality of access to resources, and they recognized that the concentration of wealth in the new industrial economy was as dangerous as the concentration of wealth in the slave economy. Their solution was to require direct election of senators—so industrialists could not buy up legislatures to pick the man they wanted—along with regulation of railroads, lower tariffs, a graduated income tax, easier credit, better working conditions, and higher wages.

When the votes were counted in the midterm election of 1890, it turned out that the newspapers, letters, barbecues, lectures, and picnics had done their work, educating those on the periphery of politics about the grand issues of the day. The Alliances had carried South Dakota and almost the whole state ticket in Kansas, and they held the balance of power in the Minnesota and Illinois legislatures. In Nebraska and Iowa, they had split the Republicans and given the governorship to a Democrat. They controlled fifty-two seats in the new Congress.

By 1892, reformers had joined together as the People's Party, or the Populists. Claiming that the nation had been "brought to the verge of moral, political, and material ruin," they warned that businessmen had bought and paid for politicians and the media to concentrate the nation's wealth in their own hands. "The fruits of the toil of millions are boldly stolen to build up colossal fortunes for a few, unprecedented in the history of mankind; and the possessors of these, in turn despise the Republic and endanger liberty."[10]

Voters agreed, and they returned Cleveland to the White House. They also put Democrats in charge of both houses of Congress for the first time since before the Civil War.

This was a revolution Republicans could not abide, and they howled that Cleveland would crash the economy. Their repeated warnings that rich men should get their money out of the stock market before the Democrats took over sparked a financial panic just days before Cleveland took office. Ignoring that the crash had happened on their watch, Republicans told voters that the recession, with its unemployment, business failures, strikes, and desperation, was entirely the fault of the Democrats, and in the midterm election of 1894, voters reversed the landslide of 1892, putting Republicans back in charge of Congress.

In the presidential election of 1896, it was the Democratic candidate, William Jennings Bryan, who sounded like Lincoln. "There are those who believe that, if you will only legislate to make the well-to-do prosperous, their prosperity will leak through on those below," Bryan said. "The Democratic idea, however, has been that if you legislate to make the masses prosperous, their prosperity will find its way up through every class which rests upon them." Republican William McKinley won the election, but a new generation of Republicans recognized that voters demanded change.[11]

They found a way to create that change thanks to a long-brewing war in Cuba. The Spanish-American War would enable young Republicans like Theodore Roosevelt to rework liberalism to meet the extraordinary concentrations of wealth and power made possible by industrialization.

In 1898, younger Republicans joined Democrats in demanding that the United States help the Cubans in their struggle against the island's Spanish colonizers. If indeed the country was as strong and moral as their elders claimed, they insisted, it had a duty to come to the rescue of the people of Cuba. The businessmen who were eager to make sure sugar production on the island wasn't disrupted objected to intervention, but politicians like Roosevelt worried that such focus on moneymaking was ruining the United States. "We will have this war for the freedom of Cuba," Roosevelt told Republican operative Mark Hanna, shaking his fist at Hanna at a public dinner, "in spite of the timidity of the commercial interests!"[12]

Intervention in Cuba enabled younger Americans like Roosevelt to rebrand the American cowboy. After the Civil War, Democrats had created the cowboy to represent a white man who worked hard, stood alone, and dominated those around him. The Spanish-American War redefined the image of the cowboy as a man who represented a brotherhood and who valued fairness for all. Given permission to raise his own regiment, Roosevelt emphasized that his men came from every part of the country and from every walk of life: Harvard men and Indigenous Americans, northerners, southerners, white, Black, rich, and poor. Any man who was hardworking and independent, who "demanded only to . . . be judged on [his] merits," could represent America as one of Roosevelt's cowboys. The press called his regiment the Rough Riders, after the cowboys and gunfighters in Buffalo Bill's Wild West Show.

Spanish forces surrendered less than three weeks after the Americans arrived. The new cowboy seemed to represent a new America, and Roosevelt took that image into government. *The New York Times* wrote that his career showed young men that "there is a higher and nobler ideal than the acquisition of fortune, and that service to one's country is the first duty of patriotic citizenship."[13]

If the U.S. was going to spread its system overseas, it seemed imperative first to clean up that system at home. Explicitly adjusting Abraham Lincoln's vision to the modern world, turn-of-the-century progressives believed in protecting an individual man's ability to rise. But while the Lincoln Republicans were committed to protecting equality before the law and to making sure individuals had access to resources, they saw no reason to create legislation addressing poverty, since they believed removing rich monopolists from power would do the trick. When they established the Bureau of Refugees, Freedmen, and Abandoned Lands to address starvation in the postwar South, they put it under the War Department to indicate that it would be temporary.

Thirty years later, the progressives knew that protecting individuals required a strong government that regulated business and supported social welfare.

When an assassin murdered President McKinley and put Roosevelt in the White House, the new president helped Americans expand the meaning of liberalism. In the years of the early republic, liberalism had meant government restraint to keep from intruding on a man's liberty. The Civil War Republicans had expanded that definition to mean a government that protected individuals by defending equality before the law and equal access to resources. Progressive Era reformers expanded that concept yet again, understanding that the federal government must restrain the excesses of big business that were crushing individuals.

That conviction was bipartisan. In the early years of the twentieth century, progressives in both parties regulated business to stop corrupt industrialists from increasing their profits by adulterating milk with formaldehyde and painting candies with lead paint, for example; cleaned up the sewage systems and tenements in cities; protected public lands; invested in public health and education; raised taxes; and called for universal health insurance. They ratified the Sixteenth Amendment protecting the income tax and the Seventeenth Amendment providing for the direct election of senators.

They sought, as Roosevelt said, to return to "an economic system under which each man shall be guaranteed the opportunity to show the best that there is in him."[14]

CHAPTER 29

The Road to the New Deal

Progressives were able to protect the rights of individuals, but that had been possible largely because Black Americans and immigrants had been cut out of the vote, making it hard for opponents to attack progressives as socialists. Women's rights activists helped them avoid that accusation, too, by arguing for their inclusion in society not as people inherently equal to men but as wives and mothers.

But others continued to try to expand American equality by defending civil rights. In 1909, a coalition came together across race and gender lines in New York City to establish the National Association for the Advancement of Colored People. To form the group, Black Americans including journalist Ida B. Wells-Barnett, suffragist and educator Mary Church Terrell, African Methodist Episcopal Zion Church bishop and civil rights advocate Alexander Walters, and sociologist W. E. B. DuBois joined with white reformers like suffragist and socialist Mary White Ovington, Jewish immigrant Henry Moskowitz, and journalist William English Walling, the wealthy socialist son of a formerly enslaving family, along with settlement house workers like Florence Kelley and Lillian Wald.

They chose as their founding date February 12, Lincoln's birthday, vowing "to promote equality of rights and eradicate caste or race prejudice among citizens of the United States; to advance the interest of colored citizens; to secure for them impartial suffrage; and to increase their opportunities for securing justice in the courts, education for their children, employment according to their ability, and complete equality before the law."[1]

Turning those principles into reality, though, would require expanding the concept of American liberal democracy once again. This time, though, it would be the Democratic Party, the party that had initially tried to replace the principles of the Declaration of Independence with the hierarchical ideology of white supremacy, that would expand those rights. By the time the NAACP organized, that change was already under way.

Curiously, the expansion of the idea of liberal democracy grew in the Democratic Party from a backlash against the determination of former Confederates to reduce their Black neighbors to a state as close to enslavement as they could. By 1878, southern Democrats had effectively disenfranchised Republican voters, Black and white, and turned their region into a one-party state. With the help of this powerful southern bloc, Democrats had taken control of the House of Representatives in 1875, in the midst of a recession, and in 1879 they took control of the Senate. Because of the seniority system in Congress, this meant that former Confederates held key positions. Retaking control of Congress, they believed they had a mandate to get rid of the power of the federal government to protect civil rights, recreating the hierarchical society the United States had utterly rejected fifteen years before or destroying the government in the process.

Determined to get rid of the new nationalism and restore states' rights as the law of the land, they refused to fund the government. One southern representative told *The New York Times*, "The great blunder of our section was in abandoning our seats in Congress in 1861." That would never happen again, he said; they would stay in Congress and control both the South and the North.[2]

Republican president Rutherford B. Hayes and House minority

leader James A. Garfield of Ohio recognized that an extremist faction in Congress forcing its will on the country by holding government finances hostage was a form of revolution. If the extremists' tactics worked, this would be only the first of their demands, and the country would fall, as one Democrat said, under "the absolute despotism of . . . irresponsible and unrestrained" partisans.[3]

Popular opinion swung behind the Republicans, and the former Confederates backed down. Caving to the extremists destroyed the Democrats in the upcoming election, when Republicans reversed their recent losses and put Garfield, now famous for his stand against those who wanted to defund the government, into the White House on a platform of protecting Black rights.

It was clear to Democratic leaders that the expanding demographics of the late nineteenth century had left the principles of the southern extremists behind. While much of the white South was looking backward, the rest of the country was full of new voices speaking unfamiliar dialects and languages, and new music, like ragtime and cowboy songs. The nation's streets, offices, factories, and schools were full of people who wore clothes from other countries and ate foods that native-born Americans found exotic. New books and journalism told the story of life from Chicago's streets or the Mexican border, or on an Indian reservation, keeping the country alive to the exciting possibilities of a multicultural world. Those determined to keep control of the country and force those around them to conform to their world, by violence if necessary, were out of step with the modern era.

So Democrats began to turn their focus to the northern, urban wing of the party, embracing the multicultural themes emerging from the new northern cities. These "New Democrats," led by New York reformer Grover Cleveland, still emphasized the importance of local government and the dangers of a strong federal government, but they cared less about white supremacy than about supporting workers and farmers in the new industrial economy. Their shift worked: in 1884, voters put Cleveland into the White House. His candidacy had attracted a number of Republicans—dubbed "Mugwumps"—who opposed their party's swing behind big business.

Cleveland's inauguration in 1885 was widely interpreted as a moment of racial reconciliation, an occasion illuminated by the fact that in his years as New York's governor, he had broadened Black appointments to office and desegregated the New York City police force.

Democrats' focus turned away from the racial animosity of the South to the northern cities, especially New York City. The Tammany Hall political machine had called the shots in New York City for decades, but the increasing corruption of its leaders led "Boss" Richard Croker to step down in 1902. His replacement, Charles Murphy, faced the problem of retaining the loyalty of his working-class voters within the bounds of legality.

To figure out what voters wanted, Murphy and the new crop of urban Democratic politicians he cultivated turned to the expertise of female settlement house workers, the nation's first secular social workers. Women like Frances Perkins, who had worked with Jane Addams at Chicago's Hull House, explained to men like Tammany Hall's James Farley the needs of workers for fair pay, workplace protections, and a basic social safety net. At the same time, Farley focused on equality before the law, insisting in 1926 that Black boxer Harry Wills had the right to challenge the white heavyweight champion Jack Dempsey, and refusing to let Dempsey fight white challenger Gene Tunney in New York City until Dempsey fought Wills. Farley paved the way for Black Americans to find their way to the Democratic Party in the North.

Farley rose through the ranks of the Democratic Party to become its kingmaker. He backed New York governor Al Smith, who was a close associate of the NAACP's Moskowitz, for the presidency in 1928, marking the first time a Catholic son of immigrants ran as a major-party candidate for the White House. Farley went on to run Franklin Delano Roosevelt's gubernatorial and later presidential campaigns.

Even before women had the right to vote, Farley insisted that their voices were crucial to the democratic experiment, and his protégés endorsed that opinion: Smith had helped Perkins organize a factory investigating commission after the 1911 Triangle Shirtwaist Factory fire to look not simply at fire dangers but also at long hours, low wages, child labor, overwork, and "almost everything you could think of that had been in agitation for years," as Perkins later recalled. When FDR became president, Perkins became the first woman in a presidential cabinet.[4]

Farley brought together a powerful coalition of Catholics, women, Black Americans, and workers to back progressive state laws. In many ways, FDR's New Deal was the urban Democratic experiment of the 1920s applied to the whole nation. Democrats used the federal government to regulate business; provide a basic social safety net, largely through work programs; and promote infrastructure, much as city bosses had pioneered.

The New Deal liberal consensus, expanded under Democratic president Harry Truman, his Republican successor, Dwight Eisenhower, and the presidents of both parties who followed them, reordered American society in the ways people like Perkins had hoped. It created what economists called the "great compression," in which wealth and income distribution became much more even, dramatically reducing economic inequality. Between 1945 and 1960 the nation's gross national product jumped 250 percent, from $200 billion to $500 billion.

After World War II, the Servicemen's Readjustment Act, more popularly known as the G.I. Bill, helped 51 percent of veterans— 7.8 million—get vocational training or a college degree. It added 450,000 engineers, 180,000 medical professionals, 360,000 teachers,

150,000 scientists, 243,000 accountants, 107,000 lawyers, and 36,000 clergymen to the economy. The benefits of the plan went primarily to white men—although technically eligible, Black and Brown men and women were largely excluded—but the movement of formerly poor white men into the middle class created a vacuum that moved everyone upward, while unions helped to solidify the power of workers.[5]

The G.I. Bill also helped about four million veterans buy homes, which in turn boosted first the building trades and then the production of new services and home goods as those houses filled with children. "Wonderful news!!" read one commercially produced card to congratulate new parents in 1962, "for the diaper service . . . greeting card publishers . . . Toy Shops . . . orthodontist . . . infants wear department . . . carriage makers . . . milk man . . . super market . . . pediatricians . . . furniture manufacturers . . . shoe salesman . . . department stores . . . congratulations!"[6]

Across the economy, incomes doubled from 1945 to 1970. The era was characterized by affluence: single-family homes with cars, good public education, steady jobs, electricity, plumbing, toys, television, health care, and a secure old age. Meanwhile, a strongly progressive tax code spread the costs of repaying the wartime debt and funding the new social services evenly. The top marginal tax rate during Eisenhower's administration was 91 percent, and the effective tax rate for the highest incomes was 70 percent. The corporate tax rate peaked at 52.8 percent in the late 1960s.[7]

New Deal programs often excluded Black and Brown Americans to cater to southern Democrats whose votes FDR needed, but the New Deal marked yet another expansion of liberal democracy. While it focused on protecting white male heads of household, it suggested that Black Americans, people of color, and women should have a say in their government and its benefits, however imperfect the early days of that expansion turned out to be.

CHAPTER 30

Democracy Awakening

I n the 1930s the New Deal coalition demonstrated that the government could promote the welfare of the people, thus establishing the liberal consensus. At the same time, the expansion of rights to women and Black and Brown Americans, as well as to other minorities, set in motion the undermining of democracy that is still under way.

Since the 1980s, political figures eager to get rid of that liberal consensus have gained power by denigrating it. Ignoring the fact that expanding equality was entirely consistent with the principles the Founders had put in the Declaration of Independence, they have suggested that doing so rejected America's historical ideals. And although the liberal consensus bolstered economic prosperity and shared it more widely than ever before, they claimed it stunted economic growth.

The demands of Black and Brown Americans for inclusion in the nation's political system after World War II forced the nation to grapple with the true meaning of democracy. President Dwight Eisenhower pushed the passage of the Civil Rights Act of 1957 primarily to protect the voting rights that were, theoretically, already established. And once James Meredith had pushed him into backing desegregation, President John F. Kennedy advocated a stronger civil rights bill. Just five days after Kennedy's murder, his successor, Lyndon B. Johnson, told Congress: "No memorial oration or eulogy could more eloquently honor President Kennedy's memory than the earliest possible passage of the civil rights bill for which he fought so long."[1]

Although southern white men passionately defended their right to rule over their Black neighbors through state legislation, LBJ, for all his love of his native state of Texas, wanted none of that. "We have talked long enough in this country about equal rights. We have talked for one hundred years or more. It is time now to write the next chapter, and to write it in the books of law," he said.[2]

Congress considered a civil rights bill in early 1964, while Black and white Americans demonstrated their support for civil rights by integrating formerly segregated spaces. On June 18, when Black and white people jumped into a whites-only swimming pool at the Monson Motor Lodge in St. Augustine, Florida, the hotel's owner, James Brock, poured acid into the pool. The water diluted the acid enough that the swimmers were not injured, but local law enforcement officers arrested them. News crews covered the incident. For a number of Americans, seeing a white man pour acid into a swimming pool to drive out Black people was the last straw.[3]

The next day, Republican Everett Dirksen of Illinois, the Senate minority leader, managed to deliver enough Republican votes to Majority Leader Mike Mansfield of Montana to break a Senate filibuster. Arizona senator Barry Goldwater, who said, "I am unalterably opposed to discrimination or segregation on the basis of race, color or creed, or on any other basis," voted against ending the filibuster, saying he believed it was "a grave threat to the very essence of our basic system of government, namely, that of a constitutional republic in which 50 sovereign states have reserved to themselves and to the people those powers not specifically granted to the central or Federal Government."[4]

The Senate passed the bill on June 19 and sent their version back to the House two days before three voting rights workers, Black

Mississippian James Chaney and white, Jewish New Yorkers Andrew Goodman and Michael Schwerner, disappeared near Philadelphia, Mississippi. As rage over the three missing men grew, Johnson pressured the House to pass the bill.[5]

It did. Johnson signed the Civil Rights Act of 1964 into law on July 2.

Just before he wrote his name, Johnson addressed the American people on television "to talk to you about what that law means to every American."

Keenly aware of the bill's timing, he noted: "One hundred and eighty-eight years ago this week, a small band of valiant men began a long struggle for freedom. They pledged their lives, their fortunes, and their sacred honor not only to found a nation, but to forge an ideal of freedom—not only for political independence, but for personal liberty; not only to eliminate foreign rule, but to establish the rule of justice in the affairs of men."[6]

That was a triumph, but "those who founded our country knew that freedom would be secure only if each generation fought to renew and enlarge its meaning. . . . Americans of every race and color have died in battle to protect our freedom. Americans of every race and color have worked to build a nation of widening opportunities. Now our generation of Americans has been called on to continue the unending search for justice within our own borders."

Johnson celebrated that the bill had bipartisan support of more than two thirds of the lawmakers in Congress and that it enjoyed the support of "the great majority of the American people."

He emphasized that the law "does not restrict the freedom of any American, so long as he respects the rights of others." He took on the old trope that Black Americans wanted "special treatment" and said that the law simply made sure those people the Founders had declared were created equal would now "also be equal in the polling booths, in the classrooms, in the factories, and in hotels, restaurants, movie theaters, and other places that provide service to the public."

"Its purpose is not to punish. Its purpose is not to divide, but to end divisions—divisions which have lasted all too long. Its purpose is national, not regional. Its purpose is to promote a more abiding commitment to freedom, a more constant pursuit of justice, and a deeper respect for human dignity."

Most Americans wanted to do what was right, he said, and it was time for them to assert their power. "My fellow citizens," he said, "we have come now to a time of testing. We must not fail."

Johnson had a vision of a "Great Society" that would eliminate poverty and racial injustice once and for all. While FDR's New Deal had used the federal government to address the greatest economic crisis in U.S. history, leveling the playing field between workers and employers to enable workingmen to support their families, the country was enjoying record growth in 1964. Far from simply saving the country, LBJ could afford to direct it toward greater things.

In May 1964, Johnson outlined his plan in a graduation speech at the University of Michigan, and the administration immediately turned to addressing issues of civil rights and poverty. After Congress passed the Civil Rights Act, it passed the Economic Opportunity Act of 1964, which created an Office of Economic Opportunity to oversee a whole series of antipoverty programs, and the Food Stamp Act, which helped people who didn't make a lot of money buy food.[7]

Republicans ran Barry Goldwater against Johnson for president in 1964, calling for rolling back business regulation and civil rights to the years before the New Deal. But voters who quite liked the new system gave Democrats such a strong majority in Congress that Johnson and the Democrats were able to pass eighty-four new laws to put the Great Society into place.

They cemented civil rights with the 1965 Voting Rights Act protecting minority voting, created jobs in Appalachia, and established job-training and community-development programs. The Elementary and Secondary Education Act of 1965 gave federal aid to public schools and established the Head Start program to provide comprehensive early education for low-income children. The Higher Education Act of 1965 increased federal investment in universities and provided scholarships and low-interest loans to students.

The Social Security Amendments of 1965 created Medicare, which provided health insurance for Americans over age sixty-five, and Medicaid, which helped cover health care costs for those with limited incomes. Congress advanced the war on poverty by increasing welfare payments and subsidizing rent for low-income families.

But the government did not simply address poverty. Congress took on the rights of consumers with new protective legislation that required cigarettes and other dangerous products to carry warning labels, required products to carry labels identifying the manufacturer, and required lenders to disclose the full cost of finance charges in loans. Congress also passed legislation protecting the environment, including the Water Quality Act of 1965, which established federal standards for water quality.

Congress also endorsed LBJ's aspirations for beauty and purpose with the National Foundation on the Arts and Humanities Act of 1965. This law created both the National Endowment for the Arts and the National Endowment for the Humanities to make sure the era's emphasis on science didn't endanger the humanities. In 1967 it would also establish the Corporation for Public Broadcasting, followed in 1969 by National Public Radio.[8]

"For better or worse," Johnson had told the University of Michigan graduates in 1964, "your generation has been appointed by history to . . . lead America toward a new age. . . . You can help build a society where the demands of morality, and the needs of the spirit, can be realized in the life of the Nation."[9] He urged them to make equality a reality and to end poverty.

"There are those timid souls who say this battle cannot be won; that we are condemned to a soulless wealth," he said, but he disagreed. "We have the power to shape the civilization that we want. But we need your will, your labor, your hearts, if we are to build that kind of society."

The Great Society programs changed America. Forty million Americans were poor in 1960, but by 1969 that number had fallen to twenty-four million. That prosperity was shared by white and nonwhite people more fully than ever before. Black school attendance increased by four years; twice as many Black people found work in professional, technical, and clerical occupations; the Black unemployment rate fell 34 percent, and median Black family income rose 53 percent. In 1960, 55 percent of Black Americans lived below the poverty line; by 1968, the number was 27 percent. In the decade after 1965, infant mortality fell by one third thanks to new medical and nutritional programs. In 1960, 20 percent of Americans had no indoor plumbing; by 1970, that number had fallen to 11 percent.

Women's lives, too, became more integrated into the United States. In 1950, women made up about one third of the total labor force; by 1980, they made up more than 40 percent, growing at a rate dramatically faster than that of men. In 1965, the Supreme Court defended their equality by recognizing the constitutional right of married people to use contraception; in 1973, it similarly protected the right to abortion.[10]

Opponents of the Great Society programs picked up forty-seven seats in the House and three seats in the Senate in the 1966 midterm elections, and *U.S. News & World Report* wrote that "the big bash" was over.[11]

But the nation seemed poised to embrace its multicultural history.

The big hit of 1971 was the sitcom *All in the Family*, in which Archie Bunker, a working-class white man from Queens, New York, fought with his feminist daughter and hippie son-in-law, who supported the liberal consensus. The African American series *Sanford and Son* debuted in 1972 and was so popular it drove its competition, *The Brady Bunch*, off the air in 1974. That year, *Chico and the Man* introduced a Latino veteran trying to help an alcoholic Anglo-American widower adapt to the Hispanic neighborhood that had surrounded his garage. Popular culture seemed more accepting of differences, more willing to believe in redemption.

That openness meant those opposing the liberal consensus seemed out of step, people who would be left behind. The Archie Bunker types seemed to be a dying breed, and modern Americans could afford to be charitable toward them, just as they had been toward the Confederates whose ideology the modern Archie Bunkers shared.

That charity extended even toward President Richard M. Nixon, who had begun the process of unwinding the liberal consensus by turning Americans against one another for political power and who had eventually used the power of the government to try to keep himself in office. When Republicans demanded Nixon resign on August 9, 1974, or face impeachment and conviction, his replacement, Gerald Ford, pardoned him to try to bring the country back together and avoid a "prolonged and divisive debate over the propriety of exposing to further punishment and degradation a man who has already paid the unprecedented penalty of relinquishing the highest elective office of the United States."[12]

Finally, it seemed that, with the post–World War II revision of liberalism to include the defense of civil rights and welfare legislation, the U.S. was on track to be the multicultural democracy the Declaration of Independence had hinted it could become. But it turned out that while those who embraced the new America were laughing at

Archie Bunker, those who distrusted it saw him as a spokesman. Then, in 1980, Ronald Reagan echoed the divisive rhetoric Nixon had used and ran for the presidency by warning voters that government couldn't provide solutions to the problems of the day. Instead, he said, government *was* the problem.

He won with 50.7 percent of the vote.

Reclaiming Our Country

n his Farewell Address on January 4, 1981, President Jimmy Carter noted that the undermining of faith in the government's ability to deal with problems meant that Americans were turning increasingly to "single-issue groups and special interest organizations to ensure that whatever else happens, our own personal views and our own private interests are protected." This, he warned, distorts the nation's purpose because "the national interest is not always the sum of all our single or special interests. We are all Americans together, and we must not forget that the common good is our common interest and our individual responsibility."

A president who had added solar panels to the White House, he urged Americans to protect "our most precious possessions: the air we breathe, the water we drink, and the land which sustains us," and to advance the basic human rights that had, after all, "invented America." "Our common vision of a free and just society," he said, "is our greatest source of cohesion at home and strength abroad, greater even than the bounty of our material blessings."

Carter urged Americans to remember these words: "We hold these truths to be self-evident, that all men are created equal, that they are endowed by their Creator with certain unalienable Rights, that among these are Life, Liberty and the pursuit of Happiness."[1]

And yet here we are.

In the years after President Ronald Reagan took over the White

House (where he promptly removed the solar panels), a radical minority once again used the power of language and the power of their own historical myth to tear apart the concept of the common good.

Their dismantling of the liberal consensus revived a dangerous trend toward authoritarianism. First, wealth concentrated upward, leaving a large group of Americans dispossessed and angry over their downward mobility. At the same time, popular culture emphasized that those dispossessed Americans were at fault for their failure in a system they increasingly recognized was rigged. Then Republican politicians flooded the media system with propaganda insisting that tax cuts and pro-business government policies were not to blame for the dispossession of white lower- and middle-class Americans. The culprits, they insisted, were lazy, grasping, and immoral minorities and women.

Increasing numbers of Americans rejected the idea that the government could defend their interests, while those who still had faith in the system and tried to elect Democrats to office found the Republicans had increasingly diluted their votes through gerrymandering, voter suppression, the filibuster, and the Electoral College. By 2016, the Republican candidate for president was openly calling for the help of authoritarian Russian leader Vladimir Putin against his Democratic opponent. And then that candidate, Donald Trump, became president.

When Americans elected Democratic president Joe Biden in 2020, he made it clear that he intended to defend American democracy from rising authoritarianism. Throughout his campaign, he focused on bringing people in the center-right and center-left together, just as scholars of authoritarianism have called for. Biden ignored Trump and pledged to work with Republicans who believe in "the rule of law and not the rule of a single man."

On January 6, 2021, after the attack on the U.S. Capitol and on the right of Americans to choose their leaders, Biden explicitly defended traditional American values.

"Those who stormed this Capitol and those who instigated and incited and those who called on them to do so" acted "not in service of America, but rather in service of one man" who "has created and spread a web of lies about the 2020 election . . . because he values power over principle, because he sees his own interests as more important than his country's interests and America's interests, and because his bruised ego matters more to him than our democracy or our Constitution," Biden told the American people. He urged Americans not to succumb to autocracy, but to come together to defend our democracy, "to keep the promise of America alive," and to protect what we stand for: "the right to vote, the right to govern ourselves, the right to determine our own destiny."[2]

Once sworn into office, Biden set out to demonstrate that the government could work for ordinary people. He went straight to the Oval Office after his inauguration and, two days after taking office, rescinded Trump's Schedule F executive order that would have ended the civil service system and enabled a president to pack the government with loyalists. He fired the political appointees Trump had tried to burrow into the federal government, and he promised that none of his family members would work at the White House.

In his first two years in office, with a slender majority in the House of Representatives and a Senate split fifty-fifty, the Democrats managed to pass historic legislation that echoed that of FDR and LBJ, shoring up the economy, rebuilding the country's infrastructure, and investing in the future, trying to bring the disaffected Americans who had given up on democracy back into the fold.

In March 2021, Democrats passed the $1.9 billion American Rescue Plan to combat the coronavirus pandemic and stimulate the economy that it had hobbled. In November 2021, some Republicans were persuaded to get on board to pass the $1.2 billion Bipartisan Infrastructure Law to rebuild the country's roads and bridges and to install broadband in rural areas across the nation. A few Republicans also backed the 2022 CHIPS and Science Act, which invested $52 billion in the domestic manufacture of semiconductors and boosted scientific research in the U.S. And in August 2022, the Democrats passed the Inflation Reduction Act, which made historic investments in addressing climate change, expanded health coverage, reduced the deficit, and raised taxes on corporations and the very wealthy.

Biden's domestic program expanded liberalism to meet the civil rights demands Carter had identified, just as Abraham Lincoln, Theodore Roosevelt, FDR, and LBJ had each expanded liberalism to meet the challenges of westward expansion, industrialization, globalization, and anti-colonialism.

Biden and his administration centered liberalism not around nuclear families headed by male breadwinners, as had always been the case before, but around children and their caregivers. He did not manage to sell Congress on childcare and eldercare infrastructure, but the Democrats did temporarily expand the child and dependent care tax credit, pass the first gun safety law in thirty years, protect interracial and gay marriage, and pass legislation to help the millions of veterans exposed to toxic burn pits in military zones.

After twelve years on the Senate Foreign Relations Committee and eight as vice president, Biden knew that defending democracy at home meant strengthening it internationally. He and Secretary of State Antony Blinken set out to rejoin international alliances and to reinforce them. Biden brought the U.S. back into the World Health Organization and set out to rebuild NATO and other strategic alliances, while forging new ones in the Indo-Pacific region and Africa.

In his first speech to the State Department, on February 4, he emphasized that he had already spoken to "the leaders of many of our closest friends—Canada, Mexico, the U.K., Germany, France, NATO, Japan, South Korea, Australia—to [begin] reforming the habits of co-operation and rebuilding the muscle of democratic alliances that have atrophied over the past few years of neglect and, I would argue, abuse." Once again, "America's most cherished Democratic values" would be at the center of American diplomacy: "defending freedom, championing opportunity, upholding universal rights, respecting the rule of law, and treating every person with dignity."[3]

The power of that defense became clear in February 2022, when Putin launched a new invasion of Ukraine. Putin was stymied by Ukraine's soldiers, who had trained hard in the eight years since the first Russian invasion, and by an international community that refused to recognize Russia's land grab, imposed strict and coordi-nated sanctions, and provided Ukraine with money, intelligence, and weapons.

This community stood together in no small part thanks to Biden and Blinken, and the strength in that cooperation discredited the argument that autocracy was more efficient and powerful than de-mocracy. Putin's highly praised and feared army turned out to be undertrained and poorly supplied: corrupt officials and their backers had siphoned off money intended for military readiness into mega-yachts and London flats for themselves and their mistresses.

The idea floated by Trump supporters that Russian society was more moral than democracies where LGBTQ people are considered equal was also discredited as Russian invaders committed war crimes against Ukraine's civilians. And the idea that democracies are weak was belied by Ukraine president Volodymyr Zelensky, a lawyer and former television comedian, who put on military clothes and, when offered an escape from his besieged city, responded: "I don't need a ride, I need more ammunition."

But despite the emerging defense of democracy, Trumpism did not die. Trump and his loyalists continued to insist he had won the 2020 election, while extremists like newly elected Georgia representative Marjorie Taylor Greene, who at one point called for Democratic politicians to be executed, told a right-wing newspaper that there was no difference between establishment Republicans and Democrats. She said she was eager to bring more action-oriented people like her to Congress to help Trump with his plan, "whenever he comes out with [it]."

Establishment leaders swung behind the Trump faction, especially after June 2022, when the Supreme Court, packed by then–Senate majority leader Mitch McConnell with three extremist judges, ignored the settled law they had promised to protect and overturned the 1973 *Roe v. Wade* decision legalizing abortion.

Republican leaders went on to challenge all of the court decisions protecting the liberal consensus government in place since the 1930s. If the Fourteenth Amendment did not protect abortion, the other civil rights it protected were on the table, including gay marriage, the right to contraception, and perhaps even desegregation. Also on the table was the government regulation of business.

Meanwhile, Trump's political star had begun to fall as his legal and financial troubles mounted in the years after the election. But he had radicalized the Republican Party, and Republican governors competed to pick up his voters. Unlike Trump in 2016, though, they made no pretense of embracing the Reagan Republican ideology of free markets: Florida governor Ron DeSantis, for instance, openly used the power of his office to reward political friends and punish those he perceived as his enemies and to manufacture anti-immigrant and anti-LGBTQ sentiment, much as Putin and Orbán had done before him. Right-wing thinkers began to argue openly that democracy and its values—equality before the law, separation of church and state, an independent press, academic freedom, and free markets—have undermined the human virtue of the past and must be stamped out.[4]

Crucially, those efforts depended on maintaining the right-wing myth that American history was rooted in a pure past that their opponents were destroying. Early in Biden's term, Republican operatives manufactured outrage over the alleged teaching of critical race theory in public schools. That legal theory, designed to explain why the laws of the 1970s hadn't created the equality they promised, was an upper-level law school elective that had never actually been taught in public schools. Republican-dominated legislatures passed laws forbidding teachers from teaching "CRT" or any lesson suggesting that the American system might ever have had systemic inequalities, or even lessons that might make some people—by which they meant white people—uncomfortable. Hand in hand with that censorship went a surge in book banning from the public schools and from some public libraries, with most of the banned books written by or about Black or LGBTQ people.

A history that looks back to a mythologized past as the country's perfect time is a key tool of authoritarians. It allows them to characterize anyone who opposes them as an enemy of the country's great destiny.

But the true history of American democracy is that it is never finished. It is the story of people who have honored the idea that a nation can be based not in land or religion or race or hierarchies, but rather in the concept of human equality. That commitment, along with its corollary—that we have a right to consent to our government, which in turn should act in our interest—has brought us our powerful history of people working and sacrificing to bring those principles to life. Reclaiming our history of noble struggle reworks the polarizing language that has done us such disservice while it undermines the ideology of authoritarianism.

In 1776, with all their limitations, the Founders proposed that it was possible to create a nation based not in religion or race or hierarchies of wealth or tradition, but in the rule of law. It was possible, at least in principle, they thought, to bring widely different peoples together in a system in which every person was equal before the law and entitled to a voice in government. They set out to show that it could be done.

That theory was never unchallenged. In the 1850s, a reactionary and wealthy minority tried to get rid of it altogether, insisting that true "democracy" centered power in the state governments that they controlled. Gradually, they took over the mechanics of the American government. Those nineteenth-century leaders perverted the meaning of democracy for their own ends, and they were able to do so because they created a closed media system that lied to their voters and demonized their opponents. They convinced their voters that American democracy was rooted in the states and that state legislators could determine the living conditions of a state's people, even if that meant enslaving them. They took over their party, and then their state governments, and then the national government. They believed they were the vanguard of a new system that would enable the United States to lead a world dominated by a few wealthy, well-connected, and usually white and male leaders, whose economy rested on inequality and enslavement.

But that story didn't end as the elite enslavers wished.

Men like Abraham Lincoln recognized that such a struggle was not just about who got elected to the White House. It was the story of humanity, "the eternal struggle between these two principles— right and wrong—throughout the world." Lincoln made it clear that those who wanted the right to self-determination had always had to struggle—and would always have to struggle—against those who wanted power. "The one is the common right of humanity and the other the divine right of kings. It is the same principle in whatever shape it develops itself," he said. "No matter in what shape it comes, whether from the mouth of a king who seeks to bestride the people of his own nation and live by the fruit of their labor, or from one race of men as an apology for enslaving another race, it is the same tyrannical principle."[5]

Lincoln emphasized that those trying to destroy democracy in his era were not the conservatives they claimed to be but were dangerous radicals whose version of America must be rejected. He called on his neighbors to defend equality before the law and the right of everyone to consent to the government under which they live. They must reclaim the history of America so that it would have "a new birth of freedom."

When Lincoln said those words in 1863, it was not at all clear his vision would prevail. But he had hope because, after decades in which they had not noticed what the powerful were doing to destroy democracy, Americans had woken up. They realized that the very nature of America was under attack. They were divided among themselves, and at first they didn't really know how to fight back, but ordinary people quickly came to pitch in however they could, using the tools they had. "We rose each fighting, grasping whatever he could first reach—a scythe—a pitchfork—a chopping axe, or a butcher's cleaver," Lincoln recalled. Once awake, they found the strength of their majority.[6]

In Lincoln's era, democracy appeared to have won. But the Americans of Lincoln's time did not root out the hierarchical strand of our history, leaving it there for other rising autocrats in the future to exploit with their rhetoric and the fears of their followers.

So far, the hopes of our Founders have never been proven fully right. And yet they have not been proven entirely wrong.

Once again, we are at a time of testing.

How it comes out rests, as it always has, in our own hands.

Acknowledgments

This book is part of an ongoing conversation with the many wonderful people who have, over the years, asked me questions about how we got to this place in American history, and how we can get out. They inspired this project, and I thank them for their curiosity, outrage, and hope.

With their support as inspiration, I turned to my literary agent, Lisa Adams, who helped me work through my ideas and figure out a framework for the book. It would not—could not—have been written without her. My assistant, Nicholas Stubblefield, pushed hard to help fill out those ideas when this project was in its early stages and then made sure I had some space in my schedule to write. Even his best efforts at clearing the calendar would have been fruitless if Boston College had not awarded me a sabbatical that gave this project the time it needed. And finally, once there were pages to work on, my editor at Viking, Wendy Wolf, maintained a healthy skepticism and used a ready pen to turn some very rough drafts into a real manuscript.

Books are whipped into shape by teams, and this one is no exception. Michael Bazemore, Michael Green, Anne Muntean, and Nadia Povalinska edited, corrected errors, and argued with me, improving the final product immeasurably; Julian Mortensen encouraged me to keep writing; Ken Porter resuscitated my laptop; Jason Herbert stepped in to rescue my citations when I had given up hope. Copy editor Kym Surridge cleaned up my prose; production editor Randee Marullo ushered an actual book into existence.

Family and friends cut me huge slack over the past year so I could write. I owe special thanks to my children, to my siblings and their families, and to Nancy Evans, for their patience and good humor during this marathon sprint.

For all that it's my name on the cover, Buddy Poland's good sense, humor, and love of history have been crucial to this project, and I thank him for that . . . and for all the rest of it, too.

This book really took shape in a long-running discussion with two women who have brought their own unique skills and perspectives to this moment in our democracy. Michele Rudenko's unerring sense for what matters and what works has guided this project, while Katya Partan's true brilliance as an editor—an apparently tireless editor— has shaped every phrase.

I thank you both, for everything. I hope it's a Maynard.

With such wonderful help, I should have produced a perfect book. That I did not is my fault alone.

Notes

FOREWORD

1. Heinrich August Winkler, trans. Stewart Spencer, *The Age of Catastrophe: A History of the West, 1914–1945* (New Haven, CT, and London: Yale University Press, 2015), 428; Eric D. Weitz, *Weimar Germany: Promise and Tragedy* (Princeton, NJ: Princeton University Press, 2018), 341–360; Benjamin Carter Hett, *The Death of Democracy: Hitler's Rise to Power and the Downfall of the Weimar Republic* (London: Random House UK Limited, 2019).
2. Richard J. Evans, *The Third Reich at War* (New York: Penguin Press, 2009), 260–281, 758–764; Timothy Snyder, *Bloodlands: Europe between Hitler and Stalin* (New York: Basic Books, 2010), 754–772.
3. My understanding of this process comes primarily from Hannah Arendt, *The Origins of Totalitarianism* (Cleveland: Meridian Books, 1958); and Eric Hoffer, *The True Believer: Thoughts on the Nature of Mass Movements* (New York: Harper & Row, 1951).
4. "22,000 Nazis Hold Rally in Garden," *New York Times*, February 21, 1939; Ryan Bort, "When Nazis Took Over Madison Square Garden," *Rolling Stone*, February 19, 2019.
5. Franklin D. Roosevelt, "Address Accepting the Presidential Nomination at the Democratic National Convention in Chicago," July 2, 1932, American Presidency Project, at https://www.presidency.ucsb.edu/; David M. Kennedy, *Freedom from Fear: The American People in Depression and War, 1929–1945* (New York and Oxford, UK: Oxford University Press, 1999), 244–248; Heather Cox Richardson, *To Make Men Free: A History of the Republican Party* (New York: Basic Books, 2021), 276–280.
6. Heather Cox Richardson, *How the South Won the Civil War: Oligarchy, Democracy, and the Continuing Fight for the Soul of America* (New York: Oxford University Press, 2020).
7. George Fitzhugh, *Cannibals All! Or, Slaves without Masters* (Richmond, VA: A. Morris, 1857), 353–354; George Fitzhugh, *Sociology for the South, or the Failure of Free Society* (Richmond, VA: A. Morris, 1854).
8. Economist Intelligence Unit, *Democracy Index 2016: Revenge of the "Deplorables"* (2017), impact.economist.com/perspectives/sites/default/files/The%20EIU%27s%202016%20Democracy%20Index_0.pdf; Sarah Repucci, *From Crisis to Reform: A Call to Strengthen America's Battered Democracy*, Freedom House, 2021, freedomhouse.org/report/special-report/2021/crisis-reform-call-strengthen-americas-battered-democracy.

CHAPTER 1. AMERICAN CONSERVATISM

1. Franklin Delano Roosevelt, "Message to Congress on Curbing Monopolies," April 29, 1938; "Inaugural Address," March 4, 1933; "Address Accepting the Presidential Nomination at the Democratic National Convention in Chicago," July 2, 1932; all at American Presidency Project.

2. John Robert Moore, "Senator Josiah W. Bailey and the 'Conservative Manifesto' of 1937," *Journal of Southern History* 31 (1965): 21–39; see, for example, "Price of a Balanced Budget," *New York Times*, December 8, 1937.
3. Turner Catledge, "10 Points Drafted; Attempt Made to Unite All Conservatives and Moderates on Plan," *New York Times*, December 16, 1937; "The Nation," *New York Times*, December 19, 1937.
4. Turner Catledge, "Congressmen Shun 'Coalition' Move; Democrats Balk at Appearing to Be Rebels and Republicans Cling to Party Role," *New York Times*, December 17, 1937.
5. *Chicago Tribune*, March 4, 1856, 2.
6. Franklin Pierce, "Third Annual Message," December 31, 1855, American Presidency Project.
7. *Chicago Tribune*, January 9, 1856, 2.
8. *Alton Courier*, quoted in *Chicago Tribune*, May 15, 1856, 2; Abraham Lincoln, "Sixth Debate with Stephen A. Douglas, at Quincy, Illinois, October 13, 1858," in *The Collected Works of Abraham Lincoln*, vol. 3, ed. Roy P. Basler (Ann Arbor, MI: University of Michigan Digital Library Production Services, 2001), 263; Abraham Lincoln, "First Debate, Ottawa, Illinois, August 21, 1858," in Basler, *Collected Works*, vol. 3, 333.
9. Abraham Lincoln, "Address at Cooper Institute, New York City, February 27, 1860," in Basler, *Collected Works*, vol. 3, 522–550.
10. Abraham Lincoln, "Fragment on Government," in Basler, *Collected Works*, vol. 2, 220.

CHAPTER 2. THE LIBERAL CONSENSUS

1. "Translation: Declaration of War against the United States, by Benito Mussolini, Italy, December 11, 1941," Wikisource, last modified December 28, 2016, en.wikisource.org/wiki/Translation:Declaration_of_War_Against_the_United_States,_by_Benito_Mussolini._Italy,_December_11,_1941.
2. Franklin D. Roosevelt, "June 5, 1944: Fireside Chat 29: On the Fall of Rome," audio recording, 16:34, Miller Center, University of Virginia, millercenter.org/the-presidency/presidential-speeches/june-5-1944-fireside-chat-29-fall-rome.
3. Paul C. Rosier, *Serving Their Country: American Indian Politics and Patriotism in the Twentieth Century* (Cambridge, MA: Harvard University Press, 2009), 47, 88–92; Heather Cox Richardson, *How the South Won the Civil War: Oligarchy, Democracy, and the Continuing Fight for the Soul of America* (New York: Oxford University Press, 2020), 147.
4. Danielle L. McGuire, *At the Dark End of the Street: Black Women, Rape, and Resistance—a New History of the Civil Rights Movement from Rosa Parks to the Rise of Black Power* (New York: Vintage, 2011), xv–83.
5. *Rosa Parks: In Her Own Words*, https://www.loc.gov/exhibitions/rosa-parks-in-her-own-words/about-this-exhibition/.
6. Arthur Larson, *A Republican Looks at His Party* (New York: Harper & Brothers, 1956), 10, 159.

CHAPTER 3. BRINGING THE DECLARATION OF INDEPENDENCE TO LIFE

1. Olivia B. Waxman, "How a 1946 Case of Police Brutality against a Black WWII Veteran Shaped the Fight for Civil Rights," *Time*, March 30, 2021; Richard Gergel, *Unexampled Courage: The Blinding of Sgt. Isaac Woodward and the Awakening of President Harry S. Truman and Judge J. Waties Waring* (New York: Sarah Crichton Books, 2019).
2. DeNeen L. Brown, "How Harry S. Truman Went from Being a Racist to Desegregating the Military," *Washington Post*, July 26, 2018.
3. Heather Cox Richardson, *To Make Men Free: A History of the Republican Party* (New York: Basic Books, 2021), 296–297.
4. Ignacio M. García, Héctor P. García: *In Relentless Pursuit of Justice* (Houston: Arte Público Press, 2002), 74–139; Patrick J. Carroll, *Felix Longoria's Wake: Bereavement, Racism, and*

the Rise of Mexican American Activism (Austin: University of Texas Press, 2003); "Texas Town Offers Apology to Widow," *New York Times*, January 14, 1949.
5. Heather Cox Richardson, *How the South Won the Civil War: Oligarchy, Democracy, and the Continuing Fight for the Soul of America* (New York: Oxford University Press, 2020), 158–159.
6. "The Civil Rights Act of 1957," History, Art & Archives, United States House of Representatives, https://history.house.gov/Historical-Highlights/1951-2000/The-Civil-Rights-Act-of-1957/.

CHAPTER 4. RACE AND TAXES

1. Angus Campbell et al., *The American Voter* (Chicago: University of Chicago Press, 1960); Heather Cox Richardson, *How the South Won the Civil War: Oligarchy, Democracy, and the Continuing Fight for the Soul of America* (New York: Oxford University Press, 2020), 150.
2. Heather Cox Richardson, *The Death of Reconstruction: Race, Labor, and Politics in the Post–Civil War North, 1865–1901* (Cambridge: Harvard University Press, 2001), 83–121; *Nation*, April 16, 1874, 247–248.
3. Heather Cox Richardson, *To Make Men Free: A History of the Republican Party* (New York: Basic Books, 2021), 131–137.
4. Heather Cox Richardson, *West from Appomattox: The Reconstruction of America after the Civil War* (New Haven, CT: Yale University Press, 2007), 69–77.
5. William F. Buckley Jr., *God and Man at Yale: The Superstitions of "Academic Freedom"* (Chicago: Regnery Books, 1951).
6. Charles R. Gallagher, *Nazis of Copley Square: The Forgotten Story of the Christian Front* (Cambridge, MA: Harvard University Press, 2021).
7. Richardson, *To Make Men Free*, 330–335.
8. "Westerns," *Time*, March 30, 1959.
9. Rick Perlstein, *Before the Storm: Barry Goldwater and the Unmaking of the American Consensus* (New York: Hill and Wang, 2001), 19–42.
10. Barry Goldwater and L. Brent Bozell Jr., *The Conscience of a Conservative* (Victor Publishing Co., 1960).

CHAPTER 5. NIXON AND THE SOUTHERN STRATEGY

1. John F. Kennedy, "Inaugural Address," January 20, 1961, American Presidency Project.
2. James Meredith, *Three Years in Mississippi* (Oxford: University Press of Mississippi, 2019), 45–56; BBC, "1962: Mississippi Race Riots over First Black Student," news.bbc.co.uk /onthisday/hi/dates/stories/october/1/newsid_2538000/2538169.stm; Heather Cox Richardson, *To Make Men Free: A History of the Republican Party* (New York: Basic Books, 2021), 351.
3. "JFK Told Jackie 'Nobody Can Stop' an Assassination Attempt," *Parade*, November 15, 2013; Bill Minutaglio, "Tea Party Has Roots in the Dallas of 1963," *Washington Post*, November 21, 2013; Edward H. Miller, *Nut Country: Right-Wing Dallas and the Birth of the Southern Strategy* (Chicago: University of Chicago Press, 2015), 121–128.
4. James Meredith with William Doyle, *A Mission from God: A Memoir and a Challenge for America* (New York: Atria Books, 2012), 183–184.
5. Jerry Mitchell, "Congressional Honor Sought for Freedom Summer Martyrs," *Clarion-Ledger*, February 3, 2014; Mo Banks, "Civics for Change: Freedom Summer 1964," June 17, 2022, Andrew Goodman Foundation.
6. Barry Goldwater, "Address Accepting the Presidential Nomination at the Republican National Convention in San Francisco," July 16, 1964, American Presidency Project.
7. Matthew Delmont, "When Jackie Robinson Confronted a Trump-Like Candidate," *Atlantic*, March 19, 2016.

NOTES

8. "Mississippi Burning," Federal Bureau of Investigation, fbi.gov/history/famous-cases /mississippi-burning.
9. "1964 Democratic Party Platform," August 24, 1964, American Presidency Project.
10. "Jimmie Lee Jackson," Southern Poverty Law Center, splcenter.org/jimmie-lee-jackson.
11. Lyndon B. Johnson, "Special Message to the Congress: The American Promise," March 15, 1965, American Presidency Project; Colleen Shogan, "'We Shall Overcome': Lyndon Johnson and the 1965 Voting Rights Act," White House Historical Association, whitehousehistory .org/we-shall-overcome-lbj-voting-rights.
12. Lyndon B. Johnson, "Remarks in the Capitol Rotunda at the Signing of the Voting Rights Act," August 6, 1965, American Presidency Project.
13. "Inaugural Address of Governor George Wallace, Which Was Delivered at the Capitol in Montgomery, Alabama," Alabama Department of Archives & History, digital.archives .alabama.gov/digital/collection/voices/id/2952/.
14. Mary C. Brennan, *Turning Right in the Sixties: The Conservative Capture of the GOP* (Chapel Hill: University of North Carolina Press, 1995), 122–128; Richard Nixon, *RN: The Memoirs of Richard Nixon* (New York: Grosset & Dunlap, 1978), 302–305, 312–313; Randall Balmer, "The Real Origins of the Religious Right," *Politico*, May 27, 2014; Maurice Isserman and Michael Kazin, *America Divided: The Civil War of the 1960s* (New York: Oxford University Press, 2000), 272–274.
15. Bill D. Moyers, "What a Real President Was Like," *Washington Post*, November 13, 1988.

CHAPTER 6. POSITIVE POLARIZATION

1. Joe McGinniss, *The Selling of the President 1968* (London: Andre Deutsch, 1970), 36, 41–45.
2. "Mario Savio: Sit-In Address on the Steps of Sproul Hall," American Rhetoric, https: //www.americanrhetoric.com/speeches/mariosaviosproulhallsitin.htm.
3. Kate Coleman, "The Roots of Ed Meese," *Los Angeles Times*, May 4, 1986; Clara Bingham, "The Battle for People's Park, Berkeley 1969: When Vietnam Came Home," *Guardian*, July 6, 2019.
4. *Time*, January 5, 1970.
5. Peter Baker, "Nixon Tried to Spoil Johnson's Vietnam Peace Talks in '68, Notes Show," *New York Times*, January 2, 2017.
6. Richard Nixon, "Address to the Nation on the War in Vietnam," November 3, 1969, American Presidency Project.
7. Spiro Agnew, quoted in Thomas Byrne Edsall and Mary D. Edsall, *Chain Reaction: The Impact of Race, Rights, and Taxes on American Politics* (New York: W. W. Norton, 1991), 85; Patrick J. Buchanan, "Media Memorandum for the President," May 21, 1970, Nixon Library, https://www.nixonlibrary.gov/sites/default/files/virtuallibrary/documents/jan10/025.pdf.
8. Richard Nixon, "Address to the Nation on Labor Day," September 6, 1971, American Presidency Project.
9. Jon Nordheimer, "Agnew Mellow in Talk Hailing Confederate Heroes," *New York Times*, May 10, 1970.
10. Jacob S. Hacker and Paul Pierson, "The Powell Memo: A Call-to-Arms for Corporations," Moyers & Company, September 14, 2012, https://billmoyers.com/content/the-powell -memo-a-call-to-arms-for-corporations/.
11. Linda Greenhouse and Reva B. Siegel, "Before (and After) Roe v. Wade: New Questions about Backlash," *Yale Law Journal* 120 (2011): 2028–2087.
12. Bruce J. Schulman, *The Seventies: The Great Shift in American Culture, Society, and Politics* (New York: Free Press, 2001), 44–45; Jeffrey Toobin, "The Dirty Trickster: Campaign Tips from the Man Who Has Done It All," *New Yorker*, May 23, 2008; Michael Daly, "The Despicable History of Roger Stone," *Daily Beast*, January 26, 2019; John A. Farrell, "Watergate Created Roger Stone. Trump Completed Him," *Politico*, January 29, 2019.

13. Beth Reinhard, "Bush Strategist Shares Insight on '00 Recount," *Miami Herald*, May 17, 2008.

CHAPTER 7. THE REAGAN REVOLUTION

1. Jonathan Alter, Gary Sick, Kai Bird, and Stuart Eizenstat, "It's All but Settled: The Reagan Campaign Delayed the Release of the Iranian Hostages," *The New Republic*, May 3, 2023; Peter Baker, "A Four-Decade Secret: One Man's Story of Sabotaging Carter's Re-election," *New York Times*, March 18, 2023.
2. William F. Buckley Jr., "Our Mission Statement," *National Review*, November 19, 1955.
3. "The 1960s Business and the Economy: Overview," https://www.encyclopedia.com/social-sciences/culture-magazines/1960s-business-and-economy-overview; U.S. Department of Commerce, "Family Income Advances, Poverty Reduced in 1967," Current Population Reports: Consumer Income, Series P-60, no. 55, August 5, 1968, U.S. Census Bureau, https://www2.census.gov/prod2/popscan/p60-055.pdf.
4. Mark Stricherz, "How a Little-Known Task Force Helped Create Red State/Blue State America," *Boston Globe*, November 23, 2003.
5. Josh Levin, *The Queen: The Forgotten Life behind an American Myth* (New York: Little, Brown and Company, 2019); Ronald Reagan, "Transcript of Ronald Reagan's 1980 Neshoba County Fair Speech," *Neshoba Democrat*, July 14, 2011.
6. Peggy O'Donnell, "The Settler Fantasies Woven into the Prairie Dresses," *Jezebel*, January 30, 2019.
7. Jacob Lupfer, "Shadows in the Stained Glass: Patterson and Pressler Chapel Windows Come Down," Religion News Service, April 11, 2019; Heather Cox Richardson, *To Make Men Free: A History of the Republican Party* (New York: Basic Books, 2021), 386.
8. Ari Berman, *Give Us the Ballot: The Modern Struggle for Voting Rights in America* (New York: Picador, 2016), 123; "1980 Ronald Reagan and Jimmy Carter Presidential Debate," October 28, 1980, Ronald Reagan Presidential Library and Museum, https://www.reaganlibrary.gov/archives/speech/1980-ronald-reagan-and-jimmy-carter-presidential-debate.
9. Ronald Reagan, "Inaugural Address," January 20, 1981, American Presidency Project.
10. William Greider, "The Education of David Stockman," *Atlantic Monthly*, December 1981.
11. Richardson, *To Make Men Free*, 389–408.
12. Dan Fletcher, "A Brief History of the Fairness Doctrine," *Time*, February 20, 2009.
13. "Atwater Apologizes for '88 Remark about Dukakis," *Washington Post*, January 13, 1991.
14. Michael Oreskes, "Political Memo; for G.O.P. Arsenal, 133 Words to Fire," *New York Times*, September 9, 1990.
15. Patrick Joseph Buchanan, "Address to the Republican National Convention in Houston," August 17, 1992, American Presidency Project.

CHAPTER 8. SKEWING THE SYSTEM

1. Heather Cox Richardson, *To Make Men Free: A History of the Republican Party* (New York: Basic Books, 2021), 398–399.
2. Jane Mayer, "Ways and Means Panel's Tax-Overhaul Proposal Brings 'Family' Strife to Conservative Coalition," *Wall Street Journal*, November 27, 1985.
3. Heather Cox Richardson, *How the South Won the Civil War: Oligarchy, Democracy, and the Continuing Fight for the Soul of America* (New York: Oxford University Press, 2020), 317–319.
4. Ian Millhiser, "Chief Justice Roberts's Lifelong Crusade against Voting Rights, Explained," *Vox*, September 18, 2020.
5. Adam Liptak, "Presidential Signing Statements, and Alito's Role in Them, Are Questioned," *New York Times*, January 14, 2006.

NOTES

6. Sean Wilentz, *The Age of Reagan: A History, 1974–2008* (New York: HarperCollins, 2008), 140.
7. James Reston, "Washington; Kennedy and Bork," *New York Times*, July 5, 1987.
8. Richardson, *To Make Men Free*, 403–405; "Text of Walsh Response to Bush Pardon," *Los Angeles Times*, December 25, 1992.

CHAPTER 9. A NEW GLOBAL PROJECT

1. Manuel Roig-Franzia, "The Swamp Builders," *Washington Post*, November 29, 2018; Franklin Foer, "Paul Manafort, American Hustler," *Atlantic*, March 2018; Olivia Paschal and Madeleine Carlisle, "A Brief History of Roger Stone," *Atlantic*, November 15, 2019.
2. Grover C. Norquist, "How Conservatism Stumbled after Reagan," *Wall Street Journal*, August 3, 1994.
3. Gene Lyons, "Racist 'Justice' Is Dead, but Not Gone," *Salon*, February 18, 2010.
4. "Statement of Principles," June 3, 1997, and Elliott Abrams et al. to William Jefferson Clinton, January 26, 1998, both at Project for the New American Century, archived at https://web.archive.org/web/20050203004656/http://www.newamericancentury.org/statementof principles.htm.
5. Steven Kull, Clay Ramsay, and Evan Lewis, "Misperceptions, the Media, and the Iraq War," *Political Science Quarterly* 118, no. 4 (2003/2004): 569–598.
6. George W. Bush, "Statement on Signing the Department of Defense, Emergency Supplemental Appropriations to Address Hurricanes in the Gulf of Mexico, and Pandemic Influenza Act, 2006," December 30, 2005, at American Presidency Project; Jennifer Van Bergen, "The Unitary Executive: Is the Doctrine Behind the Bush Presidency Consistent with a Democratic State?," FindLaw, January 9, 2006.
7. Steve Schmidt, "No Books, No Money. Just the Truth," *The Warning with Steve Schmidt*, Substack, May 8, 2022.
8. Steve Schmidt (@SteveSchmidtSES),Twitter, May 7, 2022, 9:12 p.m., https://twitter.com/SteveSchmidtSES/status/1523108447088128001.
9. Ron Suskind, "Faith, Certainty and the Presidency of George W. Bush," *New York Times Magazine*, October 17, 2004.

CHAPTER 10. ILLEGITIMATE DEMOCRACY

1. Martina Stewart, "Palin Hits Obama for 'Terrorist' Connection," CNN, October 4, 2008.
2. Jonathan Allen, "'You Lie!' Worth $2.7M for Wilson," *Politico*, October 15, 2009.
3. Christopher W. Schmidt, "The Tea Party and the Constitution," *Hastings Constitutional Law Quarterly* 193 (2011): 193–252.
4. Bill O'Reilly, "Obamacare and Socialism," Fox News, January 27, 2017.
5. Ian Millhiser, "Chief Justice Roberts's Lifelong Crusade against Voting Rights Explained," *Vox*, September 18, 2020; Tim Lau, "Citizens United Explained," Brennan Center for Justice, December 12, 2019.
6. Robert Mueller, "Address to the Citizens Crime Commission of New York," Federal Bureau of Investigation, January 27, 2011, https://archives.fbi.gov/archives/news/speeches/the-evolving-organized-crime-threat.
7. Elise Labott, "Clinton Cites 'Serious Concerns' about Russian Election," CNN, December 6, 2011.
8. David Daley, *Ratf**ked: The True Story behind the Secret Plan to Steal America's Democracy* (New York: Liveright, 2016), xxi–xxii.
9. Michael Grunwald, *The New New Deal: The Hidden Story of Change in the Obama Era* (New York: Simon & Schuster, 2012); Jonathan Capehart, "Republicans Had It In for Obama before Day 1," *Washington Post*, August 10, 2012; Jason M. Breslow, "The

Opposition Strategy," PBS, January 17, 2017; Greg Sargent, "Biden: McConnell Decided to Deny Us Cooperation before We Took Office," *Washington Post*, August 10, 2012.

10. Adam Jentleson, *Kill Switch: The Rise of the Modern Senate and the Crippling of American Democracy* (New York: Liveright, 2021), 17–21.

11. David Frum, "Norquist: Romney Will Do as Told," *Daily Beast*, February 13, 2012.

CHAPTER 11. **A SNAPSHOT OF AMERICA**

1. Patrick Radden Keefe, "How Mark Burnett Resurrected Donald Trump as an Icon of American Success," *New Yorker*, December 27, 2018.

2. Adam Gabbatt, "Golden Escalator Ride: The Surreal Day Trump Kicked Off His Bid for President," *Guardian*, June 14, 2019; "Here's Donald Trump's Presidential Announcement Speech," *Time*, June 16, 2015.

3. John B. Dunlop, "Aleksandr Dugin's Foundations of Geopolitics," Europe Center, Stanford University, tec.fsi.stanford.edu/docs/aleksandr-dugins-foundations-geopolitics.

4. Jane Mayer, "The Danger of President Pence," *New Yorker*, October 16, 2017; Heather Cox Richardson, *To Make Men Free: A History of the Republican Party* (New York: Basic Books, 2021), 339, 463.

5. "2016 Republican Party Platform," July 18, 2016, American Presidency Project; Rosalind S. Helderman, "Here's What We Know about Donald Trump and His Ties to Russia," *Washington Post*, July 29, 2016.

6. Sharon LaFraniere, "Trump Adviser Said to Have Pursued Saudi Nuclear Deal as He Sought Administration Role," *New York Times*, July 29, 2019; Jim Rutenberg, "The Untold Story of 'Russiagate' and the Road to War in Ukraine," *New York Times Magazine*, November 2, 2022; *Report of the Select Committee on Intelligence*, 116th Congress, 1st sess., vol. 5: 82–83, 318–380; Special Counsel Robert S. Mueller III, *Report on the Investigation into Russian Interference in the 2016 Presidential Election*, March 2019, vol. 1: 6–7, 128–141.

7. Richardson, *To Make Men Free*, 464.

8. Thomas E. Patterson, "A Tale of Two Elections: CBS and Fox News' Portrayal of the 2020 Presidential Campaign," December 17, 2020, Shorenstein Center on Media, Politics, and Public Policy.

9. Trump was hardly the first candidate to grasp the power of social media, though he arguably wielded it more effectively than either his predecessor or successor. This was evident in memos sent to the Biden team by former Obama strategists David Axelrod and David Plouffe to expand Biden's digital efforts. Brian Schwartz, "Obama Campaign Bosses Plouffe and Axelrod Urge Biden to Beef Up Digital Operations to Battle Trump," CNBC, May 4, 2020; Michael J. Socolow, "It Didn't Start with Facebook: Surveillance and the Conmmercial Media," We're History, May 1, 2018; Olivia Solon, "Cambridge Analytica Whistleblower Says Bannon Wanted to Suppress Voters," *Guardian*, May 16, 2018; Nicholas Confessore and David Gelles, "Facebook Fallout Deals Blow to Mercers' Political Clout," *New York Times*, April 10, 2018; Andy Kroll, "Cloak and Data: The Real Story behind Cambridge Analytica's Rise and Fall," *Mother Jones*, May/June 2018.

10. Roberta Rampton and Dustin Volz, "Trump, without Evidence, Says Illegal Voting Cost Him U.S. Popular Vote," Reuters, November 27, 2016.

11. "Full Text: 2017 Donald Trump Inauguration Speech Transcript," *Politico*, January 20, 2017.

CHAPTER 12. **A SHOCKING EVENT**

1. Yashar Ali, "What George W. Bush Really Thought of Donald Trump's Inauguration," *New York*, March 29, 2017.

2. Elle Hunt, "Trump's Inauguration Crowd: Sean Spicer's Claims versus the Evidence," *Guardian*, January 22, 2017.

NOTES

3. *Meet the Press*, "Conway: Press Secretary Gave 'Alternative Facts,'" NBC News video, 3:39, January 22, 2017.
4. The film *Gaslight* is an adaptation of Patrick Hamilton's 1938 stage production, *Gas Light*.
5. See, for example, Brian Stelter, "This Infamous Steve Bannon Quote Is Key to Understanding America's Crazy Politics," CNN, November 16, 2021; Richard Stengel, "Domestic Disinformation Is a Greater Menace Than Foreign Disinformation," *Time*, June 26, 2020.
6. Julia Ioffe (@juliaioffe), Twitter, May 19, 2022, 9:05 p.m., twitter.com/juliaioffe/status /1527500693283684366.
7. Stephanie Akin, "The Other 'Steve' in the White House," *Roll Call*, February 13, 2017.
8. Carrie Johnson, "Trump Fires Acting Attorney General for Refusing to Defend Immigration Order," NPR, January 30, 2017; Dahlia Lithwick, *Lady Justice: Women, the Law, and the Battle to Save America* (New York: Penguin Press, 2022), 17–38.
9. Caitlin Dickerson, "'We Need to Take Away Children,' the Secret History of the U.S. Government's Family-Separation Policy," *Atlantic*, August 7, 2022.
10. Diana Bruk, "Here's the Full Transcript of Gloria Steinem's Historic Women's March Speech," *Elle*, January 21, 2017.

CHAPTER 13. RUSSIA, RUSSIA, RUSSIA

1. Office of the Director of National Intelligence, *Assessing Russian Activities and Intentions in Recent US Elections*, January 6, 2017, https://www.intelligence.senate.gov/publications /assessing-russian-activities-and-intentions-recent-us-elections.
2. Tom Hamburger et al., "Manafort Offered to Give Russian Billionaire 'Private Briefings' on 2016 Campaign," *Washington Post*, September 20, 2017.
3. Jim Rutenberg, "The Untold Story of 'Russiagate' and the Road to War in Ukraine," *New York Times Magazine*, November 2, 2022; *Report of the Select Committee on Intelligence*, 116th Congress, 1st sess., vol. 5: 82–83, 318–380; Special Counsel Robert S. Mueller III, *Report on the Investigation into Russian Interference in the 2016 Presidential Election*, March 2019, vol. 1: 6–7, 128–141.
4. Jane C. Timm, "Trump on Hot Mic: 'When You're a Star . . . You Can Do Anything' to Women," NBC News, October 7, 2016.
5. Michael S. Schmidt, "Trump Invited the Russians to Hack Clinton. Were They Listening?," *New York Times*, July 13, 2018.
6. Michael Crowley and Tyler Pager, "Trump Urges Russia to Hack Clinton's Email," *Politico*, July 27, 2016.
7. *Report of the Select Committee on Intelligence*, 116th Congress, 1st sess., vol. 5: vi.
8. Matt Apuzzo, Maggie Haberman, and Matthew Rosenberg, "Trump Told Russians That Firing 'Nut Job' Comey Eased Pressure from Investigation," *New York Times*, May 19, 2017.
9. Nastasha Bertrand, "Trump's Top Targets in the Russia Probe Are Experts in Organized Crime," *Atlantic*, August 30, 2018; Nicholas Fandos and Michael S. Schmidt, "Trump Tweets Lengthy Attack on F.B.I. over Inquiry into Possible Aid to Russia," *New York Times*, January 12, 2019.
10. Mueller III, *Report on the Investigation into Russian Interference in the 2016 Presidential Election*, vol. 1.

CHAPTER 14. THE STREETS OF CHARLOTTESVILLE

1. Joseph Fronczak, "The Fascist Game: Transnational Political Transmission and the Genesis of the U.S. Modern Right," *Journal of American History* (December 2018): 563–588; NPR Staff, "When the Bankers Plotted to Overthrow FDR," NPR, February 12, 2012; Sally Denton, *The Plots against the President: FDR, a Nation in Crisis, and the Rise of the American Right* (New York: Bloomsbury, 2012), 171–217.

NOTES

2. Associated Press, "18 Months in Jail for White Supremacist," *New York Times*, October 19, 1993.
3. Jason Wilson, "Ruby Ridge, 1992: The Day the American Militia Movement Was Born," *Guardian*, August 26, 2017.
4. John C. Danforth, "Interim Report to the Deputy Attorney General Concerning the 1993 Confrontation at the Mt. Carmel Complex, Waco, Texas," U.S. Department of Justice, July 31, 2000.
5. Amanda Marcotte, "The Clinton BS Files: Conspiracy Theorists Paint the Branch Davidian Mass Suicide as Murder at the Hands of the Clinton Administration," *Salon*, September 19, 2016.
6. David Willman, "McVeigh Lashed Out at Government in '92 Letters," *Los Angeles Times*, April 27, 1995.
7. Ryan Lucas, "Who Are the Oath Keepers? Militia Group, Founder Scrutinized in Capitol Riot Probe," WBUR, April 10, 2021.
8. Aaron Blake, "Cliven Bundy on Blacks: 'Are They Better Off as Slaves?,'" *Washington Post*, April 24, 2014.
9. "Oregon Militia in Standoff with Feds Names Themselves," CBS News, January 4, 2016.
10. Rosie Gray, "Trump Defends White-Nationalist Protesters: 'Some Very Fine People on Both Sides,'" *Atlantic*, August 15, 2017.
11. Eric Bradner and Maeve Reston, "Joe Biden Takes Trump Head-on over Charlottesville in Announcement Video," CNN, April 25, 2019.

CHAPTER 15. THE FIRST IMPEACHMENT

1. House Committee on the Judiciary, Impeachment of Richard M. Nixon, President of the United States, 93d Cong., 2d Sess., H.R. Rep. No. 93-1305, at 6–11 (1974).
2. Kyle Cheney, "Schiff Accuses Top Intel Official of Illegally Withholding 'Urgent' Whistleblower Complaint," *Politico*, September 13, 2019.
3. Donald J. Trump (@realDonaldTrump), Twitter, September 24, 2019, 2:12 p.m., https://twitter.com/realDonaldTrump/status/1176559970390806530.
4. "Read Trump's Phone Conversation with Volodymyr Zelensky," CNN, September 26, 2019.
5. "Document: Read the Whistle-Blower Complaint," *New York Times*, September 26, 2019; "U.S. Government Information: Whistleblower," Library, University of California, San Diego, ucsd.libguides.com/usgov/whistleblower.
6. Donald J. Trump (@realDonaldTrump), "Rep. Adam Schiff illegally made up a FAKE & terrible statement, pretended it to be mine as the most important part of my call to the Ukrainian President, and read it aloud to Congress and the American people. It bore NO relationship to what I said on the call. Arrest for Treason?," Twitter, September 30, 2019, 8:03 a.m., https://twitter.com/realDonaldTrump/status/1178643854737772545; Tamara Keith, "'Treason,' 'Spy,' 'Coup': As Impeachment Talk Intensifies, So Does Trump's Rhetoric," NPR, October 5, 2019; Tim Elfrink, "Trump Suggests Pelosi, Schiff Committed 'Treason,' Should Be Impeached," *Washington Post*, October 7, 2019.
7. "Impeachment Inquiry, House Hearings: Ambassador Kurt Volker and National Security Aide Tim Morrison," C-SPAN, November 19, 2019; "Read Trump's Phone Conversation with Volodymyr Zelensky"; Kenneth P. Vogel and Michael S. Schmidt, "Trump Envoys Pushed Ukraine to Commit to Investigating Biden," *New York Times*, October 3, 2019.
8. Michael D. Shear, "Key Moments from the First Public Impeachment Hearing," *New York Times*, November 13, 2019; Benjamin Siu and Anne Flaherty, "Key Players in the Trump Impeachment Probe and What They Testified to Congress," ABC News, December 4, 2019.
9. Donald J. Trump (@realDonaldTrump), Twitter, November 15, 2019, 10:01 a.m., https://twitter.com/realDonaldTrump/status/1195356198347956224; Sharon LaFraniere, Kenneth P.

Vogel, and Peter Baker, "Trump Said Ukraine Envoy Would 'Go Through Some Things.' She Has Already," *New York Times*, November 15, 2019.

10. "Read Alexander Vindman's Opening Statement on Trump and Ukraine," *New York Times*, October 29, 2019.

11. Igor Bobic, "'We Are F**CKED': New Book Reveals How GOP Senators Bailed Out Trump during 1st Impeachment Trial," *HuffPost*, October 7, 2022; Rachael Bade and Karoun Demirjian, *Unchecked: The Untold Story behind Congress's Botched Impeachments of Donald Trump* (New York: William Morrow, 2022).

12. Dareh Gregorian, "Schiff's Powerful Closing Speech: 'Is There One among You Who Will Say, Enough!'?," NBC News, February 3, 2020.

13. Roll Call Vote 117th Congress—1st Session (2021), United States Senate, senate.gov/legisla tive/LIS/roll_call_lists/vote_menu_117_1.htm.

14. David Corn, "Here's How Trump's Russia 'Hoax' Led to Death and Destruction in Ukraine," *Mother Jones*, February 24, 2022; Bess Levin, "Trump Just Comes Out and Admits to Entire Ukraine Scam," *Vanity Fair*, February 14, 2020.

15. Bill Kristol (@BillKristol), Twitter, February 1, 2020, 11:09 a.m., twitter.com/BillKristol /status/1223639550209200129?ref_src=twsrc%5Etfw.

CHAPTER 16. DESTABILIZING THE GOVERNMENT

1. Michael E. Miller, "Nixon Had an Enemies List. Now So Does Trump," *Washington Post*, August 19, 2018; Gabriel Sherman, "'It's Payback Time': With Acquittal Certain, Trump Plots Revenge on Bolton, Impeachment Enemies," *Vanity Fair*, February 3, 2020.

2. Peter Baker et al., "Trump Fires Impeachment Witnesses Gordon Sondland and Alexander Vindman in Post-Acquittal Purge," *New York Times*, February 7, 2020.

3. Jonathan D. Karl, "The Man Who Made January 6 Possible," *Atlantic*, November 9, 2021.

4. Jonathan Swan, "A Radical Plan for Trump's Second Term," *Axios*, July 22, 2022; Eric Katz, "If Trump Is Reelected, His Aides Are Planning to Purge the Civil Service," *Government Executive*, July 22, 2022.

5. Peter Overby, "Trump's Efforts to 'Drain the Swamp' Lagging behind His Campaign Rhetoric," NPR, April 26, 2017; Josh Dawsey, Rosalind S. Helderman, and David A. Fahrenthold, "How Trump Abandoned His Pledge to 'Drain the Swamp,'" *Washington Post*, October 24, 2020.

6. Nahal Toosi and Burgess Everett, "Source: Trump Wants 37 Percent Budget Cut to State, USAID," *Politico*, February 28, 2017; United States Department of Agriculture, "Secretary Perdue Announces Kansas City Region as Location for ERS and NIFA," news release no. 0091.19, June 13, 2019, usda.gov/media/press-releases/2019/06/13/secretary -perdue-announces-kansas-city-region-location-ers-and-nifa; Merrit Kennedy, "Scientists Desert USDA as Agency Relocates to Kansas City Area," NPR, July 17, 2019.

7. Melissa Quinn, "The Internal Watchdogs Trump Has Fired or Replaced," CBS News, May 19, 2020; Tal Axelrod, "Trump Fires Intelligence Community Watchdog Who Flagged Ukraine Whistleblower Complaint," *The Hill*, April 3, 2020.

8. Kyle Cheney, "GAO Finds Chad Wolf, Ken Cuccinelli Are Ineligible to Serve in Their Top DHS Roles," *Politico*, August 14, 2020; Joel Rose, "How Trump Has Filled High-Level Jobs without Senate Confirmation Votes," NPR, March 9, 2020.

9. "Full Transcript: Trump's 2020 State of the Union Address," *New York Times*, February 5, 2020.

10. Michael Socolow (@MichaelSocolow), "On 19 July 1940, Hitler was giving a speech when he suddenly paused. He then promoted 12 Generals to Field Marshall for their work in defeating France," Twitter, February 4, 2020, 10:46 p.m., https://twitter.com/michaelsocolow /status/1224901977408266240.

CHAPTER 17. EMBRACING AUTHORITARIANISM

1. Franco Ordoñez, "Jared Kushner's Role in Coronavirus Response Draws Scrutiny, Criticism," NPR, April 4, 2020.
2. "Navy Rear Adm. John Polowczyk: 'I'm Not Here to Disrupt a Supply Chain,'" Facebook video of White House press briefing, April 2, 2020, 2:23, facebook.com/watch/?v=585 594418971772.
3. "In New Letter, Schumer Calls on President Trump to Designate a Senior Military Officer as 'Czar' for Both Production and Distribution of Desperately Needed Medical Equipment; Schumer Says Present Personnel Not Up to the Job," Senate Democrats, April 2, 2020; Donald J. Trump, "Letter to Senate Minority Leader Charles E. Schumer on the Federal Coronavirus Response," April 2, 2020, American Presidency Project.
4. Jeremy B. White, "Trump Claims 'Total Authority' over State Decisions," *Politico*, April 13, 2020.
5. Nick Cumming-Bruce, "Taking Migrant Children from Parents Is Illegal, U.N. Tells U.S.," *New York Times*, June 5, 2018.
6. Donald J. Trump (@realDonaldTrump), Twitter, April 17, 2020, 11:25a.m., twitter.com /realDonaldTrump/status/1251169987110330372.
7. Richard A. Oppel Jr., Derrick Bryson Taylor, and Nicholas Bogel-Burroughs, "What to Know about Breonna Taylor's Death," *New York Times*, March 9, 2023.
8. Donald J. Trump (@realDonaldTrump), Twitter, May 29, 2020, 12:53 a.m., https://twitter .com/realDonaldTrump/status/1266231100780744704; United States Department of Justice, "Attorney General William P. Barr's Statement on the Death of George Floyd and Riots," news release no. 20-499, May 30, 2020, justice.gov/opa/pr/attorney-general-william-p-barr-s -statement-death-george-floyd-and-riots; Homeland Security, "Office of Intelligence and Analysis Operations in Portland," April 20, 2021, at https://www.wyden.senate.gov/imo /media/doc/I&A%20and%20OGC%20Portland%20Reports.pdf.
9. "President Trump Walks across Lafayette Park to St. John's Church," YouTube video, 7:46, posted by C-SPAN, June 1, 2020, youtube.com/watch?v=5ShnqmiKLE8.
10. Paul LeBlanc, "Retired Marine Gen. John Allen: Trump's Threats of Military Force May Be 'the Beginning of the End of the American Experiment,'" CNN, June 4, 2020.
11. Peter Baker, Zolan Kanno-Youngs, and Monica Davey, "Trump Threatens to Send Federal Law Enforcement Forces to More Cities," *New York Times*, July 24, 2020.
12. Christopher Giles, "Facebook: Trump Posts Misleading Ad Using Ukraine Photo," BBC News, July 22, 2020, bbc.com/news/world-us-canada-53500610.

CHAPTER 18. REWRITING AMERICAN HISTORY

1. Barbara Sprunt and Alana Wise, "Trump Addresses Tightly Packed Arizona Crowd amid State's Growing Coronavirus Crisis," NPR, June 23, 2020; Brad Poole, "Trump Rally Fills Megachurch with Young Conservatives," Courthouse News Service, June 23, 2020.
2. U.S. Department of State, *Report of the Commission on Unalienable Rights*, July 16, 2020, state.gov/wp-content/uploads/2020/07/Draft-Report-of-the-Commission-on -Unalienable-Rights.pdf.
3. Republican National Committee, "Resolution Regarding the Republican National Platform," August 24, 2020, American Presidency Project.
4. Alana Wise, "Trump Announces 'Patriotic Education' Commission, a Largely Political Move," NPR, September 17, 2020; Exec. Order No. 13958, 85 Fed. Reg. 70951 (November 2, 2020).
5. Joseph R. Biden, "Remarks by Vice President Joe Biden in Gettysburg, Pennsylvania," October 6, 2020, American Presidency Project.

NOTES

CHAPTER 19. JANUARY 6

1. Dan Friedman, "Leaked Audio: Before Election Day, Bannon Said Trump Planned to Falsely Claim Victory," *Mother Jones*, July 12, 2022.
2. Morgan Chalfant and Brett Samuels, "Trump Prematurely Declares Victory, Says He'll Go to Supreme Court," *The Hill*, November 4, 2020.
3. Michael D. Shear and Stephanie Saul, "Trump, in Taped Call, Pressured Georgia Official to 'Find' Votes to Overturn Election," *New York Times*, January 3, 2021.
4. Ryan Nobles et al., "First on CNN: January 6 Committee Has Text Messages between Ginni Thomas and Mark Meadows," CNN, March 25, 2022.
5. Ashton Carter et al., "Opinion: All 10 Living Former Defense Secretaries: Involving the Military in Election Disputes Would Cross into Dangerous Territory," *Washington Post*, January 3, 2021.
6. Tom Dreisbach, "How Trump's 'Will Be Wild!' Tweet Drew Rioters to the Capitol on January 6," NPR, July 13, 2022.
7. Donald J. Trump, "Remarks to Supporters Prior to the Storming of the United States Capitol," January 6, 2021, American Presidency Project.
8. Kevin Liptak, "Trump's Presidency Ends with American Carnage," CNN, January 6, 2021.
9. Donald J. Trump, "Tweets of January 6, 2021," January 6, 2021, American Presidency Project.

CHAPTER 20. THE BIG LIE

1. Nate Schwartz, "Former Presidents Obama, Bush, Clinton and Carter Released Statements on the Capitol Riots. Here's What They Said," *Deseret News*, January 7, 2021.
2. "Romney Condemns Insurrection at U.S. Capitol," January 6, 2021, Mitt Romney, U.S. Senator for Utah, https://www.romney.senate.gov/romney-condemns-insurrection-us-capitol/; Editorial Board, "Hawley Should Resign. Silent Enablers Must Now Publicly Condemn Trumpism," *St. Louis Post-Dispatch*, January 7, 2021.
3. Kevin Liptak, Veronica Stracqualursi, and Allie Malloy, "Trump Publicly Acknowledges He Won't Serve a Second Term a Day after Inciting Mob," CNN, January 7, 2021.
4. Sonam Sheth, "Trump's 2nd Impeachment Is the Most Bipartisan in US History," *Business Insider*, January 13, 2021.
5. "Joseph Goebbels: On the 'Big Lie,'" Jewish Virtual Library, https://www.jewishvirtuallibrary.org/joseph-goebbels-on-the-quot-big-lie-quot.
6. Walter C. Langer, Office of Strategic Services, *A Psychological Analysis of Adolph Hitler: His Life and Legend*, Central Intelligence Agency, August 24, 1999, cia.gov/readingroom/docs/CIA-RDP78-02646R000600240001-5.pdf.
7. "Voting Laws Roundup: October 2021," Brennan Center for Justice, October 4, 2021.
8. Laurie Roberts, "Kari Lake Calls for Dismantling the FBI. No, Seriously, She Did," *Arizona Republic*, August 11, 2022.
9. Inae Oh, "Almost Every House Republican Just Voted against Protecting the Right to Contraception," *Mother Jones*, July 21, 2022; Malliga Och, "Busting the Filibuster," *Ms.*, October 4, 2022.
10. Dobbs v. Jackson Women's Health Organization, 597 U.S., 5.

CHAPTER 21. WHAT IS AMERICA?

1. Jake Silverstein, "Why We Published the 1619 Project," *New York Times*, December 20, 2019.
2. The President's Advisory 1776 Commission, *The 1776 Report*, January 2021, trumpwhitehouse.archives.gov/wp-content/uploads/2021/01/The-Presidents-Advisory-1776-Commission-Final-Report.pdf.

NOTES

3. James Henry Hammond, *Selections from the Letters and Speeches of the Hon. James H. Hammond, of South Carolina* (New York: John F. Trow and Company, 1866), 126; Heather Cox Richardson, *How the South Won the Civil War: Oligarchy, Democracy, and the Continuing Fight for the Soul of America* (New York: Oxford University Press, 2020), 31–42.
4. Robert J. Miller, "Nazi Germany's Race Laws, the United States, and American Indians," *St. John's Law Review* 94 (2020): 756.
5. Fannie Lou Hamer, "'I Didn't Know Anything about Voting:' Fannie Lou Hamer on the Mississippi Voter Registration Campaign," History Matters, historymatters.gmu.edu/d/6918/.
6. Langston Hughes, "Let America Be America Again," *Esquire*, July 1, 1936, classic.esquire.com/article/1936/7/1/let-america-be-america-again.

CHAPTER 22. DECLARING INDEPENDENCE

1. Fred Anderson, *Crucible of War: The Seven Years' War and the Fate of Empire in British North America, 1754–1766* (New York: Vintage Books, 2001), 453–457, 518–528.
2. Alan Taylor, *American Colonies: The Settling of North America* (New York: Penguin Books, 2001), 437–442; Anderson, *Crucible of War*, 572–651.
3. John M. Barry, *Roger Williams and the Creation of the American Soul: Church, State, and the Birth of Liberty* (New York: Viking, 2012), 9–78.
4. Anderson, *Crucible of War*, 668–684.
5. John Adams, "Monday August 14 [from the Diary of John Adams]," Founders Online, National Archives, https://founders.archives.gov/documents/Adams/01-01-02-0013-0001-0005.
6. "Great Britain: Parliament—the Declaratory Act: March 18, 1766," Avalon Project.
7. David Hackett Fischer, *Paul Revere's Ride* (New York and Oxford, UK: Oxford University Press, 1994), 23–24.
8. Fischer, *Paul Revere's Ride*, 25–26.
9. Mark Peterson, *The City-State of Boston: The Rise and Fall of an Atlantic Power, 1630–1865* (Princeton, NJ: Princeton University Press, 2019), 291.
10. Fischer, *Paul Revere's Ride*, 184–280.
11. Harvey J. Kaye, *Thomas Paine and the Promise of America* (New York: Hill and Wang, 2005), 17, 43, 50–56.
12. "Lee Resolution (1776)," National Archives, https://www.archives.gov/milestone-documents/lee-resolution.
13. Pauline Maier, *American Scripture: Making the Declaration of Independence* (New York: Knopf, 1997).
14. "John Adams to Thomas Jefferson, 24 August 1815," Founders Online, National Archives, https://founders.archives.gov/documents/Jefferson/03-08-02-0560.

CHAPTER 23. THE CONSTITUTION

1. "Articles of Confederation: March 1, 1781," Avalon Project.
2. Leonard L. Richards, *Shays's Rebellion: The American Revolution's Final Battle* (Philadelphia: University of Pennsylvania Press, 2003).
3. Jack N. Rakove, "Presidential Selection: Electoral Fallacies," *Political Science Quarterly* 119 (Spring 2004): 21–37.
4. "Benjamin Franklin to the Federal Convention: September 17, 1787," Avalon Project.
5. George Washington to Catharine Sawbridge Macaulay Graham, January 9, 1790, Founders Online, National Archives, https://founders.archives.gov/documents/Washington/05-04-02-0363.

6. Rakove, "Presidential Selection," 31–32; Donald O. Dewey, "Madison's Views on Electoral Reform," *Western Political Quarterly* 15 (March 1962): 140–145.

7. Heather Cox Richardson, *Wounded Knee: Party Politics and the Road to an American Massacre* (New York: Basic Books, 2010), 100–110, 142–144.

8. U.S. Census Bureau, "2020 Census Apportionment Results Delivered to the President," April 26, 2021, https://www.census.gov/newsroom/press-releases/2021/2020-census-apportionment-results.html.

9. "The Permanent Apportionment Act of 1929," History, Art & Archives, U.S. House of Representatives, https://history.house.gov/HistoricalHighlight/Detail/35513; Sarah J. Eckman, *Apportionment and Redistricting Process for the U.S. House of Representatives*, Congressional Research Service, November 22, 2021, crsreports.congress.gov/product /pdf/R/R45951.

CHAPTER 24. EXPANDING DEMOCRACY

1. Phillis Wheatley, "Letter to Reverend Samson Occum," *Connecticut Gazette*, March 11, 1774.

2. Jane Hampton Cook, "How Did John Adams Respond to Abigail's 'Remember the Ladies'?," *Journal of the American Revolution*, August 18, 2020.

3. Frederick Douglass, *Oration Delivered in Corinthian Hall, Rochester* (Rochester, NY: Lee, Man, and Co, 1852), 14–37.

4. "To Thomas Jefferson from Benjamin Banneker, 19 August 1791," Founders Online, National Archives, founders.archives.gov/documents/Jefferson/01-22-02-0049.

5. Elizabeth Cady Stanton, *Address of Mrs. Elizabeth Cady Stanton, Delivered at Seneca Falls & Rochester, N.Y., July 19th & August 2d, 1848* (New York: R. J. Johnston, 1870).

6. Alexandra "Mac" Taylor, "Elizabeth Freeman, Her Case for Freedom, and the Massachusetts Constitution," National Constitution Center, April 13, 2021, constitutioncenter.org /blog/elizabeth-freeman-her-case-for-freedom-and-the-massachusetts-constitution.

7. Jack Hisle, "The Quock Walker Case," Mapping the Great Awakening, https://people.smu .edu/mappingthega/stories/the-quock-walker-case/.

8. Martin v. Commonwealth, 1 Mass. 260, 1 Will. 260 (1805); Linda K. Kerber, "The Paradox of Women's Citizenship in the Early Republic: The Case of *Martin vs. Massachusetts*, 1805," *American Historical Review* 97 (April 1992): 349–378.

9. Worcester v. Georgia, 31 U.S. 515 (1832); Edwin A. Miles, "After John Marshall's Decision: Worcester v. Georgia and the Nullification Crisis," *Journal of Southern History* 39 (November 1973): 519–544.

10. Claudio Saunt, *Unworthy Republic: The Dispossession of Native Americans and the Road to Indian Territory* (New York: W. W. Norton, 2020), 161–170; Miles, "After John Marshall's Decision," 528–529.

11. Walt Whitman, *Leaves of Grass, 1855 Edition* (Ann Arbor, MI: Ann Arbor Editions, 2003).

12. "Owen Lovejoy," VCU Libraries Social Welfare History Project, socialwelfare.library.vcu .edu/eras/antebellum/lovejoy-owen/.

13. Franklin Pierce, "Third Annual Message," December 31, 1855, American Presidency Project.

14. Abraham Lincoln, "Speech at Chicago, Illinois," July 10, 1858, in *The Collected Works of Abraham Lincoln*, vol. 2, ed. Roy P. Basler (Ann Arbor, MI: University of Michigan Digital Library Production Services, 2001), 500.

CHAPTER 25. MUDSILLS OR MEN

1. William E. Dodd, *The Cotton Kingdom: A Chronicle of the Old South* (New Haven, CT: Yale University Press, 1920), 24.

2. James Henry Hammond, "Speech on the Admission of Kansas . . . March 4, 1858," in *Selections from the Letters and Speeches of the Hon. James H. Hammond* (New York: John F.

Trow, 1866), 169–176; Heather Cox Richardson, *How the South Won the Civil War: Oligarchy, Democracy, and the Continuing Fight for the Soul of America* (New York: Oxford University Press, 2020), 31–35; Matthew Karp, *This Vast Southern Empire: Slaveholders at the Helm of American Foreign Policy* (Cambridge, MA: Harvard University Press, 2016), 145–146; George Brown Tindall and David Emory Shi, *America: A Narrative History*, 9th edition (New York: W. W. Norton, 2013), 368.

3. Dodd, *Cotton Kingdom*, 24; Tindall and Shi, *America*, 368.
4. Dred Scott v. Sandford, 60 U.S. 393 (1856).
5. Drew Gilpin Faust, *James Henry Hammond and the Old South: A Design for Mastery* (Baton Rouge: Louisiana State University Press, 1982), 37–104, 241–245.
6. "Fifth Debate: Galesburg, Illinois," National Park Service, nps.gov/liho/learn/historyculture/debate5.htm; Heather Cox Richardson, *To Make Men Free: A History of the Republican Party* (New York: Basic Books, 2021), 31–32.
7. Glenn C. Altschuler and Stuart M. Blumin, *Rude Republic: Americans and Their Politics in the Nineteenth Century* (Princeton, NJ: Princeton University Press, 2000), 63.
8. Richardson, *How the South Won the Civil War*, 43; Karp, *This Vast Southern Empire*, 234–235.

CHAPTER 26. OF THE PEOPLE, BY THE PEOPLE, FOR THE PEOPLE

1. Justin Smith Morrill, Cong. Globe, 37th Cong., 2nd Sess., 1194 (1862); Heather Cox Richardson, *To Make Men Free: A History of the Republican Party* (New York: Basic Books, 2021), 53–54.
2. Heather Cox Richardson, *The Greatest Nation of the Earth: Republican Economic Policies during the Civil War* (Cambridge, MA: Harvard University Press, 1997), 103.
3. Abraham Lincoln, "Address Delivered at the Dedication of the Cemetery at Gettysburg," *The Collected Works of Abraham Lincoln*, vol. 7, ed. Roy P. Basler (Ann Arbor, MI: University of Michigan Digital Library Production Services, 2001), 18–23.
4. Heather Cox Richardson, *West from Appomattox: The Reconstruction of America after the Civil War* (New Haven, CT: Yale University Press, 2007), 8.
5. "Thoughts from an Assassin: The Journal of John Wilkes Booth," National Park Service, https://www.nps.gov/foth/learn/historyculture/thoughts-from-an-assassin-the-journal-of-john-wilkes-booth.htm.
6. Richardson, *West from Appomattox*, 56–57.
7. Richardson, *West from Appomattox*, 78–120.

CHAPTER 27. AMERICA RENEWED

1. Heather Cox Richardson, "We Are All Americans: Ely Parker at Appomattox," *We're History*, April 9, 2015, werehistory.org/ely-parker/.
2. "Confrontations for Justice," National Archives, https://www.archives.gov/exhibits/eyewitness/html.php?section=3.
3. Minor v. Happersett, 88 U.S. (21 Wall.) 162 (1875).
4. Mae M. Ngai, *Impossible Subjects: Illegal Aliens and the Making of Modern America* (Princeton, NJ: Princeton University Press, 2004), 38.
5. Horatio Alger Jr., *Ragged Dick, or Street Life in New York with the Boot-Blacks* (Philadelphia: John C. Winston Company, 1868).
6. Booker T. Washington, *Up from Slavery: An Autobiography* (New York: Doubleday, Page, and Company, 1907); Charles Alexander Eastman (Ohiyesa), *The Soul of the Indian* (Boston: Houghton Mifflin and Company, 1911); Zitkála-Šá, *American Indian Stories* (Glorieta, NM: Rio Grande Press Company, 1976).
7. George W. Williams, *The History of the Negro Race in America from 1619 to 1880: Negroes as Slaves, as Soldiers, and as Citizens* (New York: G. P. Putnam's Sons, 1882).

8. "A Legal Brief for Ida B. Wells' Lawsuit against Chesapeake, Ohio, and Southwestern Railroad Company before the State Supreme Court, 1885," Digital Public Library of America, dp.la/primary-source-sets/ida-b-wells-and-anti-lynching-activism/sources/1113.
9. United States v. Wong Kim Ark, 169 U.S. 649 (1898).
10. Michael McGerr, *A Fierce Discontent: The Rise and Fall of the Progressive Movement in America* (Oxford, UK: Oxford University Press, 2003), 99–104.
11. "A Look Back on 100+ Years of Advocacy," National Consumers League, https://nclnet.org/about-ncl/about-us/history/.
12. McGerr, *A Fierce Discontent*, 25–29.
13. Nat Love, *The Life and Adventures of Nat Love, Better Known in the Cattle Country as "Deadwood Dick"* (Los Angeles: Nat Love, 1907), 147.

CHAPTER 28. A PROGRESSIVE AMERICA

1. David Nasaw, *Andrew Carnegie* (New York: Penguin Books, 2007), 361–362.
2. Andrew Carnegie, "Wealth," *North American Review* 148 (1889): 653–664.
3. *Chicago Tribune*, January 10, 1884; Allan Nevins, *Grover Cleveland: A Study in Courage* (New York: Dodd, Mead, 1962), 342–345.
4. Carnegie, "Wealth."
5. Grover Cleveland, "State of the Union, 1888," December 3, 1888, American Presidency Project.
6. *Frank Leslie's Illustrated Newspaper*, December 14, 1889, 330; December 21, 1889, 354; January 4, 1889, 387; Heather Cox Richardson, *To Make Men Free: A History of the Republican Party* (New York: Basic Books, 2021), 174.
7. "Her Strange Power," *Topeka State Journal*, March 31, 1891.
8. Platform of the Northern Alliance, in John D. Hicks, *The Populist Revolt: A History of the Farmers' Alliance and the People's Party* (Minneapolis: University of Minnesota Press, 1931), 125, 428–430.
9. Gregg Cantrell, *The People's Revolt: Texas Populism and the Roots of American Liberalism* (New Haven, CT: Yale University Press, 2020), 262.
10. "Populist Party Platform of 1892," July 4, 1892, American Presidency Project.
11. "Bryan's 'Cross of Gold' Speech: Mesmerizing the Masses," History Matters, historymatters.gmu.edu/d/5354/.
12. Theodore Roosevelt, *The Rough Riders* (New York: Modern Library, 1999), 3–5; Richardson, *To Make Men Free*, 199–205.
13. *Indianapolis Sentinel*, quoted in *New York Times*, July 4, 1898; T. St. John Gaffney, in *New York Times*, August 22, 1898; Richardson, *To Make Men Free*, 203.
14. Theodore Roosevelt, "The New Nationalism," in *The New Nationalism* (New York: Outlook Company, 1910), 3–33; Richardson, *To Make Men Free*, 231, 235.

CHAPTER 29. THE ROAD TO THE NEW DEAL

1. "NAACP: A Century in the Fight for Freedom," Library of Congress, https://www.loc.gov/exhibits/naacp/.
2. *New York Times*, April 4, 1879, 5.
3. Heather Cox Richardson, "Lessons from the First National Shutdown," *New York Times*, December 18, 2013.
4. "Lecture by Frances Perkins," September 30, 1964, Remembering the 1911 Triangle Factory Fire, trianglefire.ilr.cornell.edu/primary/lectures/; Matthew and Hannah Josephson, *Al Smith: Hero of the Cities, A Political Portrait Drawing on the Papers of Frances Perkins* (Boston: Houghton Mifflin Company, 1969); David M. Kennedy, *Freedom from Fear: The American People in Depression and War, 1929–1945* (New York: Oxford University Press, 1999), 258–272.

5. Heather Cox Richardson, *To Make Men Free: A History of the Republican Party* (New York: Basic Books, 2021), 286–292; Glenn C. Altschuler and Stuart M. Blumin, *The G.I. Bill: A New Deal for Veterans* (New York: Oxford University Press, 2009).
6. Richardson Family Archives, by permission.
7. Richardson, *To Make Men Free*, 352.

CHAPTER 30. DEMOCRACY AWAKENING

1. Lyndon B. Johnson, "Address to a Joint Session of Congress," November 27, 1963, American Presidency Project.
2. Johnson, "Address to a Joint Session of Congress."
3. NPR Staff, "Remembering a Civil Rights Swim-In: 'It Was a Milestone,'" NPR, June 13, 2014.
4. "Text of Goldwater Speech on Rights," *New York Times*, June 19, 1964.
5. Kent Germany and David Carter, "Mississippi Burning," Miller Center, University of Virginia, millercenter.org/the-presidency/educational-resources/mississippi-burning.
6. Lyndon B. Johnson, "Radio and Television Remarks upon Signing the Civil Rights Bill," July 2, 1964, American Presidency Project.
7. Lyndon B. Johnson, "Remarks at the University of Michigan," May 22, 1964, American Presidency Project; Maurice Isserman and Michael Kazin, *America Divided: The Civil War of the 1960s* (New York: Oxford University Press, 2000), 110–111.
8. Isserman and Kazin, *America Divided*, 103–126; Joshua Zeitz, *Building the Great Society: Inside Lyndon Johnson's White House* (New York: Viking, 2018).
9. Johnson, "Remarks at the University of Michigan."
10. Karen Tumulty, "The Great Society at 50," *Washington Post*, May 17, 2014; Thom Hartmann, "Dear Republicans: We Tried Your Way and It Does Not Work," *Hartmann Report*, May 26, 2022; for right to contraceptives, see Griswold v. Connecticut, 381 U.S. 479 (1965); for right to abortion, see Roe v. Wade, 410 U.S. 113 (1973).
11. *U.S. News & World Report*, quoted in Mary C. Brennan, *Turning Right in the Sixties: The Conservative Capture of the GOP* (Chapel Hill: University of North Carolina Press, 1995), 119.
12. Gerald R. Ford, "Proclamation 4311—Granting Pardon to Richard Nixon," September 8, 1974, American Presidency Project.

CONCLUSION. RECLAIMING OUR COUNTRY

1. Jimmy Carter, "Farewell Address to the Nation," January 14, 1981, American Presidency Project.
2. Joseph R. Biden, "Inaugural Address," January 20, 2021, American Presidency Project.
3. Joseph R. Biden, "Remarks on United States Foreign Policy at the Department of State," February 4, 2021, American Presidency Project.
4. Zack Beauchamp, "The Intellectual Right's War on America's Institutions," *Vox*, November 19, 2021.
5. Abraham Lincoln, "Seventh and Last Debate with Stephen A. Douglas at Alton, Illinois," in *The Collected Works of Abraham Lincoln*, vol. 3, ed. Roy P. Basler (Ann Arbor, MI: University of Michigan Digital Library Production Services, 2001), 315.
6. Abraham Lincoln, "Speech at Peoria, Illinois," October 16, 1854, in Basler, *Collected Works*, vol. 2, 282.

Index

INDEX

INDEX